Complexity Demystified

A guide for practitioners

Patrick Beautement
Christine Broenner

'Yes, this has been a visit to Damascus that I shall not easily forget. I begin to see dimly what the civilization of a great Eastern city means, how they live, what they think; and I have got onto terms with them.'

Gertrude Bell (1868-1926)

Produced in Association with
The *abaci* Partnership LLP

Published by:
Triarchy Press
Station Offices
Axminster
Devon. EX13 5PF
United Kingdom

+44 (0)1297 631456
info@triarchypress.com
www.triarchypress.com

A catalogue record for this book is available from the British Library.

Cover design and image by Heather Fallows ~
www.whitespacegallery.org.uk

ISBN: 978-1-908009-24-1

CONTENTS

Patrick

For my late father, Alan Beautement

Christine

For my family

ACKNOWLEDGEMENTS

We would like to acknowledge the other members of The *abaci* Partnership LLP who have all contributed ideas that have helped shape the book – including former members Anthony Alston and Lorraine Dodd. We particularly thank current partner Merfyn Lloyd for his ideas on complexity-worthiness and for his encouragement that 'this is a book which has to be written'.

We would like to thank Eileen Conn of Living Systems Research for allowing us to quote her and use her 'Social Eco-Systems Dance (SESD) model in Figure 2. We are grateful to Professor Carmel Martin of Trinity College Dublin for permission to use her quote. We would also like to thank all the participants at the ECCS Workshop we held in Warwick in 2009 for their enthusiasm and insight.

In regard to the case studies we owe our thanks to a number of people who contributed material and provided comments and permissions. For Slum Upgrading in Cameroon we thank Peter Gijs van Enk of Intervolve; for the Journalism in Lebanon background and quotes we thank Robert Holloway, Director of the AFP Foundation; and for Deepwater Horizon we thank Graham Sutliffe, Geoscience Consultancy Services, for his technical expertise in checking the facts. Concerning the Lost Town Project, we would like to thank Rachel Bosworth of EEDA and the architects Anne Niemann and Johannes Ingrisch.

We would like to thank Dr Craig Cassells and Frances Sutliffe for their detailed and helpful reviews of the drafts of the book. Special thanks go to our editor at Triarchy Press, Alison Melvin, for patient encouragement and thoughtful and constructive comment.

A particular thank you to Professor Brian Collins for providing a foreword and for his support and enthusiasm for our work.

Patrick Beautement, Christine Broenner, May 2011.

FOREWORD

Complexity is all around us, we create it, and we are part of it. It should not remain a mystery, but we should not assume that analysis alone will allow us to understand it. Learning about complexity by engaging with issues that are complex will allow us to build a synthesis of 'world views' that is sustainable, resilient and yet adaptable. Practitioners who are engaged in dealing with complex issues across diverse domains and contexts will find this book illuminating, thought provoking and most of all useful - in guiding them to ways of moving forwards in their endeavours to understand and then exploit that understanding for greater purpose.

The authors draw on a wide range of experiences, both their own and others, to distil and then synthesise the essence of how to deal with what is called in other parts of the literature 'wicked problems'. This is a rapidly growing field of both academic and practical endeavour as we seek to understand and then cope with the complex context in which the human condition is situated. Publications in this field are rapidly growing in number and diversity and research activities across the world are stimulating both academic and practical application of a range of techniques.

This book is a very valuable and timely contribution to that body of scholarship and practice, bridging as it sets out to do and does, academic abstraction of concepts and methods and the stark reality of social, economic and physical situations. It should be on the bookshelf of anyone seriously engaged with any complex issue.

Professor Brian Collins, CB, FREng.

Chief Scientific Adviser
Department for Transport (DfT) and Department for Business, Innovation and Skills (BIS)
London, UK. May 2011.

INTRODUCTION

This book came about because we had been wrestling with something that seemed obvious to us and yet hard to understand and explain. Why is it that in human endeavour people appear, generally, to face two types of situations but mostly apply only one type of solution, a 'mechanistic' one, to both of them?

This default situation is typified by a global supermarket chain. From food production through to customer purchases most things are known, processes are harmonised and data is standardised. This is human activity turned into a highly structured, 'closed' enterprise – where the emphasis is largely on internal structures, procedures and people as process-followers and is designed and optimised to provide maximum performance, which can be measured and judged by numbers within a predetermined situation.

The second type of situation is typified by events such as a social night out with friends, community engagement initiatives, paddling down a fast river or dealing with sudden changes such as economic crises or with the appearance of novel markets. Here, most things are not known in advance and activities are more about grasping fleeting opportunities – it is about being positioned, from the outset, to be adaptive, open and able to engage with the evolving situation in order to influence and change things in the moment. This is human activity as a flow of changing experience – shaped by circumstances and events, rather than predetermined by process. Putting this rich, open-ended complexity 'to work', practically, dynamically and successfully in day-to-day contexts, is at the heart of what this book is all about.

So, what is the issue here? For the most part, current approaches use supermarket-chain-like 'reductionist thinking', inappropriately, to try to engage with the complex realities of the world. Yet, this type of thinking assumes, wrongly, that the world is like a machine: i.e. as a defined set of parts in fixed relationships, that can be taken apart and re-assembled as before without any of the interactions changing, and where the outcomes will remain the same regardless of such disassembly. Why do people do this, often inappropriately and regardless of the context, and then express surprise when they get the inevitable unintended consequences? Surely they recognise the differences between types of situations and are able to adjust their ways-of-working accordingly? It seems not. However, what we have realised is that people opt for the 'mechanistic solution' by default because, as they tell us, they lack a systematic appreciation of how to alter their practices to match reality in a defendable way.

'We need to do something differently but are not sure what to do or how to do it...' – this is a statement that we have often heard from a wide range of people struggling with real-world issues on the front-line of human endeavour. To put real-world complexity to work you need to go about things in a very different way from, for example, designed supermarket-chain approaches that are predicated on 'defining the problem' first or bounding the 'system of interest'. Such rational approaches may be good in theory but, as many practitioners know from hard-won experience and when faced with the uncertainties and dynamics of real-world situations, they are weak in practice – especially when, as a result of change, inaction is not an option and the only way to proceed is through learning-by-doing.

That there are differences between these types of everyday situations is self-evident. Yet when I (Patrick) have criticised the trend towards treating more and more of human activity as a mechanistic enterprise, to the detriment of people's ability to effect on-the-fly change, I have been challenged, rightly, to offer alternative approaches that are more appropriate. After all, in situations which are well understood and stable, the highly-structured approaches work fine. A great deal has been written about structured, system-engineered approaches which is why, instead, this Guide focuses on the open-ended situation, on the practicalities of life and changing human experience, rather than on the analysis of deterministic structures and processes of internal change. Until now, I have largely failed to articulate in a systematic way what the alternatives are for these open-ended, complex and dynamic situations. This is partly because, as some people tend to perceive 'complexity' as a difficult, sometimes even threatening thing to be eradicated rather than fostered, it has been essential to demystify it and demonstrate that complex situations offer opportunities and show how their largely untapped benefits can be successfully obtained. With the understanding that has been developed, this Guide indicates clearly how to engage with the 'complexity for free' out there, which is largely still 'up for grabs' in open-ended situations, and how to exploit it effectively in your context.

When Christine joined The *abaci* Partnership and we started to work together, she brought with her a breadth of practical experience from around the world about how people bring about sustainable change in their lives. This lent weight to these thoughts – that alternatives *were* available (some of which had been used successfully in individual cases), but that there needed to be a systematic way of working out, over time, how to change what to do in practice, proactively or reactively, as circumstances evolve. As a result, we pooled our ideas and organised a workshop for practitioners – people who work with complex realities in their day-to-day work – and complexity scientists at the European Conference on Complex Systems (ECCS) in September 2009. The aim of the Workshop was to try to articulate more clearly the issues that needed to be addressed if what had been learned about change and real-world complexities were to be 'put to work' in practice.

Who are practitioners in our terms? We have come across them working in banks, sponsor and donor agencies, humanitarian aid programmes, land-use planning, transportation, energy and environmental planning, emergency response, healthcare, event management (e.g. London Olympic Games 2012), climate change and sustainable development, in the manufacturing and service industries, the military, peacekeeping and security, logistics, etc. – but this list is by no means exhaustive. Indeed, the variety of people who are practitioners is as diverse as the complexities of the real world that they work with. Their position, usually at the cross-over between aspiration and achievement, enables them to see where, how and why good intentions succeed or fail as they try to bring about beneficial change, often in challenging practical circumstances. The Workshop certainly exposed many interesting insights[1] and these, along with other similar ones voiced at meetings such as complexity seminars and those organised by development aid workers, also confirmed that people face major challenges in complex situations. Fundamentally, practitioners could put complexity to work in some situations but, when asked to justify their approach (by auditors, donors and those to whom they are accountable), they could not articulate why they did what they did in a way that was defendable in the face of rationalist demands for tangible, target-driven outcomes – that is, they lacked a systematic expression of how to deal with practical realities.

Despite support in this regard being available to practitioners from the work of complexity scientists most of it is in a theoretical form (e.g. lists of classifications of phenomena, tips and tricks, etc.). Complexity science seems to offer a 'new way of working', which raised many expectations among practitioners, but they have since found out that complexity science is hard to use in practice as it does not indicate what people might need to *do* differently in specific contexts. It was evident to us that this gap between theory, experience and current practice needed to be bridged – people wanted to know what to do differently in an integrative way, in practical terms, and were looking for feasible alternatives and ideas on suitable approaches and techniques.

So we decided to write this book to offer practical solutions – in fact, an integrative approach that provides a systematic appreciation of how the complexity that underlies practice works in reality. Why? Most importantly, because practitioners have told us in no uncertain terms that they are looking for ways to do things differently across all forms of human endeavour – they want to 'Put Complexity to Work' properly. This Guide is designed to fulfil this need. At its simplest, our

---

1   Summarised in a White Paper issued by The *abaci* Partnership - see www.abaci.net

Approach is about appreciating, engaging with and focusing on the dynamic phenomena already active in the world and on shaping and influencing them to gain advantage from the opportunities they offer. This book provides a clear framework for practitioners, based both on an analysis of insights, which we have derived, from complexity science and from practical experience, for working out how to apply a range of different techniques to bring about change in real-world contexts.

This Guide is also suitable for other professionals currently employing 'mechanistic thinking', such as economists, engineers, and technologists, as well as for academics and university students, who might wish to work in a different, more dynamically adaptive and flexible way, by bringing these insights into their real-world deliberations. The Guide will support their ability to collaborate with interested professionals and stakeholders by providing a set of useful concepts and techniques based on a well-founded terminology. The book is also for people who have heard about complexity science, who see that its insights could be useful to them but want the terms used demystified and to be shown pragmatic, real-world examples of how to put the insights to work in practice.

We would be very interested to receive your comments. Please email us at research@abacipartners.co.uk

PB/CB, Tewkesbury, UK, 2011.

PART ONE – Demystifying Complexity – The Rationale for an Alternative Approach

'The thinking that got you where you are, is not going to get you where you want [need] to be. Anyone who has never made a mistake has never done anything new.'
Albert Einstein (1879-1955)

'I cannot say whether things will get better if we change; what I can say is they must change if they are to get better.'
Georg Christoph Lichtenberg (1742-1799)

CHAPTER 1: 'PUTTING COMPLEXITY TO WORK' – THE BIG IDEA

'For every complex problem, there is a solution that is simple, neat
and wrong.'
H.L Menken (1880-1956)

'If we do not change our direction, we are likely to end up where
we are headed.'
Chinese Proverb

WHAT IS COMPLEXITY?

We all know that the world is complex but, before we go any further in this Guide, we have to acknowledge that the term 'complexity' causes difficulties. It means different things to different people and has also become rather a fashionable word to use – you will find it interspersed here and there in many speeches and articles.

So, what is complexity? Well, it depends on who is asking the question. The term is used in a variety of ways, from very different perspectives or viewpoints, and this may be why people, especially professionals, struggle to communicate with each other. A rather amusing example of this occurred at a workshop involving doctors and some military people where, for about ten minutes, a serious discussion had been underway about 'operational complexity' until it became clear that the doctors were talking about complex procedures in operating theatres and the military about the procedural complexities of the theatres in which they operated – but for a short time the discussion made some sort of sense to both parties!

We must accept the ambiguity of the everyday ways in which people talk about complex things and complexity, such as, 'I found those instructions really very complex', or 'There was just so much going on, the complexity of it defeated me'. These descriptions are very subjective but they are in a language that reflects the realties of the practitioners' world – rich and expressive, communicating emotion and concern – and is shaped by individuals' experiences, viewpoints and context. This Guide copes perfectly well with such 'imprecision' – it is part of the complex reality that we all embrace. Not for us taxonomies of pre-defined labels, which some methods require, or lists of metadata items 9000 items long that are mandated as the only way to describe things. The real world simply cannot be categorised like this.[2]

---

2   For proof of this, have a look at the 'Cyc Program' of The Cyc Foundation which has been
    running for nearly thirty years and is still nowhere near finished in its task of 'labelling' the
    world. See http://cyc.co.tv

We realised that one very important step in demystifying complexity and 'putting it to work' is to acknowledge this inevitable variety in the ways in which complexity is described and to accommodate it in our Approach. Though it is important to use language clearly, in practice it is not something we should get too obsessed about as it is just a fact of life that people use these terms in non-technical ways. To provide coherence in this Guide, we could have used only the terms that complexity scientists have developed to label complex phenomena from an academic point of view. These terms have, to some extent, been adopted by practitioner communities to describe, for example, the emergence of natural phenomena, the co-evolution of businesses and markets, or the resilience of vulnerable people to natural disasters. However, there is a very important issue here – in every real-world situation these phenomena occur concurrently and are always present to some degree. As we mentioned in the Introduction, the terms are incommensurate with practitioners' needs as they do not discriminate between separate types of situations, which might need to be handled in different ways, but rather discriminate between phenomena. This is one reason why complexity scientists have found it hard to engage with practitioners – the terms they use get in the way. We address this dilemma in the Guide not by using the terms directly but by drawing upon the thinking of complexity science to inform the design of the Approach and techniques that we have developed for the practitioners we described in the Introduction. We've embedded an understanding of the academic thinking that 'explains' real-world phenomena into our design. As we have done the translation for you, you do not need to be a complexity scientist to use the solutions in this book!

And, so that we can be clear in the Guide as to the way that 'the same' complex phenomena can be described, we differentiate four different ways of talking about complexity: as it is naturally; as academics see it generally in theory; as it is seen objectively when in some context; and as experienced subjectively by people as follows:

A. We use the term **'natural complexity'** to refer to complexity as it is in the real world – an expression of the phenomena[3] that arise, unadorned by any particular set of abstractions or terminology. Natural complexity exists regardless of the presence of human beings, yet it provides the backdrop to people's activities – the medium in which people must function. It is what we all engage with, whether or not we can perceive or understand it; it is an ever-present force that is continually generating novelty – where things are happening at all scales and time-horizons. Everyday examples of natural complexity are

---

3   Complex phenomena include things as varied as: swarming in an ants' nest, people suddenly turning against their leaders, unexpected surges in power systems, the financial crisis, hurricanes etc.

manifested in the ecosystems we are all part of, in the laws of nature that determine what humanity can do, and in the givens and dynamics of the geographical and virtual spaces people share. Natural complexity generates the phenomena that people 'put to work' because it *can* be influenced, if you know how, though we don't mean here that you have to take on the raw forces of nature to make it happen. Despite some popular perceptions to the contrary, natural complexity is not a thing to be suppressed – a wild untameable random chaos – it represents the everyday phenomena which people can, and do, routinely use and without which humanity wouldn't exist.

> 'Clouds are not spheres, mountains are not cones, coastlines are not circles, and bark is not smooth, nor does lightning travel in a straight line... Nature exhibits not simply a higher degree but an altogether different level of complexity.'
> *Benoit Mandelbrot (1924-2010)*

B. We have coined the term **'academic complexity'** to refer to the descriptions and explanations of natural complexity that are provided by complexity scientists using the abstractions of scientific terminology (e.g. emergence, co-evolution etc.). For example, complexity science has established four **'axioms of complexity'** that underpin the emergence of complex phenomena. In essence, they are that complexity arises because, in some **environment**, there are **components** that **interact** at levels of time and scale and whose activities results in the **phenomena** practitioners observe. Academic complexity talks about these axioms and their implications in scientific rather than practical terms, such that the 'so-what' implications of complexity largely remain opaque to non-specialists. However, tremendous progress has been made in understanding the underlying mechanisms of complexity and in identifying, labelling and researching the variety of patterns and phenomena that arise. Research on complexity science has been driven by institutions like that of the Santa Fe Institute[4] in New Mexico in the USA, which, in our opinion, still leads the discipline. From the point of view of practitioners and this Guide, academic complexity *per se* does not help people understand what, specifically, they have to do in practical terms. Nevertheless academic complexity has established an understanding of complex phenomena and has provided a rich source of inspiration and insight for this book. However, please note that this Guide is not a 'complexity book' *per se* – if you are looking for a detailed discussion of complexity, what it is, how it comes about and so on, there are many excellent specialist publications on the topic.

---

4   See http://www.santafe.edu/library/ – Santa Fe makes all its research work publicly available.

The following two ways of talking about complexity are necessary because, without them, we cannot reflect sensibly on the activities of practitioners. The first we call '**contextual complexity**'[5] because it provides an objective perspective on the realities of the context. The second we call '**experienced complexity**' as it describes the realities from the subjective view of practitioners themselves. For practitioners the starting point is not complexity science and its terminology but the natural context and people's experiences and perceptions of it. The key point here is that where complexity science might label a situation as complex, if people's experience of the features of a situation is that it is simple then for the purposes of practice it is! A key part of putting complexity to work is in both recognising that these two 'types' of complexity exist *and* in being able to reflect on the differences and synergies between them – and we'll start explaining how to do this practically in Chapter 4.

C. So, '**contextual complexity**' refers to the types of phenomena manifested in the particular situation with which practitioners are concerned, and describes in objective terms, as far as possible, the context in which they are arising. In practice and in this Guide we follow Jack Cohen and Ian Stewart's assertion (see their book *The Collapse of Chaos*) that it has become a kind of myth that complexity on complexity begets only further complexity. If this were true, and complexity was additive in this way, then people would have no choice but to deal with this overwhelming 'über-complexity' in their lives. Yet, self-evidently, for practitioners in a natural context, the underlying causes and complexities are 'hidden' and can, for all intents and purposes, be largely ignored. What matters when appreciating contextual complexity are the features,[6] the patterns and discernible simplicities of the context that can be worked with in practice. These are identified by considering the situation from the widest possible range of perspectives and viewpoints, and factoring in the givens arising from natural complexity. We fully appreciate that, in philosophical terms, such 'objectivity' will always have a subjective element. However, you cannot put complexity to work without a careful consideration of the givens and unavoidable realities

---

5   Note that the term 'contextual complexity' was also coined by Cynthia Kurtz and David Snowden in 'The new dynamics of strategy: sense-making in a complex world' as part of their Cynefin Framework. The meaning they attach to the term, though not identical with ours, is complementary to it.

6   We will use the term 'feature' to refer to emergent phenomena or patterns which are tangible to an actor in a context. For example, because cats have different senses from people they will discern features that we cannot and vice-versa. Software agents will 'discern' features in cyberspace that are hidden to human beings and so on. In other words, there is no single, universal set of features – it depends on capability, perspective and context.

of the contextual complexity that exist whether one likes it or not. In practice, this translates into being honest about the things in the world that one cannot know, becoming aware of the things that at first didn't seem important in a specific context, and acknowledging that there is no direct way around some of the factors – they 'just are'.

D. Lastly then, **'experienced complexity'**. This concerns the real-world realities that are experienced subjectively by individuals, or by communities or institutions in a context and are described in terms that make sense to the subject, given their abilities, experience and viewpoint. These descriptions can range from common-sense observations (sadly, an undervalued, yet powerful natural ability) of the phenomena to ones that can be highly complicated and contrived. Many are 'co-constructed' realities built up in a social context into a set of prejudices or 'habits' of thought. One can hear examples in the street: 'This is how we've always voted – father said it was only right...' or 'Climate change – it's all the scientist's fault...' or worse 'But isn't this what all *sensible* people think?' When we look at practitioners' experiences we will show that, far too often, experienced complexity is considered to the exclusion of the viewpoints of others and of the different perspectives on the context ('The boss says it's like this, so we better go along with it'). The Approach we have developed is specifically designed to expose the possibilities, opportunities and contradictions that might otherwise remain hidden. Of course, experienced complexity is different for each observer and depends very much on the natural complexity of a particular context. One person may find a situation 'routine' (because they have experienced it before), whereas another may find it very scary (think of surfing on the sea for the first time). In the wise words of Marcus Aurelius (121-180 AD) 'The colour of one's thought dyes one's world...' So, no single 'objective' world-view exists in the world of practitioners' realities, there is no basis for forming a 'single absolute view of the truth'. One has to work with the messiness, the diversity of experiences of different people – accept it, engage with it and move on.

Let's summarise the ways of talking about complexity with an example. A child is pouring out milk for a cat and does this perfectly competently because, for the child, the discernible features in this natural context are 'simple' and self-evident (experienced complexity). Yet for complexity scientists there is turbulent flow in the milk and massive underlying complexity in the bodies of the child and the cat and a myriad interactions with bacteria in their environment and so on (academic complexity).

One of the Big Ideas in this Guide is that, whatever the complexities of the world in theoretical terms, practitioners can only work with the real-world phenomena, the simplicities, that they can perceive, experience and engage with – so the focus has to be on working out what can be influenced and changed in practice. Because practice is, *de facto*, determined by changing context, then what to do differently in a specific instance can't be determined in advance as it depends on circumstances. The Guide helps you come to a level of understanding, through comparing contextual complexity and experienced complexity, about the drivers of and the nature of change in the context. Then you can work out how to engage appropriately in practice in a way that puts the underlying complexity to work. In this Guide, we partner with, you, the reader as you know your situation and can answer the 'it depends' question based on your experience as you go through the book.

What Does it Mean to 'Put Complexity to Work'?

At its simplest, Putting Complexity to Work (PCtW) is about focusing on the dynamic phenomena already active in the world and concentrating on how to shape and influence these through being able to continually match capabilities[7] to context as you go along on-the-fly.[8] Here's a simple example. Think of a class of kindergarten-age children. How is their day going to pan out? You can't know in detail because it depends on whether the children slept well the night before, came with a slight snuffle or have left their favourite toy at home, for example, and also on what happens hour-by-hour. The teachers are definitely practitioners in our terms, dealing with the real-world realities of the children's moods and actions – and certainly the contextual complexity will be dynamic! The teachers will 'put complexity to work' and influence that dynamic by encouraging positive behaviour, creating experiences, playing games and having fun, while at the same time promoting some education, damping down any unwelcome conduct by the children and comforting those who are crying. The teachers won't do this according to a fixed programme but will adapt their approach as the circumstances change and concurrently with the overall intent of play and education. The teachers may change the context by 'seeding the space' with singing, dance, craft, interesting objects, reading stories or changing the type of activity say by taking the children outside. In these ways they are fundamentally affecting the individual children and what they are doing, but without necessarily telling

---

7   In this Guide 'capabilities' are all-encompassing and include: people, skills, knowledge, experience, information, toolsets, machines, infrastructures and so on. Note there is a difference between ability and capability e.g. 'I have the ability to read' as opposed to 'I am capable of reading two books a day'.

8   Things that are done on-the-fly occur concurrently with the changing context, without having to stop the dynamic.

each child what to do, step-by-step, or by getting them to follow a standardised 'educational checklist'. By working directly on the phenomena of play manifested in this context, the teachers achieve their aims and do so without imposing an arbitrary timeline.[9] This example is a microcosm of human society at large and a perfect illustration of the topic of this book.

Such an approach is in contrast to the 'usual one' that, in general terms, involves planning how you want the world to be and then trying to 'impose' that plan on the world whilst keeping it fixed as the world changes. It is not uncommon for people to talk about 'starting with a clean sheet' – which is an admission that messy realities must be swept away before their method can work, as Naomi Klein points out in her book *Shock Doctrine*. However, let's make clear that there are occasions when highly engineered, structured approaches, in their true sense, are appropriate – the trick is knowing how and when to change approaches as circumstances change. For example, the USA's Saturn V rocket would never have got to the Moon without using engineering techniques that were adequate for the parameters of space flight – until Apollo 13 of course! It is also clear, as happened with NASA's Challenger Space Shuttle disaster in 1986, that there are situations where letting go of structured approaches inappropriately would be a bad idea.[10] A great deal has been written about these structured, system-engineered approaches and this is why, instead, this Guide focuses on the practicalities of life and on changing human experience. We talk about practice, behaviours, transitions and transformations in the real world as they are happening – and especially how to enable appropriate 'complexity-aware' behaviour in general, whether by individuals, groups, organisations or institutions.

For people who say 'What is different here from what I do already?' we say that **we are actually focusing on events in the real world – and on how to adapt and affect the conditions of practice with the changing context.** This is what is different about this Guide; we provide an approach for systematically and effectively achieving this in reality. We are not interested in just changing things internally, especially not through a year-long business-change initiative using process-modelling/reengineering to deal with so-called 'internal complexity'; there has been more than enough written about that already. Our interest is in all aspects that are involved in sustaining effective practice – by developing,

---

9   It is not possible to determine in advance how long it might take to change the dynamic of play or some aspect of a child's development. An arbitrary timeline would be to state that learning to read should take no more than two years.

10   Richard Feynman's book *What do you care what other people think?* describes how the engineers were asked to 'Put on their Managers' Hats' and remove their objection to the launch taking place in conditions which were too cold, but where NASA wanted to be seen to succeed.

adapting, matching and employing appropriate capabilities. We are interested in the external manifestations of practice and in engaging with and contributing to the wider community. In the kindergarten example, the teachers have a set of strategies and principles they use for changing the classroom dynamic. For instance, they may direct what happens top-down by issuing specific instructions, or by quietly encouraging individual children to do things that change the play from the bottom-up. They may also influence peer-group dynamics so that the children themselves self-organise or self-regulate what they do based on their experienced complexity. These concepts and techniques are a subset of the wider, complexity science-inspired set that we have used to formulate the Putting Complexity to Work Approach described in this book. You will notice, in Chapters 6 and 7, similar principles and strategies being used in the various case studies where we will show how, given the relevant capabilities, our Approach can be employed across many domains of human activity.

What our experience has shown us, and what we have heard first-hand from practitioners over many years, is that to put complexity to work you need to be able to adopt an appropriate mindset in order to perceive and engage with these real-world phenomena *and* to change and influence them dynamically – and in the best case turn them to your advantage. In other words, there has to be recognition that there is something tangible to engage with – which you did not necessarily have a hand in creating, and that has a life of its own. Think of it like this – practitioners are on a journey of exploration where they can't predict what they may meet along the way and where they may need to go next. So, because the 'what to do differently' at any particular point can't be defined in advance, **the Guide can't be like a recipe book; its more like a travel guide, and we have to collaborate with you, the reader because you understand your context**, **your journey and what you are trying to achieve**. Or, if one likened this to surfing, you can stand on the beach as long as you like observing and planning (which, in a way, is necessary) but, in the end, you have to get out on the waves to do the surfing! As John le Carré says 'A desk is a dangerous place from which to view the world'. In truth, we have all seen situations where companies, despite all their market research have, when it came to it, missed the big wave of opportunity[11] – partly because they didn't know what they were looking for and partly because they were not set up for transition from the static state of observing to the dynamic experience of doing. Being able to make and sustain that kind of change is a key part of putting complexity to work.

One thing to acknowledge here is that, for many practitioners, this is not a new insight – as indicated in the Introduction. They are and always will be dealing with

---

11   We don't always give specific examples – some companies are very sensitive about their name/brand being cited in this way as they struggle to cope with the turbulence it creates – we know that you know who we mean!

everyday complex realities in all sorts of practical ways and have been successfully engaging with their contextual complexity, often through making common-sense decisions and taking responsibility for their own actions. Despite the considerable achievements of these practitioners, many have recognised that some things should be done differently – especially in the kind of open, dynamic and uncertain situations that are labelled as 'complex'. In the last few years there has been no shortage of similar examples where politicians, economists, legislators, bankers and military leaders have publicly pleaded for new approaches.

If you search the Internet, there are many companies offering solutions to enable customers to 'cope with complexity', 'deal with complexity', 'manage complexity' and so on, and many books 'explaining' complexity. It is surprising how many of them, in what is a symptom of the industrialised, reductionist view of the world, offer solutions that claim to 'control complexity' as if they can have ownership of it, or power over it on their terms, or are able to suppress it. All this is in total disregard of the fact that complexity science has shown this to be impossible and real life has taught us all the folly of these ways. Some of the most notable examples of these failures to understand natural complexity have been seen in ecology – such as in the unwise introduction of rabbits into Australia, with the ensuing devastation of grazing land that followed, and the subsequent, clumsy attempts to control the rabbits by introducing the myxomatosis disease. Despite these lessons, few companies see natural complexity as either important or as a positive dynamic that, with practical assistance, can be exploited. Such biases affect how people approach a situation and how they design and select the tools and techniques to use in practice. For example, here is a quote from a Wordpress Blog: 'Complicatedness may or may not be dangerous – I would not know for I have no definition. But excessive complexity can kill systems!' Apart from the difficulties with terminology that we have pointed out earlier, the writer clearly has a basic assumption – complexity bad, no complexity good – which then probably colours subsequent thinking, inquiry and action.

As spoken of in the Introduction, in human endeavour people seem, generally, to face two types of situations – those which are open, dynamic, event-driven, human-centric and deal with natural complexity on its own terms, and those which are treated as if they are closed, stable, predictable, process-driven, organisation-centric and which shy away from engaging with nature. Yet people mostly apply the structured, closed 'institutional solution' regardless of the context and then express surprise at the unintended consequences that result when the situations are very complex. To illustrate why this Guide is needed and what it offers over what already exists, it is instructive to examine these two 'extremes' in more detail.

The closed, process-driven type of situation is typical, say, of call centres or global supermarket chains. Up front, assumptions are made (often unspoken) about the benign and predictable nature of the world. From food production through to customer purchases most things are assumed to be known, processes are harmonised and data is standardised. The default solution is to apply end-to-end planning and rational decision-making so that the enterprise is accountable, predictable, engineered and 'professional' – whatever the activity – from interrogating the tags on the ears of the cows, through to tracking the barcodes on the commodities for sale and monitoring customers' preferences through their loyalty cards. This is human activity turned into a 'mechanistic enterprise' – designed and optimised to provide maximum performance within a predetermined situation where all are assigned defined roles.

The second, open type of situation is typified by events such as a social night out with friends, community engagement initiatives, paddling down a fast river or dealing with sudden changes such as an economic crisis or with the appearance of novel markets. This is an open, unbounded situation, where most things are *not* known in advance and activities are more about grasping fleeting opportunities – it is about being positioned, by design, to be adaptive and able to engage with the changing situation to gain advantage – it is where standardisation would be stifling and diversity a valuable source of creativity and innovation. This is human activity as a flow of changing experience – shaped through circumstance and in practice, not determined by process, even in the face of the unexpected and unpredictable.

While both situations could be described as 'complex', there are differences between them that are self-evident. Table 1 characterises open and closed situations and illustrates the differences between seeing the world as 'closed' systems that are focused on detailed processes, such as in the global supermarket chain mentioned previously, and seeing things as 'open' situations, such as in the kindergarten example. It is these complex open situations and the ways-of-working that practitioners use that are the concern of this Guide.[12] Most importantly, where there is a tendency to perceive 'complexity' as a thing to be eliminated not fostered, we wish to demonstrate the opportunities it offers and to show clearly how the (largely untapped) benefits can be obtained.

---

12   Incidentally, there is a precedent for this duality in the human brain where the left side focuses on detail, e.g. on the things we are eating, and the right side takes notice of peripheral vision, e.g. on the big picture and on things that might eat us! See Carl Sagan's *Dragons of Eden* book, p 161.

Sees the World as Closed Systems	Sees the World as Open Situations
Usually a machine, or machine-like entity whose boundaries can be defined e.g. Supermarket chain, 'Production Line A'	Usually organic, social and/or natural situations where the boundaries can only be arbitrary/logical, e.g. a kindergarten, a refugee camp
System can be labelled, e.g. 'A bicycle' and would generally be called simple or complicated	Situation can be described, e.g. diverse tropical forest ecosystem, and would be said to be stable or evolving
Overall context seems routine/predictable; features and phenomena treated as repeatable	Overall context recognised as dynamic with features and phenomena in ever-changing tension
Planning and direction of the system, its construction and function can be handled by a single person	There can be no single locus that plans or directs all things, by definition a community, 'nurturing'
Function of the system can be controlled e.g. on/off	The situation has to be influenced and is 'always on'
Focus of attention is inward, on the parts and their relationships, the external environment is largely treated as being a stable constant factor	Strictly, there is no inward/outward, us and them; but generally the focus is on overall/outward behaviours in which the environment has essential influences
Reductionist thinking applicable – can be decomposed into individually testable parts/work-breakdown structures; is assumed that overall function = sum of the parts, i.e. linear cause-effect	Common-sense/holistic thinking is appropriate – the 'parts' are the phenomena/patterns arising from interactions at all levels over time – non-linear effects, always greater than sum of the parts
Structured methods followed which define techniques to use, e.g. process model to identify all parts, relationships and functions; aim for efficiency	Select from approaches/heuristics depending on the context/what needs to be understood/own 'role' and perspectives; aim for effectiveness
Said to be able to fully represent the system in a set of engineering drawings. Parts can be individually engineered, system is assembled in fixed order; can be re-assembled	Can only use abstractions to represent aspects/components of the situation – can never know/identify all 'parts'. Situation largely co-evolves/grows – different every time

Sees the World as Closed Systems	Sees the World as Open Situations
System performance is known and can be measured/specified in exact, absolute, terms; but, removing a single part typically causes total system failure – system is 'brittle', every part necessary	Performance is averaged, measured in behavioural terms – overall is robust, resilient and self-repairing/self-regulating regardless of presence/absence of 'parts' – individual parts not predictable/necessary
Mostly 'lean' and optimised; redundant parts are an overhead only included for safety/reliability reasons	Situation always contains 'expendable parts', hence resilience sought by opening up degrees of freedom

Table 1 – Comparison of Two Ways of Looking at The World.

By comparing the two ways we can see that dynamics are embraced and fostered in open situations, and that this implies the need for corresponding, complexity-aware ways-of-working. The general Approach to Putting Complexity to Work involves realising that, in these two types of situations, there are different types of phenomena at work that pose a variety of challenges[13] and require appropriate behaviours and capabilities to be employed. In open situations these need to be blended using approaches that will achieve effective, self-sustaining change. The blending is not about following a linear 'waterfall model' – it's about preparing for change and then engaging with the evolving phenomena.

For an organisation or entity to move towards being able to work constructively with dynamic situations in reality requires behaviours and competencies to be adapted appropriately. In general this involves:

A. Acknowledging the – clearly articulated, yet not widely understood – realities of complex situations and then dealing with the consequences by being realistic about the wide variety of patterns and phenomena

---

13   Some very nice practical examples that contrast these two approaches arise in an old BBC television series called 'The Great Egg Race'. In essence: two teams of 'engineers' were set challenges by Prof Heinz Wolff from Brunel University (UK) and, using only basic materials, the teams had to solve the challenge as best they could and construct a fully working solution. In the 19th June 1984 programme, involving Scottish Crofters and judged by the steeplejack Fred Dibner (a national treasure), the crofters' ingenuity outwits the closed thinking of the other teams. Wonderful stuff! See: http://www.bbc.co.uk/archive/great_egg_race/10805.shtml

faced, and the limits on what can be understood about them, based on experiences and intentions.

B. Knowing how to approach complex situations, being able to identify the useful features of the context and the tensions that drive the dynamics of change, and being flexible enough to match and continuously adapt the strategies used to engage with the realities of the context as they evolve – rather than following fixed, automatic repertoires of behaviour regardless of the circumstances.

C. Having 'complexity-worthy'[14] capabilities – and this also means having people available with the competence and confidence to employ these capabilities effectively. This includes the appropriate personal qualities (courage, imagination, scepticism, flexibility and open-mindedness and the ability and humility to perceive the situation from other viewpoints). Being able to adopt this open mindset is a vital enabler of success – and this means being open to change, being able to see change and to acquire the necessary information about it, being able to think about change and having the capability and practical experience to do something about change.

The guidance that we have developed in this book enables these changes in repertoires to be realised by practitioners. Later, we will go on to show, systematically, how to position yourself to deal with the various kinds of real-world phenomena that may arise. To this end, we have synthesized complexity science insights into a novel Approach which provides you with: ways of gaining a realistic appreciation of your context and the nature of change in that real-world context; an understanding of how change comes about and insights concerning what can be done about it; a practical Approach and techniques for putting those insights to work; and an indication of how to access and employ appropriate 'capabilities' for carrying out change in practice. The Guide does this in an holistic rather than a piecemeal manner across enterprises and enables a follow-through over time and scale to gain further benefit.

---

14   This term 'complexity-worthiness' was coined by our colleague Merfyn Lloyd. In the same way that one might talk about a boat being 'sea-worthy' in that it is fit for purpose and can cope with the unexpected, such as a stormy seas.

CAN PUTTING COMPLEXITY TO WORK BE EASY?

Yes and no! Yes – because people navigate their way through crowded cities and generally manage to deal with their busy lives so, in principle, dealing with complexity is an everyday skill. For instance, missing a train has a web of consequences and options to untangle, some of which are not quantifiable. People also work actively with complexity when bringing up children or tending gardens, when participating in local community initiatives or going dancing. Have you ever thought about how effortlessly people avoid each other on the dance floor without any knowledge of other people's intentions for example? Well, at least some of us find it easy!

And No – because purposefully setting out to change aspects of the world, especially over the long-term, is an art not a science. It is more like medicine – where you work with living bodies and make judgements – rather than engineering, where you can be certain about decisions. Why do many people find this tricky to do? Well, because there are understandable tensions between what people might need to do and the authorisations, obligations and constraints that they work under – they may not have the degrees of freedom, or the kind of capabilities, or the ways and means available to put complexity to work. If it's possible to understand why these things make practice tricky is there something one can do about it – are there principles one can follow and techniques one can employ 'systematically'? The answer to the last question is yes, and we present our Approach for doing this in this Guide.

Let's look at some of the things that do get in the way of putting complexity to work. Probably the biggest stumbling block is when the givens and realities of natural complexity are not acknowledged and reflected in people's attitudes, mindsets, capabilities and in the approaches employed. We'll talk more about these 'givens' in Chapter 3 and their consequences, but here's a few of the most important ones. Number one is the unspoken and unchallenged assumptions and biases. For example, people assume a level of predictability about the future that is not possible in practice, or they think they can accurately and precisely anticipate the reactions of complex systems when they can't. They assume it is possible to attain a high level of certainty about the behaviour of other actors and of leadership, societies, political systems etc. but, in reality, this is impractical because how can one predict human dimensions such as passion, imagination, willpower and cunning? Another example of a given came up in a discussion at our ECCS workshop about dealing with complexity, '...what is right in one situation may be inappropriate in another, we have to accept that there is no right answer'. There will be more of these contributions from practitioners in Chapter 2.

A reason why many scientific and engineering methods are not really appropriate when putting complexity to work is because they are predicated on limiting assumptions about the world, or because they set unrealistic boundaries. For example, soft-systems modelling and systems engineering, such as described in *INCOSE's System Engineering Handbook*, state that the required starting point should be to 'understand the problem', and that it is necessary to define the 'system boundary' and so on, commenting that it is unwise to proceed until you have done this. The justification being that it would be too risky to proceed without defining the task and the extent of liability. If, as often happens in the real world, it is not possible to gain such an understanding, then surely analytical paralysis will follow. But, if it is essential for practitioners to take action then these methods are, by definition, inappropriate. Cohen and Stewart (2000) use the analogy of 'looking down an upside-down funnel' from reality to the ever-expanding sub-structure and sub-sub structures of reductionist breakdown beneath. They make the point that practical understanding is not 'down there somewhere', but is to be found here, in the context where you are now. As natural systems are open, and by open we mean open – one cannot 'enclose' them within a boundary (where does one ecosystem stop and the next one start?) – so, any kind of arbitrary fencing-off is going to be limiting. Even when we move away from systems talk for a second and look to thematic maps, which represent boundaries in neat lines, one must realise that many of these lines are an interpretation of features on the ground – an approximation that does not necessarily exist in reality as depicted. The use of boundaries for analysis sometimes seems arbitrary – such as the way that crime rates are mapped to postal code areas despite the fact that criminals do not organise themselves by postcode. Hence the desire to bound the problem and treat the system of interest as if it is predictable introduces inevitable simplifications and assumptions that undermine the realities. People think they're making it easier by defining 'the problem' and then building a model, which they then believe in, but they're actually making it more difficult to understand what's going on, by excluding key aspects that would explain why the complexity comes about in the first place. It is sometimes as bad as Fyodor Dostoevsky (1811-1881) suggests:

> 'But man is so addicted to systems and to abstract conclusions that he is prepared deliberately to distort the truth, to close his eyes and ears, but justify his logic at all cost.'

The scientific method faces two challenges here. Firstly, real-world realities indicate that there are significant constraints on people's ability to observe and know about certain types of phenomena in practice. Hence, though scientific concepts or methods may be fine in theory, if you cannot gather the data you need to make them work in reality then practitioners can't use them. Secondly, externally-set targets and outcomes often result in some scientific research being done with the cheapest resources available. This can affect the conduct of the research, for example if the scope of the work is bounded and/or significant simplifying assumptions are made. Again, by definition, the output of this work, whilst providing helpful insights, cannot be 'real-world-ready' as the realities have been more or less deliberately sidestepped. We have seen many examples of this at conferences we have attended – and, worryingly, the conclusions of this research are often used to inform policy or other real-world decisions without due regard to the caveats. The 'Complexity of Global Change' Panel[15] at the ECCS '09 Conference highlighted these very issues and discussed how, if not addressed, they could limit both the ability to carry out academic research and to exploit findings concerning climate change. Though this is not a 'fault' of the scientific method *per se*, from the point of view of this Guide these limitations are factors that we have acknowledged and mitigated when developing our Approach.

Another thing that gets in the way is the 'predictability issue' – everybody seems to like certainty so much. But, as Niels Bohr (1885-1962) says, 'Prediction is very difficult, especially about the future'. In spite of attempts to predict, unexpected things happen all the time and it seems that people are not really prepared for them. The list of examples of natural or economic calamities or even personal disasters is long and we all need a way to deal with them. But the list of positive surprises that have caused tremendous changes in some people's lives is equally long – are you ready to make the best of those? One of the famous examples is the invention of SMS text messaging. According to the *ICT Facts and Figures* for 2010 by the International Telecommunication Union (ITU) the total number of SMSs sent globally between 2007 and 2010 tripled from an estimated 1.8 trillion to 6.1 trillion – a number which the Union helpfully translates into close to 200,000 text messages being sent every second. These are incredible figures that probably nobody imagined in 1992 when the first SMS was sent. With every network becoming capable of SMS in the mid-90s, and with the younger generation at that time picking up the messaging and making it part of their own defining identity, the technology became a huge success and it took the, then fairly young, mobile phone industry by complete surprise.

Engaging and influencing complex realities is also tricky because it requires flexibility in how behaviour is matched to situation. The real world is full of dynamic change where adjustments and adaptation are always needed, and this becomes very difficult when repeatability and certainty are expected and/or demanded. An example of the tension between certainty and change can be seen in attempts to 'lock-down' the Internet through policy and legislation. The richness of ways and means afforded by the Internet are huge and are manifested

---

15   The videos are available here: http://www.assystcomplexity.eu/video.jsp?video=78

through so many different types of behaviour, both human and digital, that finding a set of definitively 'clamping' intervention points for a policy is almost impossible. Another example of expected certainty and its consequences, can be seen in the logistic supply chains that provision supermarkets. These are setup so that 'just-in-time' supply[16] can be depended upon. This is achieved by optimising the links in the chain around median throughput patterns plus or minus a set degree of variance. Of course, these chains are only as strong as their weakest links and when external factors intervene, such as unexpected weather triggering people to alter their buying habits, the chains snap, and shelves quickly empty of food because resilience and 'wiggle-room' has been removed from the supply system. Once this kind of clamping down has been implemented it is hard to reverse and the removal of constraint means that the dynamics of 'the system' will now surge in an unpredictable way as natural complexity reasserts itself. However, this does not mean that removal of constraints is a bad thing *per se* – when appropriately employed as part of complexity-worthiness it creates space for possibilities and enables the flexibility and agility that is so vital for putting complexity to work in practice. As Jack Welch says, 'Willingness to change is a strength, even if it means plunging part of the company into total confusion for a while'.

What seems to cause trouble is understanding that what people do and are is part of something dynamic, something much bigger than ourselves, that has unexpected behaviour that we can't predict. Finding strategies and approaches that cater for these 'unruly' real-world phenomena is difficult. People's thinking is drawn towards step-by-step approaches – yet these are not really adequate for dealing with dynamic changes. For example, in project management, 'problem definition' and 'scenario development' are well-known steps that are not only treated as very separate entities but, once fixed, are largely untouched by dynamics and changes 'out there'. In reality, they, and all other enterprise activities, continuously interact and are interdependent. This also raises the question: who is bringing about change? As Figure 1, overleaf, shows[17] 'we', whoever that is, don't act alone. In any situation there will be many different kinds of drivers of real-world complexity that, in one way or another, influence what is going on, and appreciating this is one of the key lessons to be learned about putting complexity to work. Nothing in the world happens in isolation – change is always interdependent in all senses. What is appropriate to do in a context changes depending upon factors such as:

---

16   The wider consequences of just-in-time supply is that we now have an 'egg-shell' economy that seems to break rather easily when something 'unexpected' happens.

17   The 'PCtW' icons on the diagram represent some of the different kinds of objects and groupings that are active in the world of which 'we', as practitioners and individuals, are part.

who else is active in that context, what your relationship is to them, and their intent and complexity-worthiness. To engage effectively with these dynamics, we maintain that appropriate integrative approaches are needed and we will present ours in both theory, so to say, and in practice in this book.

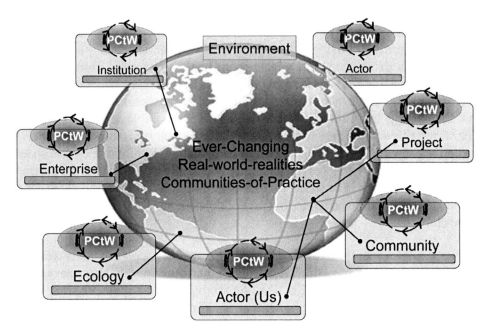

© abaci 2011

Figure 1. 'One World' – Some of the Variety of Drivers of Real-world Complexity

Apart from working with the givens of complexity and making appropriate assumptions about real life, putting complexity to work can be undermined by institutional factors. These include issues such as incentives and rewards, ethos, blame, the degree of initiative people are allowed, and so on. For example, there can be a prejudice against new ideas and ways-of-working – especially when it comes to using soft skills – involving people, tools and participatory techniques that are sometimes considered 'childish'. Yet, using these skills is a key part of 'complexity-aware' approaches and employing them effectively requires, besides the necessary mindset, a certain ethos in an organisation that promotes diversity and embraces the unexpected to trigger creativity, novelty and innovation and cross-pollination of ideas. We refer you to John Kao's book *Jamming. The Art and Discipline of Business Creativity* in which he describes the art of fostering creativity in organisations. These ways-of-working are aspects of the complexity-worthiness that we introduced earlier in this chapter.

In many working environments there are also accountability issues, which form part of the challenge for putting complexity to work. What should practitioners do with respect to 'plans', 'targets' and how to measure their success? This is no problem for results-driven sales and marketing – but the change people bring about in complex situations, given their purpose and intent, cannot always be isolated and/or measured; particularly because change often arises long after the end of a project or programme that envisaged it. And how will practitioners capture the benefits that will arise through novelty – the unexpected effects and opportunities that nobody had accounted for, or considered possible, during financial and project planning? The Approach we use in this Guide addresses this by providing alternative kinds of indicators that are suitable to use in complex and dynamic situations.

As to power-structures, some of you might have experienced what it means to literally take on the hierarchy of control structures. In Chapter 2 we will present some examples from practitioners who work directly with the supposed beneficiaries of development aid programmes yet find themselves at odds with 'the management' because of the way they do the work. We'll pick out a common theme here: practitioners find it profoundly difficult to get the message through to the donor organisations about what real life is like and what they have observed and learned in the field.[18] This is an important issue because, in the end, the donor organisations are the ones who design projects and programmes. All too often they remain fixed in their ideas – a 'communication problem' one could think. Well, that's part of the story but there is more to it than that. We know already that it requires a change of mindset and behaviour in general in order to be able to embrace complexity and to grasp opportunities. One could expect that change to come from the top – as a directive – or from outside, through public pressure from those who donate to big charities engaged in development aid. The public expects charitable donations to be spent wisely and asks for justification; people want to know whose lives has been changed, and in what way, with their money. So failure is not an option for those entrusted with the money, and when it occurs it is not good for the reputation of the aid agency or charity. Yet, even if they do fail, it doesn't seem to be a trigger for them to change their procedures in ways that enable them to acknowledge and embrace complexity more effectively.

---

18   By 'in the field' we mean on the 'front-line' of practice working 'among-the-people', such as in refugee camps, doctors' surgeries and so on – we are, generally, not talking about fields in terms of academic disciplines.

It turns out that in cases where people have tried with success to put complexity to work change did come about but not from the 'top' or the 'grassroots level', or from hierarchies, or prevailing opinions or lobbyism. Rather surprisingly, up to now, change came about mostly through the actions of a few determined individuals or groups not working at any particular hierarchical level. The secret of their success was in convincing their management, stakeholders, customers, colleagues, and bosses that, despite their different approach, they 'did not fail' in the usual terms and could also show additional unexpected benefits arising from putting complexity to work in their specific context.

So what are the benefits of a 'complexity-aware' Approach such as ours? First and foremost it is that achieving self-sustaining change is just that, self-sustaining! That means that it does not need to draw continuously on scarce resources to 'keep the project afloat' – it does that by itself. Complexity-aware approaches ensure that change is linked into the natural complexity of the local environment and to the energy, knowledge and motivation of the people who live and work there and who have taken ownership of the idea and implemented the changes. Self-sustaining change does not have to rely on outside support to keep it on track – the people involved can do that for themselves, if the conditions are suitable. Some of those involved in reconstruction in Haiti following the earthquake in 2009 have expressed concerns that are worth considering in this light, as for example Matthew Price reports on 12 January 2011 under the heading 'Haiti earthquake: One year on' or the aid worker Ian Rodgers on the same BBC news site on 11 January 2011. They seem to be asking: 'Are there too many aid agencies who, through busily 'implementing programmes', have taken the initiative away from the people themselves?' Or, 'Are the agencies waiting for the people to take up an initiative that they actually didn't have in Haiti before the earthquake?'. We examine the issues surrounding 'enabling conditions' for change in Chapter 3.

Concerning self-sustaining change then, we accept that it is not always easy to bring about – but complexity-aware approaches are better than many of the alternatives offered that don't stand a chance of success from the very beginning. Why? Because they take little account of the natural dynamics of everyday life, either ignoring or even destroying them, and instead impose a solution that must show 'benefit' within an arbitrary timescale. Often, these solutions will be implemented by a project team who come from outside the context and so, without local engagement, the project fails within weeks or months of the team leaving. Such outcomes do, sadly, occur far too often. We can say this based not just on our experience – it is also backed up by our analysis of other practitioners' observations. We have included these in Chapter 2 which is devoted to the opinions and experiences of the people working day-to-day with complex realities out there in the real world.

One key benefit of our Approach is that it exploits opportunities that would not be accessible to people using closed, structured, step-by-step approaches. As a simple example, think again of the surfer – standing on the beach gets you nowhere in surfing terms, you have to get out to sea to catch the 'big one'. And even if you do get out there, you cannot surf whilst following an instruction manual, you have to be capable and experienced enough to 'catch it' when it comes!

PUTTING IT TO WORK – WHAT'S NEEDED?

Although practitioners are getting on with the job of dealing with complexity, we have concluded from their comments and the discussion above that one could do more if the following issues, which would otherwise inhibit people's ability to gain value from complex situations, were addressed:

- become more accepting of the givens and realities of natural complexity and be prepared to challenge unspoken assumptions about how we all think the world is;

- acquire more appropriate mindsets, approaches and techniques;

- develop skills in being open to, and able to sense and work with, change and opportunity;

- move away from an understandable, but unrealistic, desire to measure at all costs;

- accept, and become comfortable with, the inevitability of uncertainty and unpredictability;

- appreciate that risk-averse behaviour, which tries to avoid 'failure', may stifle the opportunities for learning and advancement that come from the exploration of possibilities;

- examine and challenge power games and institutional structures that, though part of everyday office politics, will damage practitioners' abilities to bring about change in practice in the field;

- become more adept at dynamically matching behaviour to actual situations and at changing what is done on-the-fly;

- improve abilities such that they are more suited to practice and less focused on process, and more suited to open real-world situations rather than closed institutions – in other words, improve complexity-worthiness by building on the common-sense things that people do well already.

These are really just 'tips and tricks' which is why, right from the start of the Guide, and outlined in the Introduction, our aim has been to provide a pragmatic Approach that would address these issues. For the systematic appreciation of how change works in practice, the Approach consists of complementary parts interacting in dynamic loops: a conceptual framework ('the Framework' from now on) that provides the integrative aspects of the Approach; a set of Elements that enable the various aspects of putting complexity to work to be considered; and a pragmatic explanation of how to employ these in practice. Our Framework, by incorporating insights from complexity science, enables practitioners to describe the dynamics of their context and, because dynamics are on-going, what constitutes appropriate change. It also enables the differences and tensions, which can be accommodated, mitigated, leveraged or influenced, to be traded-off in order to be able to work out the available options. And, as one needs complexity-worthiness so that you can match and employ capabilities appropriately to the changing circumstances, our Approach addresses that need directly. In the next chapter we'll look in more detail at the experiences of practitioners in the community-of-practice who are bringing about self-sustaining change in the real-world.

CHAPTER 2: THE PRACTICAL NEED

'News, almost by definition, is unpredictable, unexpected. Even routine, scheduled events often contain unpredictable elements and when they do it is those elements which tend to define the event. There is a lot of information out there, but the bits we seize tend to be the unexpected.' *Robert Holloway, AFP Foundation. Speaker at the ECCS 2009 Workshop 'Putting Complexity to Work – Supporting the Practitioners'.*

'One group I want to draw your attention to are the frontline workers who are trapped in between that bureaucratic top-down and actual interface with the community. Dare I say, having been trained in the NHS as a GP about twenty years ago and coming back to work more recently, I feel that the heart and soul of general practice have been squeezed out by targets, by rules, by computerisation – and therefore to work like I used to work when I was in the NHS twenty years ago takes an enormous amount of effort, because the system is driving you towards numbers, diseases and processes as opposed to community engagement. I think the frontline workers in policing, in teaching, in medicine, are really the frontline everyday community engagement people and need to be empowered to actually really engage [with real-world realities] again.' *Professor Carmel Martin, Visiting Professor, National Digital Research Centre, Trinity College, Dublin. Participant at the ECCS 2009 Workshop 'Putting Complexity to Work – Supporting the Practitioners'.*

'Social Sciences were developed at the height of the Industrial Revolution, when Victorians thought they could control everything and could know everything. Social Scientists developing their theories back then were influenced by that mechanistic thinking. 20th Century technology and thinking has enabled us to see how the world is in fact a dynamic complex system. We are trapped in the limited mechanistic approach and need to change the way we do things. Whatever party is in government, we need a more sensitive government. It should be a nurturing part of our culture and not a 'Big Brother' part.' *Eileen Conn, MA (Oxon) FRSA MBE, Living Systems Research. Speaker at the ECCS 2009 Workshop 'Putting Complexity to Work – Supporting the Practitioners'.*

Let's now give the floor to the practitioners themselves – a wide range of professionals acting at different levels of decision-making and coming from a variety of working domains. The quotes above illustrate the range of issues that come to the fore when practitioners talk about the complexity of their work. These practitioners, whom we have met at many different forums, have articulated their experiences and explained in their own language why engaging with dynamic situations can be tricky. They have also listed the lessons they have learned from trying to do something differently. We have listened to these practitioners and have collected and synthesized their observations about the features they encounter in their own working context and the complexity issues they recognise and have to deal with.

Our compilation of practitioners' narratives has continuously expanded over the years. We made our observations in circumstances as varied as being a member on the board of a local civic society, from fruitful encounters with decision-makers (such as those developing transport policy), at business strategy meetings set up by the Santa Fe Institute Business Network, at workshops on topics such as 'Terrorism and Tourism' etc. organised by the London School of Economics' Complexity Group, at seminars organised by the development aid community on 'Complexity and Strategy' and 'Complexity and Evaluation', at UK Regional Enterprise Network conferences, and in the field.

It might not surprise you to find out that across the various domains in which practitioners work they had similar kinds of experiences when dealing with complexity and when trying to 'do things differently', and many common issues were raised. Some of these are apparent in the situations described in the quotes at the beginning of this chapter – such issues may be familiar to you from your own environment. This selection gives a strong impression that even when practitioners work in completely separate disciplines, on different issues within a variety of real-world realities, their experiences are equivalent. It is very interesting to learn that investment bankers struggle with the same sorts of dynamic patterns as conservation groups, for example. However, it is also worth noting the converse – that because they were operating in different domains with different ways-of-working, certain issues were on the agenda for some domains but not for others. These observations highlight the importance of context as a driver – a fact that is acknowledged throughout this Guide and which is implicit in the Approach for Putting Complexity to Work that we present in this book.

In order to draw on and examine these cross-domain deductions more closely, we ran a workshop called 'Putting Complexity to Work – Supporting the Practitioners', at the European Conference on Complex Systems in 2009 in Warwick, UK. We felt it would be particularly helpful to bring together theory and practice and invited both practitioners and complexity scientists. It was a great success and practitioners were able to learn about how to harness the insights coming out of complexity science more effectively, and complexity scientists understood the need to provide better practical, relevant support to practitioners in their day-to-day work. The material developed by the participants during the Workshop – in discussions, reflections and group work – has provided a rich source of inspiration in developing this Guide. Independent of their profession or engagement, the attendees identified similar groups of issues concerning practice during the Workshop and we have used these groupings as a guiding structure for this chapter.

WHAT IS COMPLEXITY, HOW DO WE RECOGNISE IT?

The way in which people perceive, recognise and understand whether situations are complex is diverse and thought to depend largely on their mindset, background, assumptions about the World and the context of their task. Hence, in our Framework, we have included an element where these perceptions and perspectives on the differences between what is simple, what is complicated and what is complex are considered. In our view, how people label the phenomena they experience will be different to the way academic complexity labels the same situation and so academic definitions are not helpful in practice. However, due to the lack of systematic options available to establish whether a situation is 'complex', specific requests have been made for a kind of 'symptom sorter' that helps practitioners quickly understand what kind of phenomena they are facing. You'll see in Chapter 4 that our Approach provides this by enabling practitioners to reflect about what to do and how to do it within the changing context.

Among those practitioners who have turned to complexity science in the search for pragmatic support there is a tendency to feel that they have to relate things to complexity science literature and to the 'tips and tricks' now widely advertised. They do this regardless of relevance, because they seem to feel that this gives their views 'authority'. We also notice that there seems to be a drive to 'translate' the everyday realties that people perceive into complexity theory terminology and then to try and explain them using this academic thinking. We are all familiar with relevant terms like 'Emergence' or 'Resilience' from everyday life – not least because these terms have frequently and increasingly found their way into recent newspaper and other media coverage about economic crises, epidemics, technology failures, tsunamis, earthquakes, snowstorms and other natural catastrophes around the world. The terminology has also gained a certain level of popularity and now regularly pops up in professional domains such as law, accountancy, in business management jargon and even on waste management sites. People have expressed their unease and insecurity at using this terminology in their work, as the words, concepts, (imagined) consequences and implications to some seem quite 'big' and difficult to grasp. They feel this even more so when they realise that complexity science does not immediately offer corresponding 'solutions' in relation to the terms; for example, how to go about becoming resilient or what to do to deal with emergent phenomena. The tendency of practitioners to translate from 'my complex reality' to 'complexity science-speak' is unnecessary in our view – as practitioners, especially frontline workers, often do recognise and understand the issues surrounding the complexity they face in their own context very well. They articulate and describe them in their own terms in ways that are perfectly adequate and usable for developing approaches, strategies and options. They contrast the contextual complexity with their experienced complexity and have developed effective ways of interacting with various issues arising from the dynamics and features of their tasks – mostly through applying common sense, and doing that with confidence is a virtue!

Practitioners have made a clear request for complexity science terms to be demystified and more clearly explained in a language that they can use. We certainly hope that, by the end of Chapter 4, you will feel that we have achieved this – by distinguishing academic complexity from real-world contextual and experienced complexity, and by providing a Framework that practitioners can use to describe their situation in everyday language as a basis for more effective and appropriate practice. Practitioners do not have to be 'impressed' by complexity science terminology in a way that would overwhelm them – we've selected the relevant terms, have clarified them and then picked out the insights that flow from them as part of the Approach we describe in this Guide.

Practitioners have also recognised that people have, largely, built their own 'complexity' – as they label it – through the various organisations, structures, rules, languages, views, abstractions and contrivances. In some situations, by ignoring natural complexity or by failing to appreciate their contextual complexity, businesses have been forced to become overly complicated 'internally' to compensate for the fact that they cannot deal with natural complexity other than by adding more rules and processes.[19] These in turn create situations that are experienced as complex and many of the practitioners we have talked to feel that 'we don't know how to make sense of our own complexity', that 'we lack pragmatic whole-system understanding', including how to engage with the situation in the real world. Such statements point at the experienced complexity of 'ourselves', the inner life of enterprises, individual projects and organisations, how people see and organise themselves, how things are set up,[20] what it is people think

---

19   A good example of this would be the introduction of increasingly draconian controls and sanctions to ensure that processes are followed 'correctly' to the letter – regardless of whether this deals with the real issues, the ones that experienced practitioners would identify. It is thought that Toyota Motor's 'sticking accelerator pedal' problem was of this type as Leo Lewis in his article 'Smoking gun memo reveals Toyota workers' safety fears' published in *Times online,* 11 Mar 2010, reports.

20   This theme will be picked up further in the complexity-worthiness explanations in Chapter 5.

they do and what they think their own role is in the bigger picture. Often what people have described as complex is actually a set of self-imposed difficulties and complications, but people have started trying to deal with them as if they are the kind of natural complexity phenomena that complexity science studies. Instead, these complicated rules and processes, labelled as complex when they are actually not, have inhibited people's ability to engage with the dynamic phenomena necessary for successful practice. The way to reduce this so-called 'created complexity' is to become more complexity-worthy – then many of the internal complications become redundant and opportunities become more apparent. Dealing with a sometimes vast range of real and perceived manifestations of this created complexity is a big challenge to many practitioners that one of the dynamic loops within our Framework, which we call 'Reflecting on Realities', is there to expose.

THE NECESSARY DIVERSITY OF VIEWS AND PERSPECTIVES

'For me, a landscape does not exist in its own right, since its
appearance changes at any moment.'
Claude Monet (1840-1926)

It is recognised among practitioners – though this experience varies from domain to domain – that in dealing with complex realities the diversity of perspectives and viewpoints[21] across stakeholders and actors must be accepted and employed. Comparing the various perspectives from different levels and scales and from multi-disciplinary viewpoints when considering a challenge or opportunity can deliver valuable insights. Following the start of the financial crisis in 2009, the new UK Coalition Government appealed to all levels of society to offer suggestions and ideas for improving services and saving money.[22] This was much more than just a community engagement survey, it was an attempt to discover insights that could only be revealed by people with a viewpoint that comes from being close to an issue in the way that a government cannot be. In doing this, the new Government was, in a way, trying to understand their contextual complexity. It is interesting to note that Government departments had not been able to collect this information through their institutions using their standard procedures – which says something about the kind of structural mismatch between government and community that we discuss later.

---

21 Viewpoints relate to the experienced complexity of individuals and/or entities of any type – 'How does the context seem to me/us from our viewpoint?'. Perspectives are various ways of looking at complex realities – i.e. economic, political etc. – that would be needed as part of developing and sustaining an appreciation of contextual complexity.

22 A website was launched: http://www.hm-treasury.gov.uk/spend_spendingchallenge.htm (as at Jan 2011).

The importance of understanding the context goes further: some aid projects or social policies have failed not least because, in scoping the issues to address, projects are often subject to external narratives that don't embrace local perceptions, realities and givens and are, therefore, ill-informed. Too often the way the problems are described, and the objectives are framed, impose outside meanings on local reality. A consequence is that externally-proscribed processes are assumed to be the way forward but without having the local knowledge, which is part of the contextual complexity, they cannot accommodate the realities of what enables or hinders change in the specific context being considered.

An issue often raised is how to deal with the fact that there are multiple stakeholders and multiple visions. How does one capture these visions from the real-world and how does one go about balancing them? Practitioners who work directly with communities 'on the ground' have learned that in complex situations outcomes can best be achieved by participation, i.e. that the people of the community, the 'beneficiaries' of a project, are probably best placed both to understand the dynamics of their environment and, in the end, are often the ones who can make the changes required most effectively. A good example, quoted by Amanda Ripley in her article, 'In Case of Emergency' (*The Atlantic* September 2009 issue), is this post-hurricane Katrina comment by the then (as of 2009) new FEMA head, Craig Fugate, who says 'We tend to look at the public as a liability. [But] who is going to be the fastest responder when your house falls on your head? Your neighbor.' A few years ago, Fugate dropped the word victim from his vocabulary, 'You're not going to hear me refer to people as victims unless we've lost 'em. I call them survivors.' There are a lot of examples of successful ways of capturing what we call context and of 'diagnosing' and of 'visioning' developments and scenarios with the help of participatory methods. In the development aid world these techniques have been used more systematically. Richard Chambers, in a very thorough chronology and analysis with many personal observations, describes their development and impact over the last few decades in his book *Revolutions in Development Inquiry*.

Accepting that externally imposed interventions are not the only way to bring about change is essential. This means that practitioners need to employ an approach which allows for: the collection of multiple narratives; the capture of potentially diverging values and the, sometimes conflicting, interests of 'the others'; the development of common ground in a language that is meaningful to the shared context; and feedback which informs the design of interventions. For us, this 'with and among-the-people' way of working is an essential part of practice. Practitioners know that the alternative, which is usually to commission reports by external consultants, may meet the conditions of 'the process', but rarely provides beneficial change in reality.

Practitioners have stated that ethics, trust and confidence-building are important in any collaborative approach and that a way of determining what is 'rightness' in a complex situation must also be factored into any analysis. But 'right' for whom? We refer you to an anecdote from Robert Holloway, which features in one of our case studies in Chapter 7, about a workshop with journalists in the Lebanon. He described the power of trust in bringing about change – specifically how the collaboration of the journalists, who came from different religious and political backgrounds, was fostered by the trust that built up gradually between them. The importance of trust is also underlined by Greg Mortenson. He has succeeded in the difficult endeavour of building schools in remote rural regions of Pakistan and Afghanistan, in order to promote the education of boys, and especially of girls.[23] Through gaining the trust of Muslim leaders, military commanders, government officials and tribal chiefs he managed successfully to achieve this. Greg Mortenson recounts in the book he wrote with Oliver Relin, *Three Cups of Tea: One Man's Mission to Promote Peace One School at a Time*, about when he was told the Balti[24] proverb 'The first time you share tea with a Balti, you are a stranger. The second time you take tea, you are an honoured guest. The third time you share a cup of tea, you become family' (p150). He learned that building relationships and getting to know one another was as important as building projects.

As a contrast, after the earthquake in Haiti in 2010, the deteriorating situation and the outbreaks of cholera undermined trust and confidence in aid agencies. In India, microfinance initiatives have faltered[25] because people, thinking that they are being exploited, have stopped repaying loans. Similarly, following the monsoon floods of 2010 in the Indus valley of Pakistan, accusations of political manipulation of the aid effort caused unrest and made a dreadful situation worse. Practitioners are aware that there is an understandable difficulty in building trust and allowing for emotions in a systematic way. Indeed, the word 'systematic' seems out of place when talking about ethics, values and human feelings but, as they are a key driver in any situation, they must be considered fully. This challenge is enhanced when working in foreign countries or with multi-cultural stakeholders, where different cultures and their, possibly unfamiliar, values and behaviours are the given reality to be factored in. Examples of successfully engaging with different

---

23 See for example Jonathan Foreman's '*Pakistan: Free to Learn*' for an introduction to Mortenson's work.

24 The Balti people live in Baltistan, which is in the Kashmir region of Pakistan.

25 For a discussion of this see the article 'India Microcredit Faces Collapse From Defaults' by Lydia Polgreen and Vikas Bajaj in the *New York Times* of 17 Nov 2010.

cultures can be found at each and everybody's doorstep[26] so you can probably read about great examples close to home in your local newspaper.

The capability needed for understanding different viewpoints and values and for building trust in complex situations could be described as a transdisciplinary[27] one, as it is largely about purposefully engaging with people who are probably *not* like-minded in order to gain insight from this variety. Practitioners are looking for support to improve their understanding of how to adapt to such conditions in their own context. This is partly about finding people who are effective working as facilitators at the interface between these various views, disciplines and perspectives and partly about appreciating the extent and value of this diversity to practice.

ENABLING EFFECTIVE COMMUNICATION AND COLLABORATION

'Whoever is not acquainted with foreign languages knows nothing
of his own.'
Johann Wolfgang von Goethe (1749-1832)

Good communication using appropriate language and behaviour for balanced negotiation are *essential* when working in challenging contexts. Practitioners feel that developing common ground and compatible modes of communication, language and negotiation techniques with the 'communities-of-interest' involved in specific contexts is important. They appreciate the need for cross-disciplinary approaches out of the knowledge that neither one person nor one group can assemble the understanding and capabilities necessary to alter a context in such a way that brings about sustainable change. Developing common ground and rich understanding of each other requires alternatives to the standardised taxonomies often used – such as ways of expressing the issues in terms that are relevant to all those who are sharing the real-world context, regardless of the artefacts used.

---

26   The 'Concrete to Coriander' project in Birmingham, UK, is one of these examples, portrayed by Caroline Beck in her article 'Home Comforts' in *The Garden* (August 2009 issue). The project aims at the integration of Bangladeshi women, who were often isolated because of lacking English language skills, into the wider community. The project turned a derelict car park in the city into a community garden where vegetables and, not to forget coriander, a vital ingredient of Bangladeshi cuisine, are grown. Part of the produce is taken to fairs and horticultural shows to sell, boosting the women's self-confidence.

27   Transdiciplinarity as described by Basarab Nicolescu in his *Manifesto of Transdisciplinarity*. Nicolescu says that trandisciplinarity 'concerns that which is at once between the disciplines, across the different disciplines, and beyond all discipline. Its goal is the understanding of the present world, of which one of the imperatives is the unity of knowledge.' (p44) He argues that reality is not something that exists on only one level, but on many, and that only transdisciplinarity can deal with the dynamics brought about by the action of several levels of reality at once.

Comments like 'We are spending a lot of resources [as a result of] having the wrong conversation' are often heard. In this particular case[28] it comes from the health sector and relates to how conversations between patients and doctors (to establish causes of pain reported by the patients) can lead to resources being wasted if only the physical causes of pain are considered. Recognising that pain can also be related to stress or socioeconomic conditions would allow doctors to have different conversations with their patients such that they, the patient and the healthcare system, apply more appropriate interventions.

A wide range of culture-dependent techniques for exploring contexts, for carrying out thought experiments and capturing issues are employed by practitioners and we will give some examples in the case studies in Chapter 7. Metaphors are often used, although some practitioners feel that they simplify matters too much. Innovative methods for multimedia documentation and communication, including stories, and alternatives to written reports such as audio, photography and video, are proposed in support of developing shared understanding with stakeholders. Importantly, these exchanges are as much about 'the people' educating the practitioners about their context as they are about the practitioners explaining what they intend/would like to do.

It is also recognised that there are many 'domains of discourse' to be accommodated (e.g. directing, ordering, agreeing, influencing). These arise because in communication between individuals, even in relaxed situations, there are overtones of status, position, power and expertise that flavour the conversations. When authority figures are present, people may say what they think they ought to say, not what they really think, either to gain favour or to avoid a rebuke. The domains of discourse affect how people communicate because they shape the atmosphere. Conversation in a business meeting can be quite bland and rather straightforward; when receiving directions people are generally attentive; when problem-solving as a team things can get noisy and animated. So, especially in challenging situations, one must be sensitive to these overtones and be prepared to influence them if the mode of discourse is inappropriate, especially – to mention them again – in culture-sensitive situations and/or with stakeholders and business partners from, or in, foreign countries. All of us know people who only communicate in one way and then complain that they cannot get their colleagues to do what they want. In community engagement, turning up to lecture 'ordinary people' on what they should do is almost certainly going to lead to disinterest, resentment or even hostility. Practitioners have, in this context, also noted the lack of good facilitators – people who are able to let opinions, ideas and topics emerge while guiding people effectively through the 'process'.

---

28 We refer to a paper by Pruscia Buscell titled 'Complexity and Change on the Reservation' in *emerging – The newsletter of the Plexus Institute*, p10.

The people we spoke to emphasised that developments such as the Internet offer new ways for people to organise (i.e. ways that simultaneously recognise commonality and difference) and communicate – with all the advantages and annoyances that computers can generate. News travels around the world in seconds and can be accessed worldwide through the Internet – and it's easy to press 'Reply to All' on an email when you didn't mean to! Picking up on this point, enterprises and institutions are very wary of mistakes in their 'domain of discourse' where this might lead to their brand being damaged. Social networking sites offer a chance for special-interest groups to pop up overnight and pillory some unfortunate executive whose company has just made a mistake. This ability for totally novel (compared to pre-Internet days) social structures to emerge has extended both the natural complexity of the real-world and hence the contextual and experienced complexity that we are all involved with. Our Approach specifically accommodates so-called cyberspace, the Internet, mobile phone networks etc., by recognising that it is a fundamental part of human life and therefore of practice – cyberspace is not, and cannot be, treated as separate from the rest of human endeavour. We are now all part of what has been termed the 'digital ecosystem' and so the 'people with whom we may organise' include software entities, 'agents' as they are called, whose motivations and behaviours are not like those of humans. Next time you get a 'People who bought this also bought' recommendation, be aware that you and others are being influenced by machine-generated information and that this is increasingly an issue when putting complexity to work!

LIMITS ON ANALYSIS, MODELLING AND VERIFICATION OF COMPLEXITY

> 'The only valid model of a complex system [that there can be] is the system itself.'
> *Murray Gell-Mann (born 1929)*

This brings us nicely on to the next issue that is often raised by practitioners. How can you quantify and validate models and tools for analysing real-world complexity? Under pressure to deliver predictable and repeatable results based on hard data a lot of practitioners' discussions revolve around which tools, models and techniques to use for various tasks. In complex situations, this becomes a difficult issue, or shall we say 'a bit more complicated'. When we ask the questions: Is real-world complexity as we have described it computable? If not, which techniques and tools are appropriate? we get very distinct observations. Here's one from the research side:

> 'Our models are being over-interpreted and misinterpreted. They
> are getting better; I don't want to trash them *per se*. But as we
> change our predictions, how do we maintain the credibility of
> science? We need to drop the pretence that they are nearly perfect.'
> *Lenny Smith, quoted in Pearce, F. (2007)*

This is an interesting comment in itself in that it puts the responsibility for the inadequacies of modelling on the users rather than on the models themselves: that they are '... being over-interpreted and misinterpreted'. In practice, there is a drive 'to quantify at all costs', and 'to predict' – not least because numbers are 'defendable' to the management and the decision-makers. Practitioners recognise that this drive for tangible outcomes can create distorted perceptions. It causes people to look for approaches that use indicators that, on closer inspection, turn out to be inappropriate for the context and consequently give 'wrong' significance to events. However, models do have their place. For example, the Santa Fe Institute's Steve Lansing has been dealing with issues such as rice growing in Bali and has used agent-based modelling to show that the strategies, based on social and religious controls, used by local farmers to determine planting times were robust and appropriate. The data was used not to tell the farmers something they already knew but to 'prove' to government officials that their centrally-imposed scheme was causing damage, and this persuaded the government to withdraw the scheme. The challenge for practitioners then is that they have been getting contradictory advice from the complexity science and modelling communities about the utility and limits of computability. Here's a view, also from the academic side, which we feel puts the case clearly:

> 'We do not have any idea how the people in our models will adapt
> to change and this is not new. The very fact [that] a generation ago
> we thought we could treat cities [as if they are] in equilibrium is
> testament to the limits of our knowledge. But I believe that what
> this is showing is that we need new forms of intelligence system
> to deal with the future where we will have many different models
> running in parallel, mediated by a context the seeks to 'inform'
> rather than 'predict'. The quest is to find the appropriate milieu in
> which to act this way.'
> *Prof Michael Batty at ECCS 09*

Many practitioners express the view that the utility of modelling for complex environments in practice is constrained by assumptions and other limits. Its use is complicated by the variety of boundaries that are introduced by the (hierarchical) levels and by the scales in time and space that have to be embraced in complex environments. In many environments in which people live, and where one tries to intervene and 'help', the realities are emergent, non-linear and unpredictable.

Practitioners who experience this as normal working conditions have learned to stop thinking in a deterministic way and accept that trial and error along the way may be better, and that mindset changes are required accordingly. One has to live with the fact that most real-world patterns, phenomena and behaviours are unpredictable – that they are beyond the so-called 'prediction-horizon' and are, by definition, 'unknowable' with certainty. In Chapter 3, we'll talk more about this horizon and why uncertainty is a fact we have to live with, and not an opinion to be dismissed, and what this means for practice in Chapter 6.

Concerning the quantification and validation of models and tools, practitioners feel that part of the problem is the mindset and the language used such as 'optimum', 'validate', 'prove', 'targets'. This language of 'success and failure' needs to change to one that recognises that it is in the nature of complex environments for phenomena to arise that cannot be 'measured' in this way. The idea of 'targets' itself needs to adapt – what are targets in complex situations and what is the relationship between targets? The measurement and the defensibility of the results and indicators that practitioners present in their work are very vital to them, but if targets cannot be expressed as tangible outcomes then different kinds of metrics are required. The mindset that has to be adopted must lead both to the formulation of targets appropriate to the change that can be achieved, and also to an understanding of the potential significance of relationships between what may sometimes seem to be conflicting targets. For example, the manager of a football (soccer) club may wish to maximise profit for the shareholders and an obvious way of doing this would be to cut back on player salaries. If the options were modelled using financial criteria, an optimum solution might be determined and targets set accordingly. However, determining the exact effects of these targets on player morale and performance would not be possible. Even the fact that the modelling had been done at all might be enough to change outcomes for the club because players might become disillusioned. Clever managers would consider some of these hypotheses in their head and come up with trade-off strategies such as offering the players incentives for improving their own, and the clubs', future themselves. Such incentives may have non-financial aspects, such as fame and celebrity status, that would be outside the scope of a money-based model.

What about the practicalities of this? Well, coping with the non-linearity of events and phenomena over time – i.e. that they do not always 'unfold' in a systematic way – is a big challenge. And a big opportunity! What kind of tools and techniques can one use to engage with non-linearity? How does one get from linear to non-linear thinking, from always using the same key variables for predictable outcomes independent of the context? And, how do we characterise a problem in order to choose a tool? Is there a tool for the problem? These are not new questions. Practitioners already have a good grasp of how to select toolsets that are appropriate for various phases in a project or for an on-going enterprise and have been using them in various domains with great success. In Chapter 5, as part of our Approach, we will be providing some 'appropriateness strategies' for selecting techniques for use in complex environments, which can augment those that practitioners already use.

THE EFFECTS OF FEEDBACK, FAILURE AND LEARNING

It is well understood that social phenomena underpin collaboration and purposeful activity. Practitioners in various contexts are very aware, in principle, of how feedback and learning in organisations comes about and how failure is handled. As a result, they have seen both good and bad examples of organisational and institutional engagement with communities, i.e. with the social phenomena with which practitioners are concerned. They know that things can be done better and are asking the question – How would you set out to create 'nurturing organisations'? (we answer this in the next sub-section). However, in addressing this topic one must factor-in the many others previously mentioned, such as: enabling feedback in dynamically-changing contexts, fostering trust to provide a space for negotiation, leaving room for 'error' which enables active learning from failures, engendering and recognising the value and utility of 'informal' (human-scale) interactions and adopting an appropriate mindset and language (e.g. of respect, recognition, power and incentives). Practitioners clearly perceive this as a challenge – not least because these factors are all interwoven. So rather than treating them as 'single issues', practice must include the necessary realisation that there will be many interdependencies with other relevant factors all of which contribute to what we called complexity-worthiness earlier.

Let's look closer at feedback and learning. Practitioners who pay specific attention to feedback and learning are those who are working with project and programme evaluations, for example in development aid or the health sector. In practice, these evaluations are, for the most part, kept separate from actions; and reflection on actions or learning from the specific context is often not carried forward to enable the question, 'have we made any difference?' to be answered in terms of the value/quality and 'goodness' of outcomes for the beneficiaries. Instead, what tends to happen is that the evaluation measures whether the project management has been successful in terms of the project methodology proscribed and whether the predetermined objectives were achieved. You may have seen the email going around with the story of a manager who used the 'Managing Successful Programmes' approach to organise a birthday party. He ended up rewarding the person in charge of the 'Implementation' Work Package because, by ensuring that beer was drunk according to a strict schedule and jokes were told in the right, predetermined order, at the right place and right time, people were so bored that they went home early and so money was saved. Incidentally, the party organiser got her bonus, too, for following the set method in a professional manner. This is a parody, but we have all seen exactly this type of thing happen in too many organisations and projects for it to be in any way funny any more – in fact it is shameful that it actually happens at all.

Nevertheless, there is the recognition, among those working in the field with actual beneficiaries, that evaluations can provide an holistic appreciation of the lessons learned, and that the learning benefit can be fed back to donors so that evaluation outputs *can* shape and influence both the proposal and the implementation of effective activities, projects and programmes. Those practitioners who work with public funding feel under pressure to be seen to spend money with demonstrable results in short timescales. Accountability remains a critical factor for a lot of practitioners and this points at the issue of power and control. Who in the end decides about approaches? The practitioners we have talked to also mention the important role that inhibiting or enabling rules, established within organisations and throughout project and programme lifetimes, can have on their success.

An example of an attempt to deal with this is from a government acquisition project. In essence, it was about changing to a more 'on-demand' way of working and away from one in which spending profiles were defined ten, twenty or even thirty years ahead. In the original process, funding and accountability were tightly tied into tranches of money, only available during a specified window of time and with specific conditions attached to each window – which meant that every year there was a panic to 'get the money spent' or there would be contrivances to move the money around. Whilst this process could work well in a predictable world it cannot in reality. The solution proposed and being prototyped at the time of writing is to move to a situation where packets of funding are tied not to arbitrary timelines but to outcomes measurable in practitioners' terms. Such an approach is flexible and enables trade-offs to occur between those accountable for the overall funds, the project managers and the practitioners. It does, however, require that acquisition approaches become more agile throughout and shows that this kind of organisational change is not without its challenges. That the changes are going ahead indicates what can be achieved when the issues are considered holistically.

So, in contexts where funding institutions or customers request clear results, practitioners feel that it is important to highlight examples of people already demonstrating adaptive, flexible approaches that succeed and deliver. In practice this obviously works better in some cultures, political systems and organisational structures than in others. Alternative ways of 'measuring' social change and development have been presented by Dee Jupp and Sohel Ibn Ali in their publication *Measuring Empowerment? Ask Them. Quantifying qualitative outcomes from people's own analysis* which describes an example from a social movement in Bangladesh:

> '... which managed to find a way to measure empowerment by letting the members themselves explain what benefits they acquired from the Movement and by developing a means to measure change over time. These measures, which are primarily of use to the members, have then been subjected to numerical analysis outside of the village environment to provide convincing quantitative data, which satisfies the demands of results-based management.' (p13)

What is necessary according to the practitioners is to – in one way or the other – make evaluation part of the entire project and to involve the stakeholders in the evaluation, so that there is a possibility for continuous learning and adaptation of developments influenced by constantly changing circumstances. This leads us on to consider how this kind of thinking can be spread across, between and outside organisations.

DYNAMICS OF STRUCTURES AND ORGANISATIONS

How to create nurturing organisations? If governmental, institutional and organisational structures are inhibiting – what are the consequences? Practitioners characterise these structures as too rigid, ossified, or clamped, which consequently inhibits the human-scale activities of concern to them. An important aspect in practitioners' daily work, especially of those directly engaged with communities, is how these formal structures of organisation and ways-of-working relate to 'informal' social forms of organisation, which are often (wrongly) dismissed as insignificant just because they do not present themselves with a structure that matches with those that government, institutions and organisations expect to engage with. Think of the Hurricane Katrina example again where the mismatch between the rigidly organised structure of FEMA, the Federal Emergency Management Agency (in the USA), and the conditions on the ground made engagement impossible. FEMA personnel waited until the US National Guard had brought about the kind of 'order' that would allow FEMA to start doing its job – the fact that survivors had to endure two weeks of misery while FEMA waited for the 'right' conditions is an indication of the size of the structural mismatch.

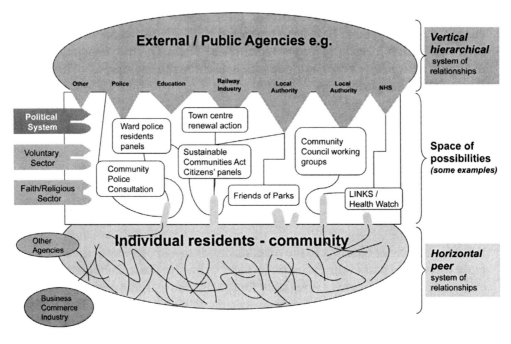

External / Public Agencies e.g.

Vertical hierarchical system of relationships

Other   Police   Education   Railway Industry   Local Authority   Local Authority   NHS

Political System

Voluntary Sector

Faith/Religious Sector

Ward police residents panels

Town centre renewal action

Sustainable Communities Act Citizens' panels

Community Police Consultation

Friends of Parks

Community Council working groups

LINKS / Health Watch

Space of possibilities *(some examples)*

Other Agencies

Individual residents - community

Business Commerce Industry

Horizontal peer system of relationships

© 2010 Eileen Conn Living Systems Research

Figure 2 – Social Eco-System Dance (SESD) Model showing the 'Space-of-possibilities'.

Being able to demonstrate the (potentially damaging) consequences of this kind of mismatch to policy makers and managers is an important concern for practitioners. On the one hand, there is structure in government, institutions and organisations which, it is assumed, will be found in other groups as well – which is not necessarily the case. On the other hand, because community groups are fluctuating phenomena they do not have conventional types of 'graspable' structures. This asymmetry between the 'top-down' and the 'bottom-up', as they are often referred to in terms of relationships and organisational dynamics, is well described by Eileen Conn in her paper 'Community Engagement In The Social Eco-System Dance – Tools for Practitioners'. She contrasts the horizontal relationship of fluid informal networking between peers in the community 'world' with the detailed structured regulation of the vertical hierarchical world of organisations, and illustrates it in her Social Eco-System Dance Model shown in Figure 2. Among practitioners there is a strong feeling that defendable alternatives need to be offered about how to work in the space-of-possibilities between communities and other structures, and with the 'intermediaries' in that space, and how to connect with them for mutual benefit. We hope, through this Guide, to help with the development of a better understanding of how to do this.

Why do these 'rigid, ossified, clamped' structures come about and why are they defended so strenuously in the face of clear evidence of the damage they may be causing? As we mentioned in Chapter 1, there are quite a few examples of difficult situations from practice where any attempt to apply a less mechanistic, more open view of the world in practice has been blocked outright. It may be that managers and decision-makers, who cling to the reductionist approach instead of addressing reality, feel threatened in their position and in their credibility. Power is manifested in five types of relationships that practitioners might find in their context. Rupert Smith in his book *The Utility of Force* defines them as: positional (I'm the boss), expert (I'm the doctor), referent (I am your champion, hero-worship, I'm a celebrity), reward and punishment ('justice') and 'people-power'. In the following chapter we will look at the reasons why such power dynamics arise.

Practitioners also express a clear difficulty with the mechanistic views of how people (have to) operate in organisations (e.g. the 'machinery of government!'), especially when these views underpin entire organisational cultures. Fixed structures are said to inhibit dialogue, lower motivation, take away responsibility, discourage initiative, cause disengagement and undermine the establishment of working partnerships. Hence, to some managers, the following quote might seem demanding:

> 'Don't tell people how to do things, tell them what to do and let
> them surprise you with their results.' *George S. Patton (1885-1945)*

Inhibiting set-ups within organisations also influence how the organisation perceives itself with respect to its customers, partners, and other stakeholders outside – and anyone who doesn't seem to be a 'team-player', as defined in the organisation's own terms, or who is an 'out-of-the-box' thinker, is likely to be sidelined. This brings us back to the question of who is in the best position to achieve change – and it may not necessarily be the person formally responsible – such that enabling initiative and creating ownership of the issues at stake among the staff, participants and beneficiaries is considered important. To implement such thinking in practice – i.e. establishing dynamic partnerships without the tensions brought about by inappropriate reductionist management methods – is perceived as difficult. Though this might be seen as just another business change issue, there is more at stake than just internal end-to-end change. A successful example of 'taking people on board' and creating ownership of the overall idea is that of Samsø, Denmark's Renewable Energy island.[29][30] Here, probably the greater motivation for the people to get involved was that of being investors and financial beneficiaries. The energy conversion that was implemented from 1998 onwards changed the energy production of the entire island to almost self-sufficiency from renewable energy sources. This was achieved through a combination of community-owned onshore wind turbines, which meet the island's electricity needs, and straw, woodchips and solar power for the heating supply on the island. Lastly, to offset the emissions of the island's transport, offshore turbines were installed. In the specific context of the project, the change agents were the local people.

Remember the discussion we had on closed and open ways-of-working in Chapter 1? Understanding the differences between closed systems, such as a bicycle that largely behaves the same way every time you use it, and open systems, as in human communities, is important. These 'systems' are totally different in the way they can be understood, engaged with and influenced and practitioners know that people want to feel comfortable about going into and working with such open-ended situations. In practice it is a big challenge for an organisation accustomed to a feeling of certainty through planning and forecasting, to allow for learning, to encourage risk-taking, and to move to a state where continual adaptation to a changing contextual complexity is the norm. Such flexibility is often derided, especially where the usual artefacts like project management schedules and flow charts seem to be absent. Comments such as, Don't you have a concrete plan? Doing all that hand-waving stuff, are you? Making it up as you go along?, are likely to be heard from those who feel that it is unprofessional to, as they see it, 'not know what you are doing', 'not have a Plan B' or to be making 'U-turns'. This transition from closed to open ways-of-working is tricky at the best of times, and so we certainly do touch on it and on transformation in general, in Chapter 5 and in our case studies in Chapter 7.

HOW TO EFFECT SELF-SUSTAINING REAL-WORLD CHANGE IN PRACTICE

So, how do you bring about change in challenging environments? At the heart of the Putting Complexity to Work Approach lies the issue of concurrently 'juggling' the dynamic loops we briefly mentioned in Chapter 1. That is, to reflect on the dynamically-changing realities and on practice itself at the same time. Think of our surfer; whilst surfing and dealing with the buffeting of the waves she is also noticing: what other surfers are doing so she doesn't run into them, how the wave

---

29 Listen to this BBC World service programme for more information: http://www.bbc.co.uk/iplayer/episode/p0040kgs/One_Planet_27_08_2009/ (accessed 21 November 2010)

30 For an insight into the setup of local village meetings on the island for the implementation of the plan read Chris Turner's *The Geography of Hope. A tour of the world we need.*

is developing and whether she feels she has the capability to deal with its challenge and 'drop in' on it – to catch the wave and start the ride. This is all 'on the water' behaviour; if the surfer were on the shore she might be doing other things such as stretching exercises, getting warm again or putting on suntan lotion (well, if you happen to surf in a sunnier spot than in the UK, anyway). She also might spend time learning from other surfers, watching what they are doing, which spot they choose to go into the water, etc. But doing the wave-catching exercises on a boogie board to get a feel for the ocean – she has to do that herself.

Practitioners feel that there is a need to be able to engage with the currently active dynamics on-the-fly – where there may not be time for extensive planning – and to understand how to do this better. They think that complexity science can support them in understanding the mechanisms underlying change and transition but they have expressed the need for more assistance in how to work appropriately with a given dynamic context. Because the changes required depend so much on the context – what is 'right' in one situation may be inappropriate in another – it is not easy to make hard-and-fast general recommendations as to what needs to be done with which kinds of techniques. Accepting the 'always-on' and ever-changing nature of the situation, which we, as practitioners, are co-evolving with, means being able to identify and describe the dynamics, to appreciate what triggers and drives them and to understand the nature of their impacts on the context. The interconnectedness of the relationships within open-ended situations means that people cannot make changes without these affecting the situation itself, their own configuration, understanding and capabilities, *and* their place in the events.

For 'Putting things into Practice' practitioners expressed the need to do things differently and, as a result, are looking for a comprehensive systematic framework they could use in practice. They would want to use the framework to assemble the 'change issues' that are part of their day-to-day work and from which they could gain an appreciation of their changing context and options.

SYNTHESIS OF PRACTITIONERS' ISSUES AND NEEDS

From this review of practitioners' experiences, four complementary strands have become obvious that we will build on throughout the book:

A. **Practice is Driven by its Context and the Environment.** Fundamental to everything people do is the nature of the environment in which it is done and the contexts which people can shape to support their activities – such as when a road is closed in preparation for a street festival. Everything arises from the givens and realities of the natural complexity in which its 'components' interact and phenomena emerge. Practitioners are not immune from these fundamental drivers that must be factored into their considerations.

B. **Practice is all about Working with the Dynamics of Real-world Change.** The dynamics of challenging contexts requires practitioners to engage with the ever-changing phenomena *while they are available* if self-sustaining change is to be achieved. Given the widespread acceptance that these situations are generally transient means that they can only be influenced by affecting the 'mechanisms' that cause them to arise – be they social or environmental or a combination of these.

C. **Practice is Modified by Contemplation and Reflection, which go hand-in-hand with it**. Within dynamic contexts, specific states of contemplation and reflection about the changing situation are required. This continuous consideration of contextual and experienced complexity, and the factors surrounding the practicalities of influencing in the specific context, enables the practitioner to judge and adjust the appropriateness of options and interventions.

D. **Effective Practice Depends upon and is Augmented by Complexity-Worthiness**. It is increasingly appreciated that context-specific types of capabilities need to be available so that the various 'spaces of possibility' can be explored and the overall dynamics can be engaged with and exploited. All the other strands of practice mentioned above fall flat without appropriate complexity-worthiness.

In the next chapter we will investigate some of the insights from complexity science that practitioners have been asking about. Specifically, we will show that in many contexts complex phenomena can be explained and understood and that insights based on the understanding of these scientific explanations can form the foundation for practical solutions. We will have a look at these insights and show how they can be used in a way that addresses the issues and needs raised by practitioners in this chapter.

CHAPTER 3: COMPLEXITY SCIENCE PRINCIPLES, CONCEPTS AND TECHNIQUES

'We delight in the beauty of the butterfly but rarely admit the
changes it has gone through to achieve that beauty.'

Maya Angelou (born 1928)

Building on the practitioners' observations about complex realities, this chapter reviews, through the practitioners' lens, what complexity science can offer to practice in a form which is real-world ready. It does so because the converse, looking at practitioners and practice through the complexity science lens, would not have provided material that was directly usable. Complexity science has produced many important insights about complexity, the phenomena that arise and the underlying science that explains them. However, as these insights are couched in the language of 'academic complexity' and are often researched separately in specialist areas, they are not accessible to practitioners without the kind of interpretation and synthesis into everyday concepts that this book provides. Practitioners need to know how complexity works in their specific context – they know what it is because they deal with it every day, but they want a better understanding of what they can do about it in a practical way and on their terms.

What we will do first in this chapter is explain a bit more about academic complexity and how we intend to make use of it. We will then indicate what its insights have to say about the issues raised by the practitioners in Chapter 2. Next, as part of getting the mindset, we'll bring key insights together into a set of underpinning concepts that inform our Approach and from which stem the techniques that you can use as part of your practice when putting complexity to work effectively. In this way we'll make the link between practitioners' needs and the relevant complexity science insights and we'll then discuss what to do differently as a result.

ACADEMIC COMPLEXITY – UTILITY AND LIMITATIONS

Some complexity scientists may feel that the way to deal with complex realities is to 'teach the practitioners complexity science'. Is it necessary to become a complexity scientist to put complexity to work? Do practitioners have to learn the scientists' language in order to be able to employ insights? We think not. Effective ways of interacting with phenomena in specific complex situations have been developed in many domains and, whilst these domains are certainly not free of unintended consequences, people are not paralysed into inaction by a bewildering difficulty in understanding complexity in their context.

You may have assumed that this Guide would have started with a tutorial on complexity science and then asserted that mastering this was a necessary precursor to putting complexity to work. There are many explanations of 'complexity' available from the plethora of academic and 'pop-science' resources (see the References for a selection of them) and we felt it would be pointless to try to duplicate them here. Also, there are pragmatic reasons why 'starting with the science' would not have been appropriate for this practitioners' Guide. One is that the research focus of complexity science itself does not allow for the specific nature of the dynamics and features of the contexts in which practitioners work. In this way by, in effect, treating all contexts as if they have the same homogenous characteristics, the crucial role that context has in shaping complexity is excluded. Other reasons that we summarise here are that:

- practitioners have no option other than to embrace the unavoidable realities of the real-world environment. Scientists can make 'simplifying assumptions', to avoid/sidestep these dynamic realities – which practitioners cannot do;

- the practitioners' contexts or needs must be taken into account on their own terms – however tricky those are to engage with. Scientists would need to 'translate' from the academic to these practical terms if their work is to be both directly relevant to practitioners and ready for them to employ;

> 'More of the concepts of complexity need to be turned into practical approaches and examples more widely shared ... some of the language is terrible, terms need to be demystified or more clearly explained'.
>
> *ECCS '09 Workshop Participant*

- it is essential to cope with multi-perspective/multi-viewpoint motivations and the variety of human behaviours, values and interests, especially of non-institutional/informal actors, as these are the practitioners' main concerns. Scientists often assume, for simplicity, that human actors are homogeneous and behave in 'classes'. This means that the deductions they make from the results of their experiments are not representative of the real-world;

- the dynamically interconnected nature of real-world issues must be addressed head-on. Scientists often address issues in their scientific discipline in isolation/in the abstract and discount the wider environment;

- because it is impossible to carry out formal validation and verification of models in truly complex situations practitioners might be misled if they gave too much credence to the 'results' from modelling. Scientists can carry out test series under certain assumed conditions, whereas a field mission in a natural hazard area is almost impossible to simulate;

- even 'non-complexity' disciplines such as biology, although they do use complexity science explanations, still tend to focus on the theoretical rather than the practical.

This is why we provide practitioners with an alternative approach, which is not complexity science-centric. In Chapter 1 we coined the term 'academic complexity' to refer to the descriptions and explanations of natural complexity, and which scientists have developed and delivered in the abstractions of scientific terminology. These descriptions may provide scientists with a 'rigorous underpinning' to the topic but this is not considered helpful to practitioners. Our Approach starts from the realities of the practitioners' viewpoint and then works back into identifying and articulating the insights from complexity science that are relevant to practice.

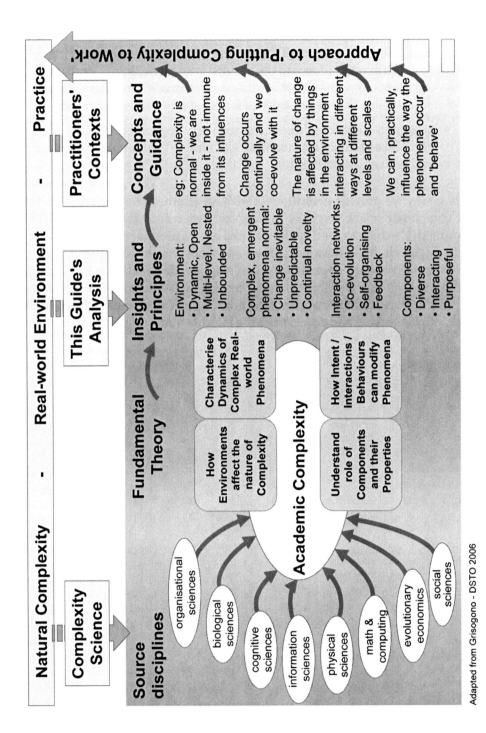

Figure 3 – Academic complexity in the Context of this Guide.

We've shown academic complexity on Figure 3 so you can see how its insights and principles are translated to form the basis of the Approach that we present in this Guide. A single unified 'Complexity Theory' does not exist. Most theoretical complexity approaches originally stem from physics and computer science in particular, but also from mathematics, ecology and biology. Other scientific subjects, such as sociology, economics and psychology, have embraced complexity science from their disciplinary viewpoint, studying and researching complex phenomena and the fundamental rules that underlie all these disciplines as well. Academic complexity is generated from the source disciplines which output insights and principles – the question is, which ones are useful to practitioners? Well, the fundamental theory underpinning these insights is linked to a taxonomy of phenomena – each of which complexity science explains separately without saying much about how they relate to each other or what the insights mean in practice for 'doing things differently'. Here's a typical taxonomy based on those developed by Eve Mitleton-Kelly in *'Ten Principles of Complexity and Enabling Infrastructures'* and elaborated on in Ben Ramalingam and Harry Jones' working paper *'Exploring the science of complexity: Ideas and implications for development and humanitarian efforts'*:

A. Self-organisation and self-regulation[31]: the tendency for order and structure in the real-world, such as clouds and forests, the asteroid belt and so on to come about spontaneously without there needing to be a plan or someone in charge.

B. Emergence: the way that dynamic phenomena, like flocking and swarming, arise, are sustained, and disperse as a result of interactions between things in a way that cannot be predicted by looking at the things in their 'static' state. The whole is always different from the sum of the parts.

C. Connectivity and Networks: that these interactions can also be thought of in terms of networks of relationships between nodes and that these networks have certain performance properties in terms of their resilience and the ways that messages propagate across them.

D. Connectedness and Interdependence: that these relationships and interactions create interdependencies that we see in nature – in symbiotic or parasitic relationships and in enterprise in the links between customers and suppliers and so on.

---

31   Part of a list sometimes indicated by the term 'self-*', where the star (*) substitutes for self-organisation, self-monitoring, self-generation, self-maintenance, self-regulation, self-sustaining, self-adaptation etc.

E. Feedback: that through these networks of interdependencies and interactions feedback can occur where actions of one type in one place can have different consequences in another place.

F. Far from equilibrium behaviour/non-linearity: where the way that emergent phenomena change is not proportional or, other than in general terms, predictable – where a relatively small input, such as the actions of a single stock-market trader, may produce disproportionate sizes or qualities of change over vastly different scales and timescales.

G. Co-evolution: is the way that any change not only affects the wider world but also affects the initiator of change, so that all co-evolve together. It means that interventions never quite work the same way twice as the world will have moved on since the last one.

Surely this taxonomy explains some of the things we all see in the real-world? Well, in a way, yes – but it leaves practitioners to put the pieces together and to work out the practical implication for their context. As Figure 3 shows, we have taken this taxonomy of insights and translated it into useful concepts and guidance and have embedded these in this book. This is very different from the many papers we have seen recently, which take a practitioner's context and then break it down under each of the types of phenomena above – the emergence that was noted, the co-evolution that was detected and so on. In a way, this is close to a type of reductionist breakdown. In this kind of research, the situation has been analysed and separate insights deduced but what difference does applying the labels 'emergence', 'non-linear' etc. make in practice if there is no synthesis of the implications and consequences?

If you consider our surfing example, practitioners and complexity scientists would think about this situation in very different ways. Complexity scientists would research the phenomena and, say, examine the types of turbulent or smooth waveforms. They would analyse and describe surfing using theories about how the surfboard might behave or work out how to model the dynamics of the collapsing wave front in relation to the beach profile underneath – in other words from an academic complexity view. In contrast, practitioners would consider how they experience this situation, what they would 'do' on the surfboard, how it affects their context and the circumstances that they find themselves in, and what are the related phenomena – such as fads in surfing and its appeal to young people. For practitioners, these sorts of things are their 'complex realities' and they understand that these generate the challenges and opportunities that they face in practice.

In addition, when merely complicated, deducible, situations are mis-classified as complex or chaotic this may lead practitioners to try to seek out and deal with an assumed complexity which isn't actually there in the context. In fact, there may just be self-generated difficulties arising from the inappropriate use of rules and procedures etc., which can be addressed in more direct ways. We deal with these issues in our Approach by providing a 'Symptom Sorting' concept to unpick these issues so that practitioners do not, as some complexity scientists want them to, need to analyse the complexity and its causes in academic terms. Instead they appreciate that, despite this underlying complexity, there are 'simplicities' evident in practice that they can work with and they are adept at doing this on their own terms (the 'child pouring milk for a cat' is an example of this). It is worth noting that practitioners deal with the 'natural context', whereas those back at headquarters in their offices tend to use rational analysis along with a 'constructed context' that they have largely developed for themselves – we'll come back to the consequences of the differences between these contexts in the case studies later in the Guide.

As an example of what rational analysis can do to practice, let's consider Shostakovich's Quartet No. 2 in A major, Op. 68. In 1941, during the Second World War, the composer Dimitri Shostakovich was evacuated from his home in Leningrad, then under terrible siege, to Kuibyshev, in the country. The Second Quartet was written at Ivanovo in 1944 in a 'House of Rest and Creativity' – a government-sponsored rustic retreat for writers and composers (see Stephen Harris' article 'Shostakovich's String Quartet No. 2'). Shostakovich described the second quartet, a passionate and deeply moving piece reflecting his dreadful wartime experiences, to the writer Daniil Zhitomirsky 'is "a valse macabre". And if it were compared to the classics, it should be compared to the Waltz from the Third Suite by Tchaikovsky' (quoted in Paul Epstein's *Notes to the Emerson String Quartet recording Dmitri Shostakovich: The String Quartets*). In contrast, here's how the piece was described in 'correct' musical terms in the programme of a concert we recently attended:

> '. . . The second theme is loud and energetic, like the first, but can be distinguished by its use of dotted rhythms on repeated neighbouring notes. The comparatively long development rises to a climax which exhibits the relentless rise in tension that is typical of Shostakovich. After this, the two themes are calmed down, the first in longer notes with pizzicato accompaniment, the second with dotted notes ironed out of its alternations. The recapitulation is short and uncomplicated... The central *Romance* begins with a cello taking over the motif, and the music then becomes more flowing with a mainly waltz-like rhythm; once again there is a rise in tension at the centre. The recitative returns at the end'
> (*Cheltenham Music Society Programme, 13th November 2010*).

Whether this analysis was written by the Takacs Quartet, who performed the piece with astonishing and wonderful expression and verve, or the Music Society, we do not know. The point we wish to make here is that, for practice, such impoverishment of expression is unhelpful as it strips out the essence of what drives human endeavour. Following on from this there is one final and very important point to make based on this quote from Richard Feynman (1963):

> 'The next great awakening of human intellect may well produce
> a method of understanding the qualitative content of equations.
> Today we cannot see that the water flow equations contain
> such things as the barber pole structure of turbulence that one
> sees between rotating cylinders. Today we cannot see whether
> Schrödinger's equation contains frogs, musical composers,
> or morality – or whether it does not. We cannot say whether
> something beyond it like God is needed, or not. And so we can all
> hold strong opinions either way.'
> *The Feynman Lectures on Physics, Volume II, p41-12*

If complexity science has almost nothing to say about the qualitative aspects that are the bread and butter of practitioners' work – such as trust, emotion, values, ethics and so on – then this is a serious limitation. These aspects are all the sorts of things that were highlighted in Chapter 2 by the practitioners as being crucially important to successful practice. It is because of this shortfall in complexity science that we have no choice but to select and translate academic observations that are useful into a form that can be applied to practice.

RELEVANT INSIGHTS AND PRINCIPLES FROM COMPLEXITY SCIENCE

In this section we aim to bridge the gap a little between these two very different ways of looking at the world. For complexity scientists, it is a universal truth that complex phenomena come about when at least these four conditions are met – these are the 'axioms of complexity', which we have mentioned before in Chapter 1. As a reminder they are:

- a suitable environment in which the phenomena can arise and be sustained – in the surfing example, the sea, the beach and their surroundings – the fundamental givens and realities;

- the 'components' or entities in the environment – in the example: objects in the sea, the water itself, the surfers and their equipment, which have suitable attributes and properties that enable them to interact with each other in novel ways;

- the interactions of the 'components' in the environment – such as the contact between the surfer and the surfboard and the board with the sea – and, where relevant, the purpose and intent that drives them;

- the dynamic patterns generated from the interactions which are persistent enough to be detectable as features – i.e. the emergence of complex phenomena appearing at different times, at different scales and in different modes (sound, light, force, signals). In the surfing example, these features include: waves, eddies and whirlpools, speech, human courage and so on.

Together these generate the phenomena of natural-complexity which complexity scientists study and which they describe in the language of academic complexity. In the 1970s, at the Santa Fe Institute in New Mexico, USA, the term 'complex adaptive systems' (CAS), was coined to describe the role of information processing in natural systems i.e. that CAS are adaptive, that their individual and collective behaviour changes as a result of experience and communications among them. CAS are complex systems that have the capability to respond to prevailing conditions, for example cells, bones, organs and muscles in a human body, fauna and flora in nature etc. CAS co-evolve with events in their environment. Their reactions and activities in turn can affect other CAS, possibly triggering activities that propagate from one entity to another. While these interactions are initiated locally between immediate neighbours, their effect can propagate widely. A precondition for the interaction and connectivity is that the elements can sense and communicate with each other at some level. A whole domain of CAS research opened up and led to the study of agents, swarm intelligence and other sorts of collective behaviour typical of life (see for example Steven Levy's book *Artificial Life*). Swarm intelligence describes collective behaviour in decentralised, self-organised, groups that are typically made up of a population of 'agents' interacting locally with one another and with their environment. Although there is normally no centralised control structure dictating how individual agents should behave, local interactions between them often lead to the emergence of global behaviour. Examples can be found in nature, such as ant colonies, bird flocking, animal herding, bacterial slime moulds and fish schooling. In the late 1990s, Graham Mathieson in his paper *'Complexity and Managing to Survive it'* extended this work to include the notion of 'complex adaptive reflexive systems' (CARS), where intent and the reflexive, self-aware, aspect that is missing from CAS research is necessary to explain the behaviour of so-called purposeful entities – such as animals, people as consumers, social groupings and even institutions (and maybe, in the future, robots). In society, human 'swarming' can be found in flashmobs, riots, in overnight Internet sensations, in fashion trends and in community practice. In a nutshell, this body of excellent and imaginative research, along with the study of causality and system dynamics, constitutes the academic complexity that we refer to in this book.

In the rest of this chapter we intend to draw out from this and other academic work some of the insights and principles that we will include in the formulation of the concepts underpinning the way our Approach is used to put complexity to work. We'll first look at the givens and realities and then, based on an extended set of the 'axioms', at the insights that follow. These include: the role of environments; the dynamics of emergent phenomena; purposefulness and intent; and 'components', their properties and interactions. We have grouped the rest of this chapter under these headings.

Fundamental Givens and Realities. The first set of insights we want to discuss arise from a point we have made before, that there are some things in the world which 'just are' – they are givens and realities about which we humans can do little. However, in practice, they form the very essence of the natural environment in which people work and so they should not, must not, be ignored or discounted. So what are some of the givens and realities and in which ways are they relevant to practitioners?

A. **Complexity is Normal.** The first one is that complexity is a normal, everyday phenomena arising from the natural world. For example, as individuals people navigate their way through crowded cities and generally manage to deal with their busy lives so, in principle, dealing with complexity is an everyday skill. Related to this is the fact that complexity offers opportunities, such as the fun of surfing or the opportunities of new markets, which people take advantage of all the time. It is such a pity that you hear people talking about complexity, chaos and the randomness of things in one voice – usually in a negative context. Such a mindset, unfortunately, precludes people from seeing the possibilities and opportunities available in the world and, instead, drives them to look 'inwards' for manufactured and contrived solutions. As there are lots of phenomena available 'for free' out there, part of the job of practitioners and communities is to look for these and turn them into an advantage, which is often about grasping fleeting opportunities. As we'll see when we talk about purpose and intent below, sometimes people feel that they need to have 'permission' to use their initiative despite the fact that they use it all the time in a common-sense way.

B. **Change is Continual and Inevitable.** Another given is that change comes about continually and inevitably – it occurs everywhere – not just out there, so we all change with our world via unavoidable co-evolution. It is complexity itself that generates this endless novelty spontaneously through emergence. Accepting this dynamic, the always-on and ever-changing nature of the situation within which we, as practitioners, are 'co-evolving' means appreciating that people cannot make a change without affecting both the situation itself and people's place in the changing events. This is one of the reasons why practitioners need to reflect iteratively on the realities of their context and on the conduct of practice in order to give space to consider what is occurring through co-evolution.

C. **Underlying Complexity can be Grasped.** Just to reiterate the given here – complexity science has indicated how these complex, emergent phenomena arise. It states that in any environment where entities, especially purposeful ones, interact then people will see complex behaviour occur at many levels and scales. Complexity science also tells us all that the nature and dynamics of these complex phenomena are fundamentally affected by the nature of the environment, and the properties and abilities of the interacting components/entities that generate those phenomena. The insight for practitioners is, then, that complexity is not a mystery, it is something people can, within limits, make sense of and do something about without having to delve into the details.

D. **Causality can be Influenced.** This leads on to the issues of causality and determinism. Generally, people have a simplistic view of them and talk in terms of finding 'the cause' of an effect, or 'the person' to be held responsible for something, or 'the cure' for a problem etc. This focus on singular or primary causes is called direct causality and is usually understood in terms of events unfolding (as if they already existed somewhere, 'ready' to be unfolded, which they are not), and with each effect inexorably determining the next, like a machine. Alternatively, so-called systemic causality thinks in terms of networks of criss-crossing causal relationships through which consequences propagate and interact – exhibiting emergent behaviours along the way. It is possible to make complex environments appear simpler by restricting the scope of attention to a particular pathway, by just considering one of our surfers at a time, for example. This thinking does not help practitioners intervene effectively in complex environments as there is no exact way of working out if side-effects or unintended consequences will arise. One must accept, therefore, that multiple interacting pathways exist in general between an event or property of a complex situation at one time, and a property of interest at some later time. Also, as the nature of this causal influence is 'many/multi-modal/multi-scale'[32] some interactions will not be apparent to observers with particular mindsets or viewpoints. In reality, there will always be aspects of the evidence that link so-called 'causal elements' together that will remain unknowable – a mystery whose causes are apparently invisible and undetectable. However, despite not being able to identify exact causes or predict outcomes with any precise certainty, complexity science insights can be used to develop techniques for influencing situations and triggering change as a way of exposing the drivers of a context and hence of discovering options and possibilities for practice. We provide an example of how these techniques can be applied in what we call the 'Landscape of Change' in Chapter 6.

E. **There are Limits to Prediction.** An underlying principle that follows is that many different options being considered may result in similar outcomes and the converse, that similar options may generate very different outcomes. This is because it is not possible to detect, observe or know all the things that are going on in reality, so exact prediction of the effect of outcomes is not possible. In 'real' complex contexts there is a distinct prediction-horizon. This prediction-horizon is a vital concept to embrace. Reliable, specific, predictions can only be made about things that are relatively static in their nature (such as the physical geography of an area, which enables predictions to be assumed to be valid a long way into the future), or highly dynamic yet certain (such as mobile phone infrastructures, which can be modelled within constraints), but only a limited way ahead before the prediction-horizon is reached. Beyond this horizon, for everything else (especially the highly dynamic and intangible such as emergency response activities – where the phenomena are on many scales and manifest themselves in many ways), individual outcomes cannot be systematically predicted at all. However, from this practitioners understand that it is possible to foresee the emergence of patterns, and/or features, in complex situations in general – such as the likelihood of disorder if a food truck arrives unannounced in a refugee camp of hungry people – where the 'causes' of the behaviour are fairly self-evident. However, in our experience, practitioners are usually not interested in trying to predict the kind of specific instances of behaviour that might vex complexity scientists. For example, consider a city where we know that the traffic accident statistics at a set of traffic lights by a bar selling alcohol will be higher on Friday and Saturday

---

32   Multi-modal, i.e. propagate via many means such as sight, sound, pheromones, physical contact etc; and, multi-scale, i.e. from the level of chemical elements to the level of human society and from milliseconds to millennia.

nights around the time that the bar closes. Again, the 'causality chain' is self-evident. However, it is a completely different class of problem to try to predict the exact instance and causal chain leading up to Mr Blogs-Smith having an accident in his Ford Ka at the same traffic lights at 2316 hours on a specific day. In reality, it is impossible in practice to predict in this way. Even 'after the fact' it may be almost impossible to work out, beyond reasonable doubt as the police might try to do, exactly why the accident occurred. The key point here is that, for practitioners, causality in relation to the emergence of patterns is of interest but causality concerning specific instances is not.[33] Which is why, in practice, practitioners just accept this and are more interested in engaging in 'a journey' and through learning-by-doing, adjusting the route and 'themselves' as they go along. The alternative is to avoid action until one is certain of what to do – which one can never be.

F. **The World is Messy.** Complexity science tells us all that capturing a full, reliable and accurate representation of the factors that generate specific complex phenomena is almost impossible. This is because most of the information required is unknowable, unobservable or too transient. Think of the surfer, or people in a crowd protesting about the 2010 austerity measures, or a bank in crisis. No single 'objective' world-view exists that can be used to form a 'model' in these dynamic situations. Which data would you need to gather? Do you know how or where you would gather it? In the world of practice, there is no basis for forming a 'single view of the truth'. The reality is that you have to work with the messiness and learn by doing – as Tom Ritchey points out in his paper *'Wicked Problems – Structuring Social Messes with Morphological Analysis'* – as a way of exploiting the diversity and opportunity that the messiness offers.[34]

G. **Effects are Non-Linear Phenomena.** Complexity science describes non-linear systems as those with a lack of proportionality between cause and effect – where small disturbances can lead to large consequences that are very sensitive to the initial conditions. This has been captured in the public imagination by the so-called 'Butterfly Effect', a metaphor coined by Edward Lorenz, where the flap of a butterfly's wings on one side of the world can, in theory, lead to a hurricane on the other. The changes can also be sudden, a catastrophe, and Catastrophe Theory has

---

33 Though for those in the headquarters, working with their constructed context, such prediction is of interest and so they should be aware of the givens and realities about the practical limitations of causal prediction.

34 Ritchey contrasts the 'wicked messes' which arise in complex situations with 'tame difficulties' posed by machines.

been developed to examine the reasons why these kinds of transitions occur.[35] The concept of non-linearity has practical relevance, because it means that the route between stimulus and desired change cannot be a rational one – the steps in-between will jump in unpredictable ways across levels and scales and will propagate by a variety of means. In science terms, there is no guarantee of there being a fully-connected graph[36] – in practical terms, this means that there can be no conventional plan mapped out in advance. Even informal interventions can be disproportionately effective – there is the example of the 'tea-lady' who turns up at a key moment in a tense office environment and, by breaking the tension with a forthright suggestion, opens up a whole new space-of-possibilities. The insight that one can only predict in general terms, as already discussed, applies here; it means that there is no way of working out, in absolute terms, whether particular courses of action are 'the right ones'. All that can be done is to have some idea of which indicators might provide the clues that suggest a need to adjust what is going on – requiring a very different, judgement-based, sense of 'rightness'. This evidence from complexity science indicates, therefore, that a target-based mindset predicated on absolute outcomes is usually flawed – because it relies on an unrealistic need for the world to be stable and predictable which, except in a few special cases, it is not.

H. **You Can't Turn Back Time.** A reality that must be acknowledged is the arrow of time (as Paul Davies discusses in his book *The Cosmic Blueprint*). In the real world, many phenomena are irreversible – such as trying to unscramble eggs or un-stir the milk from your tea. On a more profound level, it's a hard to accept but provable fact that, even if you could turn the clock back and put everything 'as it was' and start again, the outcomes would be different every time because it is impossible (in practical terms) to recreate the initial conditions, everywhere, exactly. One has to accept, therefore, that the converse is true – that because you can never be sure of the 'initial conditions' and, because of non-linearity, many of the patterns, phenomena and behaviours that arise will be unpredictable and unrepeatable.

I. **Repertoires must be Appropriate to Connectedness.** Complexity science states that the interaction between components generates the networks of 'connectedness' of the real world and that these

---

35   For more on this we recommend Roger Lewin's book *Complexity – Life at the Edge of Chaos*.

36   Where there would be a set of 'linear' connections between nodes of the graph such that there is some identifiable path between any one node and any other, and that there are no isolated, i.e. unconnected, nodes.

interactions can be influenced to change outcomes – but only if the interventions can be matched to the structure of the network of interactions. A key principle here is what complexity scientists call the law of requisite variety[37] which, in effect, states that to engage with or affect something, capabilities must match with or exceed the nature of things being affected. In other words, if you want to influence supermarket-chain-like behaviour you can do that with policy changes, economic incentives, safety rules and so on; if you want to affect the way the Amazon rainforest grows then you need very different kinds of 'capabilities'. Practically, this means that flexible systems that generate a large range of diverse options, of degrees of freedom, are better able to generate the requisite variety and promote change in their environment than those which are tightly optimised around a set of initial conditions such that they cannot generate novelty on-demand. The more options, i.e. the bigger the total wiggle-room that can be generated, the better a system is able to respond to or bring about change. The business world might easily relate to these statements when it comes to thinking about the diversification of a product line – to be able to respond to or even pre-empt changing market demands to their advantage (which at times can change very suddenly) or in order to react to economic downturns. However, this doesn't mean that you can have absolute control over what goes on – the arrow of time and predictability insights have put paid to that. Many things can only be achieved through third parties – individuals, groups, the environment itself, for example. So, sometimes 'letting go' gets results. It is a mistake to think that if you do not intervene, then change will not happen. The truth is that it probably is going to happen anyway – just not as you would prefer; it may even be better.

J. **Effects Propogate Across Scales.** Part of the complexity-aware mindset is realising that you can't control complexity because you can't have or get ownership of all the things that cause it to arise. An important aspect revealed by complexity science is the way in which influences and changes can propagate and cascade, via many intermediate levels and mechanisms, in a way that at first-sight seems counter-intuitive. For example, a well-meaning policy change may unintentionally increase poverty, potentially making people more susceptible to disease that in turn might create problems for the health sector. This 'surprising' propagation of effects occurs because

---

37 The terminology originally comes from Ashby, a psychiatrist and academic famous for his work on Systems Theory and Cybernetics, who formulated his 'Law of Requisite Variety' in his 1956 book *An introduction to Cybernetics.*.

natural networks are 'scale-free'[38] and the heterogeneous nodes that make up these networks are interconnected in a manner that facilitates rapid cascades, as illustrated by Albert-Laszlo Barabasi in his book *Linked: How Everything Is Connected to Everything Else and What It Means* and by Duncan J Watts in *Six Degrees: The Science of a connected Age*. It is not the properties of the nodes that make the networks scale-free, it's the (changing, complex and also heterogeneous) nature of the inter-relationships between them. Nodes that are highly connected with others are called 'hubs' and these play an important role and have disproportionate influence on network linkage. Scale-free networks are very resilient – the whole network will not necessarily be damaged by removing a single node, even if it is a hub node. An example of how these insights might be used comes from epidemiology. If there is an epidemic and a disease is spreading fast it is better to immunise the hub nodes first than to try to inoculate everyone – as it is via the hub nodes that the disease spreads quickly. As a corollary, unwanted effects can quickly propagate across the network via the highly interconnected nodes to parts of the network far from, for example, the initial well-meaning intervention. Realising that an effect may continue to reverberate in the environment of its own accord long after the original trigger is important. For this reason we emphasise the importance of iteration over timescales that may extend way beyond those of an initiating project.

The Role of the Environment. From a complexity science point of view, the environment here is not just the physical, geographical, one – it includes every manifestation of nature from the nano to the macro, from subatomic forces to the sweep of the universe and everything in-between – and, of course, society and cyberspace too. Some relevant givens and realities follow:

A. **The Environment Shapes the Context.** This broad definition of 'environment' owes its current form as much to things that have happened in the past as to what is currently happening. So the insight here is that practitioners need to consider more than just what is happening 'now'.[39] Think of our surfing example. What might have happened on the beach yesterday, last week, last millennia and how might that be

---

38   Scale-free networks are so called because their topology does not depend on their scale. Whether small or large these naturally-occurring networks operate in a similar way that can be exploited. The brain, human society, the Internet and ecosystems are examples of scale-free networks made of nodes with heterogeneous characteristics.

39   We covered the ancillary issues that affect performance in our 2009 paper on '*Complex Phenomena in Orchestras – Metaphors for Leadership and Enterprise*'.

relevant to the current dynamics? An example of something that would matter to practitioners is the so-called Zero-Sum Game – that there are certain resources in the world that are finite – 'If you take it I can't have it'. It is interesting, though maybe distracting, to ask what the 'natural complexity' of cyberspace is like? It certainly exists, there are certain laws, rules and givens about how it works down at the electrical, electronic and digital level and these are clearly of consequence,[40] yet they are unlikely to be a practitioner's primary concern. However, does Zero-Sum work there?

B. **The Environment has Many Facets.** As we have discovered in Chapter 2, human endeavour has added new niches and diversity into the environment. Things that people have produced that add to the complexities of the natural environment might include: buildings and devices, cyberspace and the Internet, regulations, politics, laws and policies, issues of environmental awareness, morals, cultural and ethical issues, art and so on. Of course, this is good! These are all things that are within people's gift to alter and, as is clear from the discussion above, changing them means that interactions, and therefore phenomena and outcomes, will be different. In a way this is just common sense – but if it is applied with the Putting Complexity to Work mindset it gives people many more subtle ways of bringing about powerful change in practice.

C. **The Environment Interconnects.** Co-evolution reminds us that there is no 'us' and 'them' in the environment, or even in cyberspace, and that the results of this mutual evolutionary influence propagate right out into the real world.[41] Given this, it is tricky to work out: 1) which scale to work at, 2) what the scope is of issues to address in practice, 3) what to include and exclude, and 4) what timescale(s) to do the necessary reflecting, influencing and shaping. Complexity science tells us that it is actually not possible to absolutely define these things, other than as abstract 'contrivances', because there are so many different ways in which things that are apparently bounded and separated from each other can be connected through the natural networks of interaction and reverberation. This is particularly true

---

40   An example are the articles by the *Wall Street Journal* called 'What They Know' (about privacy, etc) but which quickly drop into an extraordinary level of detail about the inner workings of mobile phones and Internet protocols, such as, for example in the one on 30 November 2010 by Julia Angwin and Jennifer Valentino-Devries titled 'Race Is On to 'Fingerprint' Phones, PCs'.

41   A simple example is the 'flashmob' where the Internet provides a way for strangers to self-organise spontaneously in the real-world – sometimes with startling effects! See: http://www.youtube.com/watch?v=SXh7JR9oKVE.

because the relationships between the nodes in the network can also change dynamically. For example, people's preferences and opinions, memberships and allegiances all change all the time. We acknowledge this in our Approach by looking at contextual complexity from different perspectives and viewpoints to identify, not boundaries as such, but degrees of connectedness and coupling.[42] The surfer's coupling to the surfboard is different to the surfer's coupling to a ship passing on the horizon. Unless the surfer is distracted by a flare going up from the ship – possible but unlikely – one can largely discount the presence of the ship from the considerations.

D. **The Environment is a Mediator.** Complexity science talks about a number of subtle ways in which change can be nudged along by manipulating the environment. One, called stigmergy, discussed by Eric Bonabeu, Marco Dorigo and Guy Theraulaz in *Swarm Intelligence. From Natural to Artificial Systems*, relates to the way that changes in the environment 'signal' the need or reason to behave differently. The 'seeding the space' strategy that the kindergarten teachers used, mentioned in Chapter 1, is an example of this type of environmental influence, as are features such as the colours used to paint rooms that have different functions (cool grey, vibrant red etc.) or where people put boundary fences. The implication for putting complexity to work is that one must consider these things as part of requisite variety, as part of the repertoire of options and as part of complexity-worthiness.

E. **The Environment is a Space of Possibilities.** The environments in which complexity is present or 'comes to pass' offer novelty and opportunity that are fittingly described as 'spaces of possibilities'. Umberto Eco, in the chapter 'The Poetics of the Open Work' in his book *The role of the Reader. Explorations in the Semiotics of Texts*, refers to the musical work 'Scambi' (Exchanges) by Henri Pousseur, a composer involved in research and development of electro-acoustic music. Eco defines the room for interpretation that Pousseur offers as a 'field of possibilities':

> 'Pousseur has offered a tentative definition of his musical work which involves the term 'fields of possibilities'. In fact, this shows that he is prepared to borrow two extremely revealing technical terms from contemporary culture. [Instead of] The classic relationship posited between cause and effect as a rigid, one-directional system: now a complex interplay of motive forces is

---

42   In this sense 'coupling' refers to strength of linking or dependency between things. This can range from the rigid, mechanical coupling of devices with nuts and bolts through to the loose coupling of intent between people with shared beliefs who may then act in similar or coherent ways.

envisaged, a configuration of possible events, a complete dynamism of structure. The notion of 'possibility' is a philosophical canon which reflects a widespread tendency in contemporary science: the discarding of a static, syllogistic view of order, a corresponding devolution of intellectual authority to personal decision, choice and social context.' (p58)

Though not a complexity scientist, 'the field of possibilities' that Pousseur describes enables a variety of choices for personal interpretation to emerge – but which also requires openness from the musician towards the dynamics of the musical piece. The insight here for putting complexity to work is that our cultural and conceptual environments are as significant for practice as the natural environment in which we are operating – and that the experienced complexity of others are also part of contextual complexity. It is important for practitioners that they understand these 'spaces of possibilities', these niches in the ecosystem of life, which is why we have a specific elements in our Approach that can be used to provide this appreciation.

Insights about the Dynamics of Emergent Phenomena. The givens and realities under this heading cover, on the one hand, the kinds of general dynamic patterns in the world and, on the other, how to work with them to change outcomes in a desired way. We'll discuss the practicalities of this when explaining the concepts and strategies for influencing and shaping dynamics below. For now we'll note the following insights:

A. **Dynamic Flows can be Influenced.** Concerning the dynamics themselves, they have a certain 'momentum' once established in a context. It just happens to be a fact that if you are working with an ongoing dynamic you cannot bring about change faster than it allows without causing potentially counterproductive dislocation. An example is the dynamic of an ecosystem, such as indigenous peoples in a rainforest, where unwise, even if well-meaning outside interventions can be catastrophically destructive to the livelihood of these people. Indeed, once local structures, dynamics and emergent phenomena are lost, they cannot be imposed from the top as an arbitrary set.[43] As we have discussed, the initial conditions can't be re-instated and, as many of them are emergent phenomena, they have to arise from local interactions that may take months or years to engender (along an

---

43   Studies, such as that by James Drake in 'Community Assembly Mechanics and the Structure of an Experimental Species Ensemble' have shown how robust an established ecosystem is to the arrival of new species. The ecosystem, over time, develops an 'identity', like an immune system, which resist intruders effectively. Drake called this the 'Humpty-Dumpty Effect' – because if you took the ecosystem apart you couldn't put it together again.

evolutionary trajectory that can't be known in advance). The insight for our Approach is that identifying, engaging with and sustaining these existing 'flows', because they are already there, is a way of bringing about change which might otherwise take years to achieve if initiated from scratch, especially when dealing with community issues. Another insight is that complexity-worthy enterprises will be competent in the use of terms and concepts related to the changing dynamics and tensions of practice, not just in the artefacts and processes of management. The flip-side of this is that it may only be possible to deal with certain established and possibly unwelcome behaviours by disrupting or possibly breaking them so that alternatives can then arise. Straightforward examples would be a business away-day for a session of 'anything goes' brainstorming or the intervention of the police to break up a riot in a street.

B. **Patterns Exist in the Dynamics.** Complexity science has a lot to say about the types of transitions between phenomena that can happen, whether triggered deliberately as part of enactment[44] and learning-by-doing, or arising unexpectedly as a result of spontaneous changes over different scales, levels or time-horizons. Figure 4 shows the pattern behind these transitions that is potentially useful to practitioners. The diagram originally came from work on cellular automata (CA), simulations of simple calculating 'creatures' interacting on a grid, by Chris Langton in 'Computation at the edge of chaos'. He noticed that the CA in his simulation behaved in a number of different ways, and classified these as shown on Figure 4. To his surprise, the distribution of their behaviours was not chance or random; it formed this distinctive graph. The sharp point at the top became known as 'Langton's Lambda Parameter'. In trying to understand this distribution he noted that the 'vitality' of his CA[45] was highest at the Lambda point where the amount of information and resources that the CA needed to interact had the effect of being 'just right'. This point has since been called the 'Edge of Chaos'[46] and the effect is a version of the 'Goldilocks Effect'.[47] The

---

44   Enactment is where, in the absence of information, you explore and discover by doing – in the way that someone might promote a 'loss leader' to see if customers like it. More of this in the strategies concept below.

45   Please do not presume that by using the word vitality we are inferring that the CA were 'alive' – it is a figure of speech to indicate their degree of effectiveness at being viable in the worlds he simulated.

46   The term 'Edge of Chaos' was coined by Doyne Farmer of the Santa Fe Institute.

47   The 'Goldilocks Effect' is more commonly used in relation of the position of the Earth in the Solar System – not near the sun and so too hot, nor too far away from it and too cold, but 'just right' (like the bowls of porridge in the children's fairy tale *Goldilocks and the Three Bears*).

Lambda point is an example of what chaos theory calls an 'attractor', a condition where behaviours repeat as a result of an area of stability developing. When conditions alter, a phase transition occurs, usually as a result of a set of pressures leading to what is called the 'tipping point' – where the previous order becomes dislocated and leads to the possibility of novel ones forming, as illustrated by Malcolm Gladwell in *The Tipping Point*. Once the transition has occurred then there will be convergence on a new 'attractor' which might be a lowest energy basin or, if there is dynamic tension, around the 'just right' point for those changed conditions. We'll say more about how to make use of these types of transitions, opportunities and dislocations in Chapter 5. The key point for the discussion in this Guide is that, unless disturbed in some way, natural complexity tends to converge on these 'just right' zones and that this tendency is a given that drives phenomena. An attractor basin example would be in the sort of product convergence that seems to have occurred with cars – many of them now look similar in shape (this is partly because of energy-efficiency considerations but also a reflection of global homogenisation and 'lean management', which avoids the financial costs of diversity).

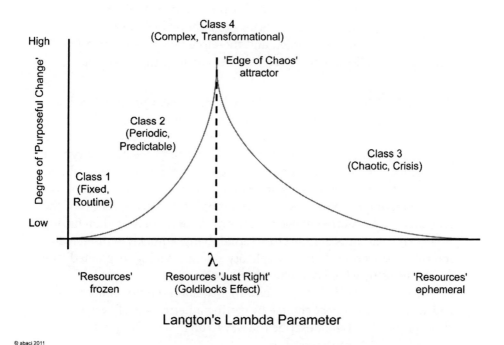

© abaci 2011

Figure 4 – Transformations at the so-called 'Edge of Chaos'.

C. **Dynamics Exist at Various Cycles.** One other reality to note about the dynamics is that, on the human scale, activities like surfing are very reactive – change and dynamic adjustments are happening millisecond by millisecond. The work of practitioners generally is more deliberative and where reflection and action go together. Iterations may occur over, comparatively, quite leisurely timescales – days, weeks or even months. Certain dynamic cycles in nature occur over hundreds or even thousands of years in human terms, yet dynamics they certainly are. Maintaining purpose and intent over such durations, say as part of climate-change considerations, does not come easily to humanity and this can cause difficulties for putting complexity to work. It is for this reason that the ability to contrast experienced complexity with contextual complexity and intent is key to exposing the tensions in and drivers of change (which, as you will see in Chapter 6, arise from the mismatch between context, intentions and possibilities). For example, a novice surfer does not understand how anyone can react quickly enough to catch a wave whereas, once experienced, it all seems easy – it's all down to perceptions.

Purposefulness and Intent. Given what has been said above about the tendency of situations to naturally converge on a 'just-right' zone, what is the significance of purpose and intent in relation to dynamic phenomena? Well, it's a simple one – it provides a way of disturbing conditions to either move the zone or trigger a phase change such that a new order, and therefore new zones, can arise. Some of the givens and realities that are relevant here include the following:

A. **Purposeful Change Does Not Come by Chance.** Complexity science provides a way of identifying the class/type of phenomena one is dealing with and so provides the basis, through purpose and intent, for selecting from a range of options for influencing, shaping and seeding the type of emergence – so that what one anticipates is more likely to come about. Hence, putting complexity to work requires a radically different emphasis from reductionist approaches – to an emphasis on an awareness of the tensions and drivers of change in real-world phenomena and on having fitness and readiness to adjust to external changes quickly without major internal dislocation. With complexity science having 'explained' the mechanisms by which complex phenomena come about, practitioners can take these insights, add intentionality, and be more aware of how and why they can affect change by getting a better feel of how to tune these properties. We'll describe the way to do this in Chapter 6.

B. **Intentions are Part of the Context.** Purpose and intent are considered by complexity science to be modifiers of the properties of the components, or of things that would affect their interactions – such as the degree of people's involvement or withdrawal – and these will change outcomes. So, part of putting complexity to work, where everything seems different depending on where you stand in relation to the situation, is to be able to appreciate issues from the points-of-view of the other actors who have their own purpose and intent. This reflection involves learning how to hold on to particular perspectives or viewpoints whilst considering the other actors' concerns and then comparing them – not always an easy skill! How the dynamics change then depends very much on how we all adjust our intentions – and if some people are not 'allowed' to change their intentions, others choose to and others are indifferent, what happens then? People have a stake in the outcomes; they will want to know that things are in their interests too – on their terms, valued in their way. They may want other transitions to occur and they will not be open and honest if the power-structures put them in a subordinate, weak position – 'participation' will set off on the wrong foot under these circumstances. As Michael Thompson indicates in his book *Organising and Disorganising*, the reality is that people have to work within a network of intentions, some of which will be hidden, yet be able to express their own intentions clearly and then, through comparison, identify synergies, opportunities and contradictions with others in the context.

C. **A Puzzle is not a Mystery.** An underlying principle that follows is that that there is a big, though often not well understood, difference between solving a 'puzzle' about facts and delving into things that are 'mysteries', such as people's intentions (see Gregory Treverton's *Reshaping National Intelligence for an Age of Information*). Puzzles deal with what one already knows and understands, such as many of the factual things about the world which can be deduced (generally to the left of the Lambda Parameter on Figure 4), whereas mysteries require the kind of inventive, creative formulation of hypotheses and, especially, multidisciplinary thinking that often seems irrational yet is required to consider purpose and intent at the 'Edge of Chaos' and beyond. The practical consequences of these differences are covered in the discussion of judging appropriateness as part of complexity-worthiness in Chapter 5.

D. Modelling Intentions needs to be done Appropriately. Though people use models to inform their thinking, another reality is the limited ability of models to accommodate issues related to purpose and intent in practice within the models. There is a theorem called 'Gödel's Incompleteness Theorem' which shows, mathematically, that all models are flawed. It states that models, such as the complex/agent-based societal ones,[48] which are 'formal systems', are incomplete and could, therefore, mislead practitioners. One of two things may happen. If the model is asked 'Is there anything else we can do?' it may answer 'No'. Gödel states that there WILL be other valid options, but that the model will not be able to reveal them (because it is incomplete). Someone may then ask: 'Is this the right answer, the right thing to do?' Again the model may say 'No'. In this case, Gödel indicates that it is possible for people to come up with valid insights – yet there will be some that the model won't be able to test or prove to be 'right'. What does this mean in practice? It means that someone may reject an option because the model tells them to reject it – not knowing that the option would work fine in reality. We can conclude that modelling is appropriate when used to inform human decision-making but not to replace it. Practitioners therefore should partner with the modellers/technocrats and question the answers that the model gives. According to Gödel's Theorem, any other use may lead to people seriously deceiving themselves – even causing unnecessary harm. Complexity science indicates that predictive modelling is too constrained by its assumptions about 'knowability' and by its limited ability to represent easily (if at all) qualitative factors such as trust and motivations, for example. We have, as a result, looked elsewhere for cross-disciplinary insights about the dynamics of these social, psychological and cognitive phenomena, for example in Fritjof Capra's *The Web of Life. A New Scientific Understanding of Living Systems*. An example of cross-disciplinary insight is also the work of Kurtz and Snowden (2003) who, with the Cynefin Framework, have developed pragmatic techniques, based on abduction,[49] to analyse so-called micro-narratives collected from people (i.e. expressions of their experienced complexity in our terms). They exploit the 'distributed cognition' of groups as a way of 'modelling' issues arising in complex

---

48   E.g. TRANSIMS, TRansport ANalysis and SIMulation Systems developed at the Los Alamos National Laboratory, see the website of the Network Dynamics and Simulation Science Laboratory at Virginia Tech.

49   Abduction being suitable for complex situations as it is 'beyond' induction or deduction in that it exploits intuition and human insight to develop plausible explanations rather than using the step-by-step 'rational' analysis of deduction. This distinction is similar to the one made earlier between mysteries (wicked messes) and puzzles (tame difficulties).

situations. Even then, for practice, people should not automatically seek scientific guidance on these matters where largely it doesn't exist but, instead, should value and give credence to human intuition and common sense.

'Components', their Properties and Interactions. Complexity science tells us all that the nature and dynamics of complex phenomena are fundamentally affected by the properties, attributes and abilities of the interacting components/entities that generate that phenomenon. Things such as the number of components, their variety, their degree of agitation or sluggishness, and the modes of interactions they can display all affect outcomes. If these 'components' are Internet blogs or social networking sites then cyberspace becomes involved again as an agent of change. Some of the givens and realities include:

A. **Components are Individually Different Yet Collectively Similar.**
A very important given is that these components are, at one and the same time, individually different yet collectively self-similar. We're sure that you have had the experience of going to a foreign country for the first time, especially one with a very different culture from the one that you are used to, and finding yourself saying about the people 'They all look the same'. Yet, as soon as you get to know a few of them, their individual characteristics enable you to pick them out of a crowd of a thousand people with no difficulty. The fact that all components are individually different, even down to each snowflake for example, means people have to accept the reality of heterogeneity – that people can't ignore difference as a driver of change. The benefit of diversity is that people are able to create novelty, innovation and change as part of effective practice. Conversely, the sort of self-similarity[50] that you will find in dendritic patterns at all scales, from the capillaries in your lungs to the network of rivers in a delta, means that people have to acknowledge the reality of the fractal, as it is called, nature of the world. Another example would be that the types of interactions between a small group of people are similar to those you would find between organisations – manifesting themselves as competition, collusion and so on. These fractal qualities are useful to practitioners, enabling them to take advantage of these universal patterns and features.

---

50   The term comes from Benoit Mandelbrot and it refers to the fact that, for example, if you cut one of the florets of a cauliflower, you see the whole cauliflower but smaller, and if you cut it again, the same thing happens.

B. **Components – Presence or Absence Makes a Difference.** The complexity science 'axioms', referred to in this chapter and earlier in the book, indicate that changes that modify the properties of the components/entities, or changes that affect their interactions, will alter the nature of the phenomena that emerge. In addition, does the presence or absence of certain entities trigger specific effects? Some entities may have to be involved in the context regardless of their apparent benefit from a practitioner's point of view; whereas others could leave without consequence. Certain mixes of entities may be required to shift the dynamics in particular ways. As mentioned above, the degree of coupling between components is another factor to consider. The aim of our Approach is to enable practitioners to gain some appreciation of how to work with these factors in suitable ways.

C. **Components have Properties that Matter.** Some of the important properties of components that would affect outcomes have been listed below. While these properties of the complexity-worthiness of components are distinct, when one of these attributes is lacking the others are much more difficult to achieve. When they are all present, however, the likelihood of success increases greatly. They include:

- Self-maintenance of 'individuality': the ability to maintain a distinct, purposeful identity[51] over time despite environmental changes through self-generation, -regulation (homeostasis) and repair (which also involves identifying 'non-self' via an 'immune system' and so on);

- Robustness: the ability to maintain effectiveness across a range of tasks, situations, and conditions by, for example, embracing diversity and avoiding single points of failure;

- Resilience: the ability to recover from or adjust to misfortune, damage, or a destabilising perturbation in the environment by exploiting the properties of networks;

- Responsiveness: the ability to react to a change in the environment in a timely manner by building-in agility and wiggle-room as innate capabilities from the start;

---

51   This self-maintenance of identity is called 'autopoiesis' by complexity science. Autopoiesis ('self' + 'production') is a term coined by the Chilean neurobiologists Humberto Maturana and Francisco Varela in the early 1970's for the necessary and sufficient properties complex systems must have to be considered to be 'alive' (see their paper '*Autopoiesis: the organization of living systems, its characterisation and a model*'). Also see the books of Capra (1989) and Levy (1993) for further description of the workings of this phenomena.

- Flexibility: the ability to employ multiple ways to succeed and the capacity to move seamlessly between them by adopting adaptive approaches by design;

- Innovation: the ability to do new things and the ability to do old things in new ways by adopting mindsets that see change as opportunity not threat.

A final point here is that complexity science indicates that entities (components) are strongly affected by those features that affect their ability (and willingness) to interact. In practice this includes such things as the ability to communicate well, using appropriate language and behaviour – and these are all part of complexity-worthiness.

PUTTING COMPLEXITY TO WORK – INFLUENCING CHANGE

To finish this chapter we'll look briefly at how these insights and principles might help practitioners in putting complexity to work. By working, appropriately, with the underlying causes of complex phenomena described above, there are plenty of degrees of freedom and options available for, selectively and pragmatically, shaping and influencing change in a context. The complexity insights and principles above tell us all that there are at least four main avenues, in principle, for influencing all types of emergence, adaptation and evolution and, consequently, change in practice over time. Influences can be made:

- *by making changes in the environment*: e.g. 'seeding', so preferred phenomena are more likely to come about (such as providing infrastructure that strengthens human livelihood) or by directly altering the geography (for example, tree-planting, irrigation schemes, landscape regeneration etc., or influencing cyberspace by setting up 'going digital' projects);

- *by changing the nature of top-down influences*: e.g. via orders, policy directives, direct interventions, assigning accessibility rights and so one;

- *by changing/manipulating self-organisation/self-regulation* (self-*) etc. 'mechanisms', eg: by influencing social drivers (such as incentives/ ethos, behavioural norms and the formation of community groups);

- *by changing the nature of bottom-up influences*: e.g. via 'the people' who can think/act locally but cause effects with potentially broad impact (e.g. the public mood, blogs, individual initiative leading to self-help campaigns).

These four general avenues for influencing change are the basis of one axis of what we call the 'Landscape of Change' for putting complexity to work which we will develop in Chapter 6 of this Guide (the other axis being based on the 'axioms of complexity' previously discussed). There are, of course, in theory, also *'doing nothing'* options, which may involve active disengagement or just letting things follow their course. Given that timeliness is a key factor in perceptions of complexity, someone who apparently 'does nothing', may in fact be playing a game with timescales over years or decades (as Machiavelli did in his political scheming).

To summarise the chapter, academic complexity provides a wide range of relevant insights for practitioners that we have now extracted and used to form the basis for an approach for 'doing things differently' in practice. In the next chapter we'll look at how these insights and concepts, which build on the observations made by practitioners in Chapter 2, have informed the design of our Approach and Framework for Putting Complexity to Work. We'll go through the Framework explaining the Elements which make up its composition, what they do and how they complement each other and enable engagement with the dynamics in real-world contexts. We'll leave the explanation of how to use it in practice to Chapter 6 and examples of its use to the case studies in Chapter 7.

CHAPTER 4: THE APPROACH, ITS DYNAMICS, FRAMEWORK AND ELEMENTS

'If you want to build a ship, don't drum up people together to
collect wood and don't assign them tasks and work, but rather
teach them to long for the endless immensity of
the sea.'

Antoine de Saint-Exupery (1900-1944)

Our Approach for Putting Complexity to Work, which we present in this Guide, consists of three complementary aspects that are used concurrently in an iterative and dynamic manner: 1) a conceptual Framework, which provides the integrative aspects of the Approach; 2) a set of Elements, which enable the various aspects of putting complexity to work to be considered; and 3) a pragmatic explanation of how to employ these in practice. These aspects and their interdependencies will be described in this chapter, which also includes further explanation about the objective of the Framework and what can be achieved with it. But there is much more to our Approach than its aspects – its application generates the intersecting dynamic loops of reflection and practice that enable continual and appropriate change to be sustained. Hence, this Guide equips you for your journey through changing circumstances, with an Approach and techniques for understanding, reasoning about and influencing various types of change in reality.

To use the Approach in practice you will need to bring along those capabilities which can be accessed and employed at the time that enable you to be complexity-worthy to some degree or other in relation to the situation. So, as part of the Approach we also give some guidance on how to estimate complexity-worthiness, and a way of working out what needs to adapt and change so as to achieve it. This adaptation is based on the nature and extent of any ongoing mismatch between capabilities available and needed in the context. Don't worry now about how the Approach works when practically applied because there will be coverage of that in Chapter 6, which then leads into the case studies in Chapter 7.

So, what's the Framework for and why is it needed? It's needed because practitioners *cannot* work with real-world realities by using set 'methods' and following a list of instructions, like a recipe-book or a car repair manual. What is required is something very different; a set of 'contemplative positions' or rules-of-thumb to take depending on the circumstances. If this is beginning to sound far too way out for you then hang on a moment – fixed instructions can't work, so what are the practical alternatives? Well, how would you teach someone to surf – how do surfers develop their skills? Partly through doing a series of exercises on land or in easy conditions, partly though building up experience by surfing on increasingly challenging waves and partly because there is a body of 'lore', of wisdom, passed from surfer to surfer about how to make the most of 'the big one' when it comes. This wisdom about how to approach surfing is encapsulated in a set of ideas (concepts) expressed as principles and guidance for action (for example, how to catch a wave), which provide a framework within which capabilities can be employed – in other words, just exactly all the things that we are covering in this Guide.

However, there is one interesting difference. As we have said before, surfing is very reactive – change is happening millisecond by millisecond and the dynamic adjustments are happening very quickly, in human terms anyway, whereas the work of practitioners (such as setting up an education programme in a very poor country) is generally more deliberative. Therefore reflection goes on in parallel with action and their iterations may occur over, comparatively, quite leisurely timescales – days, weeks or even months. Change is experienced in different ways relative to the time-horizons of the actors in their context and this is why this Guide can't be a recipe-book – we have to collaborate with you, the reader, because you understand your context. It is also why we call the Approach 'integrative' – it doesn't just integrate things into some static configuration, as you might when providing an 'Integrated approach to manufacturing', it enables continuous change in relationships, interdependencies and, hence, the interactions to be explored. The Approach is designed to ensure that novel behaviours and phenomena can be generated, experienced and employed as part of the flow of living and adapting enterprises. Note that we could have called our Approach 'holistic' but, sadly, the word is much misused these days – despite the pioneering work of Jan Christiaan Smuts who, in his book *Holism and Evolution,* defines it in practical terms, 'As Holism is a process of creative synthesis the resulting wholes are not static but dynamic, evolutionary, creative.' (p87)

One key point here is that because the world is fractal i.e. self-similar at every level, we do not need a different version of the Approach and Framework for every situation – one Framework does pretty well for most contexts, from bacterial infection in the medical domain to opinion-forming in world politics. Given the integrative Approach, the rest of this chapter will explain what the Framework consists of and you can be confident that it will address the issues and needs described previously.

We'll explain the Framework in two sections using Figure 5 for reference. The Figure expands one of the 'Actor' icons we saw in the 'One World' graphic in Chapter 1 so we can have a look to see what's going on inside one of these purposeful entities as it interacts with the environment and, through engaging in the community-of-practice, with other actors, entities and organisations participates in change.

The first section of this chapter, Dynamics of the Framework, will give an overview of the overlapping dynamic loops that can be seen in the Figure. These loops, together with a so-called 'Landscape of Change', which performs the synthesis (explained in Chapter 6), are at the heart of enabling the Approach to be integrative. The overlapping loops, shown as circles on the Figure, are about engaging in the community of practice, reflecting on that practice ('Symptom Sorting') and on the realities that affect the context (using the 'Trade-off Space'). There is also a fourth loop, complexity-worthiness.

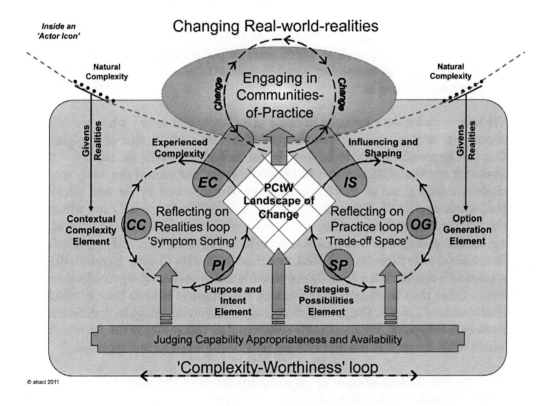

Figure 5 – An 'Actor Icon' expanded showing the Framework and Elements for Putting Complexity to Work.

The second section, Elements of the Framework, will describe each of the six Elements (shown as abbreviations in capital letters on the Figure), how they have been derived and what each is designed to do. For ease of discussion, the Elements are grouped as follows:

- Influencing and Shaping (IS), Strategies and Possibilities (SP) and Option Generation (OG) supporting the Reflecting on Practice loop, and

- Experienced Complexity (EC), Contextual Complexity (CC) and Purpose and Intent (PI) supporting the Reflecting on Realities loop.

Complexity-worthiness (shown on Figure 5 as the outer rounded rectangle) is part of the Approach – it is about what it is necessary to have so that you can use the Approach in practice and we will talk about the importance of being able to select, gain access to and employ capabilities that are appropriate to the changing circumstances. As mentioned before, complexity-worthiness, the underpinning 'glue', determines the degree to which you can put complexity to work. Note that the discussion of complexity-worthiness is so important that the whole of Chapter 5 is dedicated to it.

We have to pause for a moment to bring in an important note – when we talk about 'you' we tend to mean 'you the reader', but we are in danger of implying that the Approach is only to be used by an individual, which we are not – it works for any assemblage, enterprise or community. But, one of the really very slippery things about all this is working out who we mean by 'us' and 'them' (i.e., where applicable, appreciating the extent of self and non-self) and where the interdependencies are. Also, it's tricky to work out which scale to work at, e.g. local or global, what the scope is, what to include and exclude, and over which timescale(s) to do the reflecting. Well, as we have learned in Chapter 3, complexity science tells us all that it is actually not possible to define these things in absolute terms, other than as abstract contrivances. Practitioners have to bear in mind that memberships and allegiances change all the time and things look different from each viewpoint. We specifically accommodate this reality in the Approach where relative comparisons and shifting relationships can be incorporated.

We have designed the Approach to assist people with the important task of adopting mindsets and perspectives that are appropriate to what is being done or needs to be done in relation to dynamic change in the context. One of the real-world givens is that there is no single, all-encompassing 'right' or correct mindset – diversity is good and different mindsets reveal different things. This is a rather long-winded way of saying that if you assume, for example, that there are notional boundaries in particular places between various groups, then it does not mean that you are 'wrong' to assume they are there. However, what it does mean is that you must be able to appreciate what the consequences are of making such assumptions as they will affect your experienced complexity and therefore change the way you put complexity to work. It just so happens that this is one of the things that the Elements of the Approach are designed to do for you, by supporting iterative reflection on issues and their relationships. So let's start with the dynamics of the Framework that arise when practitioners use the Approach in a particular context and when the Framework's Elements[52] are linked up and interact with each other as part of practice.

DYNAMICS OF THE FRAMEWORK

Of course the six Elements mentioned above are not static – they interact in many ways and largely do so in a manner that we have characterised as four loops. In practice, these four dynamic, inter-related loops enable a continuously changing synthesis to be achieved, around the Landscape of Change, to keep up with the shifting circumstances. Think of our surfer; whilst surfing and dealing with the buffeting of the waves (Engaging in the Communities-of-Practice) she is also considering what line she will take along the wave front (Reflecting on Practice) whilst also keeping an eye on what other surfers are doing and how the wave is developing (Reflecting on Realities), and judging whether she feels that she has the capability (complexity-worthiness) to deal with the challenge of the 'big one'. It is clear then that these types of dynamic do co-exist in reality and so, when the Framework is applied in practice, the synthesis of its loops is, therefore, an appropriate internal (within the entity) manifestation of the changing real-world external context. Indeed, an ongoing and growing appreciation of the context reveals enablers and blockers. Overall, these iterative loops enable people to deal with change, novelty, and the unexpected and to access a wide range of opportunities by providing a means to expose and explore the mismatches and tensions that drive and contribute to change. We will now look in more detail at each of these loops in turn.

A. **Engaging in Communities-of-Practice Loop – Doing things in Practice – Achieving Change**. This loop is about doing; it's about continuously bringing about change by matching capabilities to intentions and it's about implementing the appropriate options that have been identified, 'on-the-fly', along with the dynamics of the situation and within the complexities of the context. Practice is about balancing what you are doing with what you are experiencing. If you are complexity-aware then you will be doing and noticing different types of things from someone who is not sensitive to complex phenomena as such. For example, one business might be very aware of changing trends on social networking sites and be actively involved in influencing them through opinion-formers, whereas another business

---

52 If you're wondering why we don't describe the Elements first, then the dynamics, well, you have a point – we've tried explaining it both ways round and we think this one works best for 'holistic' thinkers like practitioners.

might single-mindedly implement its goals regardless of such transient opportunities. When one does decide to engage with the 'space-of-possibilities' there are many different types of things you, or the people best placed to do it, can do. In simple terms it might be that things would go better if other people took the lead, or that one realises that it is time to take a break or even stand back completely! Suggestions for what may be more appropriate options at any particular time come in through the Influencing and Shaping (IS) Element when 'Reflecting on Practice' and using the Landscape of Change. It may be to interact with others – by collaboration, negotiation, facilitation and other types of conduct – or to alter the environment itself, say by 'seeding' the space with objects or with phenomena that influence the outcomes (as you would when you set up a room for a World Cafe[53] session), or by directly shaping the phenomena themselves (as the teachers did with the kindergarten children). This loop then is where complexity is 'Put to Work' by pragmatically engaging with things as they are in a given context as well as influencing, shaping and changing the dynamics and the phenomena along the way.

B. **Reflecting on Practice – Explore what's Appropriate**. This is one of the two 'reflecting' loops. Just to make clear, when you are reflecting it doesn't mean that everything stops while you do it, nor that the loop takes a set time or follows a set process. We are all familiar with thoughts crossing our mind as we do things – considering what's going on, trading-off strategies and possibilities and wondering about different options in relation to our capabilities and abilities and whether we are doing the 'right' thing. Or, reflecting on what needs to be done given that the context has changed, or that we wish to change it. In a project, it might be that options need to be reconsidered in the light of feedback from, or participation by, the community. As an individual it's fairly effortless to do; as a team it can work well too and, when it does, one gets a great 'buzz' of achievement – however, it's harder to work out why this happens in some circumstances and not in others. But again, that would suggest that these activities are detached in a way that they cannot be in reality. In dynamic situations you cannot put things aside part way through and then carry on from where you were – the conditions will have changed – you must reflect on the different ways of putting complexity to work that are available to you as you are actually

---

53   The World Café dialogue is a technique that embodies the idea of the harnessing 'conversations that matter' as the basis of the shaping of collective intelligence from which innovations and new ideas emerge. The World Café process is described in *The World Café. Shaping our Futures through Conversations that matter* by Juanita Brown and David Isaacs.

doing it. Also, a balancing view from reflecting on realities needs to be factored in, using the Trade-off Space (that will be explained in Chapter 6), as the comparison between experienced complexity and contextual complexity provides insights that contribute to suitable engagement in the real world.

C. **Reflecting on the Realities – Appreciating the Circumstances.** This loop is about gaining an understanding of the real world and reflecting on how change may affect the journey people are undertaking. Has there been an outbreak of disease, a change in the natural complexity, which means that the schooling programme should be suspended as it will only help spread the illness faster? Has a key middle-man withdrawn his support? If so one must consider whether one can still meet the aims without his help. This loop reflects on the environment, monitors phenomena, interactions and actors, explores the dynamics and compares understandings with intents and purposes to avoid ending up with lots of unchallenged assumptions, received wisdom, bigotry, groupthink and so on. An important part of this is reviewing perceptions of the social situation being experienced, as the perceptions themselves depend on the interactions one has with others, the relationships one can develop and sustain and the collaborations engaged in. Comparison also enables the insights[54] needed to put complexity to work to be developed – we call this 'Symptom Sorting' (it will be explained in detail in Chapter 6). Based on an understanding of the characterisations of the changing situation and 'our' purpose, it asks things such as 'Does our intent still make sense?' Conventionally, these things might be considered to be 'head-office' activities where plans are developed, models run, their results reviewed and risks evaluated. But this would be, in surfing terms, 'on-the-beach' activity, disengaged from the dynamics that we are all concerned with. Though it may be useful as part of the 'preparing for doing', it is no substitute for the doing itself. Crucially, the decisions that head-office people make should not replace those made by the people in the field, without very good reason, as the field-workers are the ones 'in-contact' with the realities in a way that head-office cannot be. This tension comes up again and again in practitioners' analyses of their work, as we reported in Chapter 2. Practitioners are seeking more effective ways of demonstrating the power of local insight, expertise and experience versus the power to override and control claimed by those in positions

---

54   Regarding motivation, discomfort, desire, appeal, curiosity, opportunity and whether to detach, reduce or increase tension, degrade or innovate, for example.

who are remote from the realities. In this regard, the utility of this loop is also to 'surface' and capture, as far as possible, what could otherwise be hidden – the 'people issues' that are the stuff of life.

D. Lastly there is a complexity-worthiness loop where, behind the scenes, appropriate capability is being adapted, adjusted, updated and made accessible to support the matching of influencing and shaping options to the realities of practice, so that an appropriate contribution to change can be made (that will be explained in detail in Chapter 5).

To get a first idea, here's a quick example of how these loops work in practice. Think of a business start-up driven by an enthusiastic entrepreneur working with a small team in a dynamic situation with a great deal of uncertainty about customers, their market and availability of finance. Whilst dealing with the need to sell products, attending meetings with banks or venture capitalists to get the funds and with the media to get the message out (i.e. the Practice) the team is also considering how their customer base is developing and what kind of feedback they are getting (Reflecting on Practice). They're also considering what competitors are doing and where the market seems to be taking them (Reflecting on Realities) and judging whether they have the edge, the agility, and the capabilities and procedures they need (complexity-worthiness) to make a success of the business in such a competitive market. We'll explain in Chapter 6 how these tensions and trade-offs can be synthesised and options generated to put complexity to work. Let's look next at how each of the Elements in these loops supports practice.

ELEMENTS OF THE FRAMEWORK

The Framework for Putting Complexity to Work contains the six Elements outlined at the beginning of this chapter. Just to reiterate, the Elements are not steps in some process – each Element relates to different aspects of overall performance and each one 'sparks' in different ways at different times. They are complementary to each other, both as part of our design and as invoked by circumstances. Together they enable the integrative Approach which is necessary to work with the various kinds of features, phenomena and situations that we all find in the world. As you iterate through the dynamic loops discussed above, the journey you make through them and via the various Elements, depends on the changing circumstances. Each Element reveals particular things that another one won't or can't – they are not separate activities happening in some sort of contrived isolation, they are states of appreciation, being or doing, and this section will explain what triggers them in a complexity-aware way. In reality, the order in which the Elements will be invoked and 'threaded together' depends on the changing circumstances and, as we'll show in the case studies in Chapter 7, the order and degree of concurrency will be different each time as situations change.

So, we'll now explain how each Element was derived, what it is for, what needs to occur for it to function, what it produces and what its utility is for practitioners. We appreciate that this section is rather technical so we've broken it up into well-signposted sub-sections. For ease of discussion, the Elements are grouped as follows. First, there will be a sub-section on the Elements that support the 'Reflecting on Practice' loop, and they are: Influencing and Shaping (IS), Option Generation (OG) and Strategies and Possibilities (SP). Next, there is a sub-section on the Elements that support the 'Reflecting on the Real-world realities' loop, and these are: Experienced Complexity (EC), Contextual Complexity (CC) and Purpose and Intent (PI). Note that some of the Elements have specific techniques or visual representations associated with them and some do not. as is appropriate. Lastly, there'll be mention of how all the Elements might come into play to support the 'Engaging in Communities-of-Practice' loop. We just need to emphasise again that the order in which the Elements are described below does not form a set process – and they should not be used in this manner. You, in your context, are the expert and will, in using the Approach, be the one best placed to find your starting point and determine in which ways to use the loops interactively.

Elements which Enable Reflection on Practice. To be able to reflect on what is happening in practice, and on the appropriateness of one's actions, one needs to consider whether the strategies formulated and the possibilities considered (SP) continue to be 'valid', whether the options being generated (OG) are relevant to the context and whether the ways in which the Influencing and Shaping (IS) are underway need to be changed:

A. **Element 'IS': Preparing for Influencing and Shaping – Adapting what is Done in Practice**. This IS Element consists of a number of context-dependent implementation activities concerned with preparing for doing, informing the doing and adjusting the doing. What practitioners get out of this IS Element is an increased likelihood that the changes that were anticipated will indeed fulfil the intent – it is all about what is practical, realisable and relevant:

    1. **Why the Element is Needed – Drivers and Underpinning Principles.** Being able to judge whether particular behaviours or interventions are suited to the situation is key to putting complexity to work successfully – its where the 'rubber hits the road' in colloquial terms. This Element provides a way of making those judgements, which then inform how things are carried out

in practice. One of the complexity science principles that applies here is that there is no way of working out, in absolute terms, whether particular courses of action are 'the right ones' – all that can be done is to have some idea of which indicators might provide the necessary clues to make the judgements required to adjust what is going on. This Element enables practitioners to work with their degrees of freedom in practical terms.

2. **What the Element does – Why it Works.** This Element is concerned, therefore, with implementing appropriate ways of bringing about or influencing change and of shaping phenomena in practice. It is also about monitoring and evaluating the changing situation as best as we can judge it, and draws upon Experienced Complexity to do this. It works because it employs complexity science-inspired techniques for bringing about change through appropriate engagement, in order to influence the changing realities. These techniques include, as we saw in the previous chapter: those that can be applied top-down, such as in giving direction; or those that tune self-organisation and self-regulation, such as incentives or peer-to-peer influence; those that work bottom-up, say through initiative; and those that modify and/or seed the environment and which work directly on the phenomena to, possibly, trigger transitions. Its visual representation is in a Landscape of Change, explained in Chapter 6.

3. **What it Produces – The Element's Utility to Practitioners.** The Element's 'outputs' – for example, things to do, capabilities to use, people to influence – are mostly of utility in the community-of-practice space, but they also inform the reflecting loops and affect all the other Elements. Its utility then is in turning all the reflecting that is happening elsewhere in the Approach, whether reactive or deliberative, into actionable insights for 'doing'.

B. **Element 'OG': Option Generation, Review and Adjustment.** The OG Element is for systematically working out appropriate ways to carry out the influencing and shaping given the dynamic context. It enables a broad repertoire of candidate behaviours and suggested interventions to be generated that support the Reflecting on Practice dynamic. What practitioners get from this is a choice of potentially 'valid' alternatives to select from, which take into account contextual and experienced complexity, risk trade-offs, intent and the capabilities which are accessible – in other words, feasible options for consideration:

1. **Why the Element is Needed – Drivers and Underpinning Principles.** This Element is needed to trade-off what practitioners would like to do with what is likely to be possible, given the circumstances, and what is viable given the capabilities and the means available – and this may include a 'doing nothing' option. It also identifies who or what might implement the options and where and when they might be activated. An underlying complexity science inspired principle is that many different options may result in similar outcomes and the converse, that similar options may generate very different outcomes – which is why people are more interested in engaging in the journey and adjusting it and 'ourselves' as they go along.

2. **What the Element does – Why it Works.** The Element uses appropriate techniques to consider, pragmatically and realistically, options for exploiting opportunities and addressing the concerns that have been raised by practitioners. It draws upon the purpose and intent and examines the strategies and corresponding possibilities that are under consideration, both from reflecting on the situation and evidenced through practice, and on the capabilities that are likely to be available. It enables practitioners to systematically weigh up these factors, about the practicalities of putting complexity to work, in a way that is consistent with the insights we have derived from complexity science.

3. **What it Produces – The Element's Utility to Practitioners.** The Element provides sets of options that might be suitable in certain circumstances and can be compared using a simple visual 'tool' called the 'Trade off Space', which we will explain in Chapter 6. This way of generating options is useful for practitioners because it gives them a candidate set which can be implemented when the conditions are suitable, not just activated in an arbitrary or pre-defined order, or at a time determined in advance. This context-sensitive way of working is flexible and has adaptive change built into it by design – which is great for dealing with uncertainty.

C. **Element 'SP': Strategy and Possibilities – Considering Possible Futures.** The SP Element is for generating and reviewing strategies and possible futures. It consists of a number of techniques that enable practitioners to balance strategy against a 'space-of-possibilities' such that intent can be modified and practice can be tailored or transformed as necessary – it is where the head-scratching tends to be done:

1. **Why the Element is Needed – Drivers and Underpinning Principles.** This Element is all about considering what could happen, however bizarre or unlikely it might seem at first glance, rather than just looking at what seems probable. Without it practitioners could miss opportunities or find themselves repeating behaviours that may have worked in the past but which may not be relevant now. An underlying principle is the big, though often not well understood, difference between solving a puzzle and delving into things that are mysteries. The Element opens up strategy formulation to include consideration of these mysteries as possibilities.

2. **What the Element does – Why it Works.** This Element is used to carry out an ongoing review of strategies, given current realities and experiences, and to formulate and explore all sorts of possible futures. It forms the basis for considering options and assessing current influencing and shaping activities. It does this by using a variety of techniques, sourced from experience, for triggering exploratory thinking. It works because it is designed to generate novelty, challenge assumptions and received wisdom and to break groupthink. and because it specifically sets out to take note of and factor in the real-world realities exposed by the Contextual Complexity (CC) Element (see below). Key to this is the ability to adopt a variety of mindsets and to deliberately set out to consider issues from a variety of perspectives and viewpoints.

3. **What it Produces – The Element's Utility to Practitioners.** The main utility of this Element to practitioners is that it provides a way of considering factors and events that otherwise might be unexpected – and of mitigating the unpredictable. It also provides a way of exploring what the various actors might do and of identifying indicators of significance and value to them. The Element is also a good way of generating novelty, sparking innovation and identifying otherwise fleeting opportunities. The strategies developed and the possibilities identified feed back into the Experienced Complexity (EC) and Influencing and Shaping (IS) Elements and inform the community-of-practice loop where options for acting in practice can be formulated within the strategy.

Elements which Enable Reflection on the Realities. One of the things we were apprehensive about when we were developing this Approach was the challenge of talking about objective and subjective realities without losing ourselves in a philosophical nightmare. We knew from our own experiences, and from what practitioners have said to us, that the differences between people's perceptions and actual realities caused a great deal of tension. Individuals, organisations or agencies would set about doing something, convinced that they had a balanced view of the world, knew what mattered, knew what people wanted and had worked out the way to 'solve it'. Unfortunately, some were poorly informed on all these counts. To put complexity to work successfully it is absolutely essential to be able to reflect on the real-world realities and on the complexities experienced in as open and robust a way as possible and to identify the differences and tensions – i.e. to do 'Symptom Sorting' which is what these next three Elements are designed to enable:

A. **Element 'EC': 'Experienced Complexity' – Subjective Perceptions of Real-world Realities.** The EC Element is for describing and illustrating the context as 'you' see it. It consists of a series of questions that trigger the articulation of the issues and enable meaningful narratives, reflecting a broad expression of perceptions, to be developed. The Element captures comparable impressions of the situation, the actors, how they relate to each other and what is significant. This representation enables current impressions to be compared with both past ones and the hypothetical future ones that would have been generated by the Strategies and Possibilities (SP) Element:

   1. **Why the Element is Needed – Drivers and Underpinning Principles.** The Element is needed as it provides the basis for contrasting one's view and knowledge of a situation with the actual contextual complexity. The way people engage with the world is coloured by what they experience and the way that they experience it – the channels through which people receive messages about the world and the degree to which they are open to such messages. Experienced complexity refers to the different ways that we experience and describe the world around us and how these experiences change over time. If, for example, we tend to notice and experience crime problems and disasters, we will tend to think of the world as an unfriendly place. If, on the other hand, we are drawn towards noticing good deeds and initiatives you might think of the world as benign, even friendly. One of the important principles here is that different people will view the same experiences in very different ways and they may learn different lessons. Also, the way one describes the experience depends on the experience itself, modified by impressions of it and the deductions or inferences made based on one's knowledge, expertise, maturity and familiarity with the situation. Someone from an arid country may say how much they really enjoy rainy

holidays in Scotland because of the novelty value. Note that the 'people' here can be communities and enterprises as well – not just individuals. A club or society might have a position on what is, and what is not, acceptable behaviour for example – these may be manifested in constitutions or rules for example. A really crucial part of experienced complexity is this: events that happen to us affect our attitudes concerning what interests us and what we most value. This in turn affects the way we perceive those events. For example, someone in an office whose printer fails during a power failure while they are trying to produce a vital customer report for the next morning might say that they had a 'dreadful day' as a result of it. Whereas colleagues in another part of the building might take the opportunity to exchange ideas and say that they had a great time and that the lack of power turned out to be very useful. Experienced complexity is, by definition therefore, highly subjective. This Element is needed to expose as much as possible of what is behind what people think and perceive of their context. Other key drivers are the types and modalities of interaction through which people experience the world. For example, via cyberspace people may experience things directly on their screens, through their use of social networking sites, or indirectly from 'recommendations' forwarded by software agents working in the background – such as the suggestions you get when typing words into search engines. The Element is designed to pick up on these experiences too.

2. **What the Element does – Why it Works**. This Element is designed to tease out 'our' subjective, possibly underdeveloped, though not necessarily uninformed, view of the environment, the actors and their behaviour (including self) and the phenomena experienced in the area of interest. An important part of people's perceptions of the context arises from the nature of the social situations one experiences – the interactions with others, the relationships developed and sustained and the collaborations engaged in, including emotions and feelings. This Element brings attitudes and opinions to the surface, whether balanced or prejudiced, and other factors that might affect behaviour and how people go about influencing and shaping in different ways. It works because many of these things, though subjective, can be intercepted and expressed in a way that informs reflecting.

3. **What it Produces – The Element's Utility to Practitioners**. This Element provides an expression and clarification of one's view, previous experience, current knowledge and impressions of the changing situation, of the environment and actors that seem

relevant in the specific context, and of the role people think others play. It is an ongoing compilation of people's observations, feelings and emotions about the context and any factors that are deemed relevant. It brings to the surface things that seem either particularly difficult and/or negative and things that are positive and inspiring. All of these responses might be important stepping-stones or 'openings' for emerging opportunities. The Element provides the necessary input for comparing one's viewpoints and experiences with the contextual complexity.

B. **Element 'CC': 'Contextual Complexity' – 'Objective' Appreciation of the Context.** The CC Element is for gaining an 'objective' understanding of the natural complexity of the context. To set the mindset for discovering and capturing information about relevant patterns and phenomena that are active in the real world, it draws on the givens and realities, described in Chapter 3, and on all the human dimensions in the context. Doing so reveals weaknesses in the appreciation of the situation and enables practitioners to challenge assumptions that might have been formed, especially if these had resulted only from experienced complexity. It also enables the possible consequences of mismatches between perceptions and reality to be put in context. What practitioners get out of this is a meaningful view of the realities and, through comparisons in the Reflecting on Realities loop, how these may affect endeavours. In the end, this Element is all about recognising and facing up to realities, however welcome or unpalatable they are:

1. **Why the Element is Needed – Drivers and Underpinning Principles.** For many institutions and organisations what goes on outside their front door, while obviously of interest, is not always their focus – sometimes with disastrous results.[55] Widely used standards like ISO 9001 (quality), process accreditation tools like Capability Maturity Model Integration (CMMI) and approaches like 'Managing Successful Programmes' (MSP) tend to be designed for quality, standardisation and repeatability of internal activities with very little involvement with what goes on outside.[56] Putting complexity to work requires a radically different

---

55 An example: in 2005 a UK airline, British Airways, treated their in-flight meal provider (Gate Gourmet) as if they were external to their enterprise. When Gate Gourmet's staff went on strike and negotiations failed, suddenly many of British Airways' flights were grounded – this outcome seemed to catch British Airways totally by surprise – as if they had thought that Gate Gourmet's contribution was external to British Airways' activities and so could be discounted.

56 These are just a couple of examples of the ones used in business change initiatives and in project management.

emphasis – an awareness of the changing real-world phenomena and an emphasis on fitness and on readiness to adjust to external changes quickly without major internal dislocation. Hence, this Element is needed because it provides a way of achieving and maintaining this relevant external focus – and the understanding necessary to be able to contrast it with the experienced complexity. It offers a return to the kind of pragmatism, built around the innate abilities of people, that is increasingly being demanded (see for example James N. Mattis' 'USJFCOM Commander's Guidance for Effects-based Operations'). In that sense it is different as it is rejecting the trend towards the increasingly obsessive collection and mining of data that, as it is believed by its proponents, provide a way of divining the future. As an intelligence expert recently said to us, 'You can have the most efficient gold mining machine in the world, but without the intellect and cunning of an expert to tell you which part of which river to put it in you're wasting your time'.[57] Complexity scientists would agree. The CC Element offers the basis for reflecting – it gives an honest account, which might reveal a picture of 'uncontested space', of possibilities that didn't seem to be there before – and gives an idea of the capabilities needed to engage with a given situation.

2. **What the Element does – Why it Works.** This Element enables practitioners to gain an objective estimation of the environment, the components that are active and the features and phenomena that are significant in a context. It enables practitioners to answer questions such as: 'Why is the environment here behaving as it is, what are the dynamics and what is causing them to come about?' The answers, by challenging people's perceptions and (often unspoken) assumptions, enable them to get their bearings about the unavoidable realities that must be factored into the considerations. This Element also considers who the other significant players are, what their intentions may be, what perspectives they may take and viewpoints they may have. All together they enable practitioners to express the situation in objective terms, based on an assessment of information gathered and on the understanding gained about the dynamics of the context.

3. **What it Produces – The Element's Utility to Practitioners.** It is through this Element that you come to understand perspectives and viewpoints relative to others – this includes appreciating their

---

57 We know that someone will say, 'In time we'll have detectors in every part of every river so then we won't need experts' and, indeed, this sort of 'brute force' approach has its place – but not in a resource-limited future world

cultural values, interests, motivations and livelihood factors. Over time, through relationships, people gain insights and lessons, and the degree to which they take notice depends on issues such as trust and emotion and the ethical and legal framework within which the exchanges are made. What is experienced is also affected by the nature and apparent influence on the situation by other actors – whether possibly or actually involved in the complex realities of interest. In addition, it is a way for practitioners to work out who has the power to influence, what types of power they have and how it is exerted. This understanding forms a basis for considering what might need to be influenced to achieve certain outcomes. This Element is where, objectively, one can consider why it is that the situation has come about, by looking at who benefits, who suffers and who or what are the driving factors in its changes (such relationships, motivations, groupings, allegiances and interactions). In short, because this Element provides a way of expressing the real-world realities it enables the 'Reflecting on Realities' dynamic to be maintained. The outputs from this Element include a description of the features of the context in terms that make it possible for them to be compared with those coming from the Experienced Complexity (EC) Element. These features include: degrees of freedom, wiggle-room, power-structures and so on. This comparison is useful to practitioners because it may reveal or highlight inconsistencies or contradictions between world-views that may be distorting decision-making and/or causing opportunities to be missed, or influencing and shaping activities that are futile or unfit. These insights inform the deliberations of the Purpose and Intent (PI) Element and help the Strategies and Possibilities (SP) Element sketch out the extent of 'wiggle-room'.

C. **Element 'PI': Purpose and Intent – Formulation, Review and Articulation.** The PI Element is for articulating desired change or intent in regard to opportunities. It consists of a series of questions that form a structured discourse to get at the heart of, and to trade-off, practitioners' own purpose, intentions and motivations in relation to what they have learned about those of the others. What practitioners get out of it are a declaration of intent, as work-in-progress, and clarifications of purpose and motivations with the related factors and influences. This enables practitioners to consider these in relation to their experiences and to the complex realities at work in the context – it is also about making clear whether change is being sought, imposed, responded to or ignored and so this informs the Reflecting on Practice dynamic loop:

1. **Why the Element is Needed – Drivers and Underpinning Principles.** Practitioners need this Element to ensure that purpose and intent are clearly formulated and expressed so that synergies, opportunities and disconnects in the context can be identified. This gets to the heart of a really important issue that we have already mentioned – if someone is going to use this Approach, who will it be and how will they define themselves in relation to the things going on in the wider environment? This sense of me/us can vary tremendously in how it is felt and manifested. A key underpinning principle has been articulated by Thompson (2008) – that purpose and intent coming from a 'boss' at the top of a hierarchy is very different to that from a disinterested worker, from a keen member of a community, from a hermit or from a criminal. Yet these intentions are not mutually exclusive; the boss can't be a boss without workers, a community relies on its individuals, even if some of them try to be hermits. Bearing these interdependencies in mind, the Element provides for an expression of factors surrounding motivations that can be considered in the Reflecting on Realities loop.

2. **What the Element does – Why it Works.** This Element is where intent is formulated, based on ideas and visions, and then iterated. It works because it uses structured discourse to ask questions such as the following ones: What is the nature of the current situation? What has caused the phenomena perceived to come about? How much can be understood about how this situation 'works' and what the viewpoints, motivations and influences of others are? (go to Symptom Sorting). What is motivating 'us' to intervene in this complex situation, what is the problem/opportunity 'we' perceive? Why did 'we' feel it was a problem – what discomforted 'us' enough to trigger 'our' involvement? What are the implicit intentions? We are intervening in order to do what? (go to Strategies and Possibilities). Who is challenging the assumptions? What is the nature of the change 'we' are trying to bring about? (go to Option Generation). What could be engaged with to shape and influence the phenomena? Given what is known about the situation, would the proposed interventions make sense – how would 'we' know if they did? (go to Landscape of Change).

3. **What it Produces – The Element's Utility to Practitioners.** The Element produces, in effect, a cognitive map of possible influences which practitioners can use to clarify the stated purpose and to formulate an intent that 'makes sense', given the experienced and contextual complexity. This cognitive map is not, and indeed

cannot be, some ponderous artefact. It is a representation that makes sense to those involved – there is no formula for what it should look like. This Element's utility is to surface intentions and give them clear articulation.

Elements to Enable Practice – For achieving Change. In reality, changes over time in the real world might trigger events which would lead practitioners to make changes in the way they engage by altering their complexity-worthiness. Or new possibilities may be thought of such that practitioners decide to make different contributions that change practice and hence the real world. This back and forth iterative reflection, indicated in Figure 6 overleaf, and the exposure of 'deltas' and tensions is fundamental to the Putting Complexity to Work way-of-working that the Approach enables. As a result, practitioners may invoke any appropriate Element within the Framework, but two Elements will be involved in practice all the time: Influencing and Shaping (IS) and Experienced Complexity (EC). Of course, they have already been mentioned in relation to the two 'reflecting' loops, but IS and EC have dual roles as already shown in Figure 5 and magnified in the Figure below. These two Elements work closely together and, in practice, most practitioners would not consider them as separate. The iteration between doing and sensing the doing is, in most situations, instantaneous. But there are situations where this is not so, where there is a temporal asymmetry[58] that our Approach must be able to accommodate. This is why we think they must be kept separate:

---

58   Let us say something has been done as part of influencing and shaping but there is no way of knowing when the expected indicator of change may arise or if at all – say someone has been asked to try to contact a missing person. In that case, the sensing that goes on within the Experienced Complexity Element may need to be sustained in a persistent way for weeks or months, i.e. the acting/responding is very asymmetric.

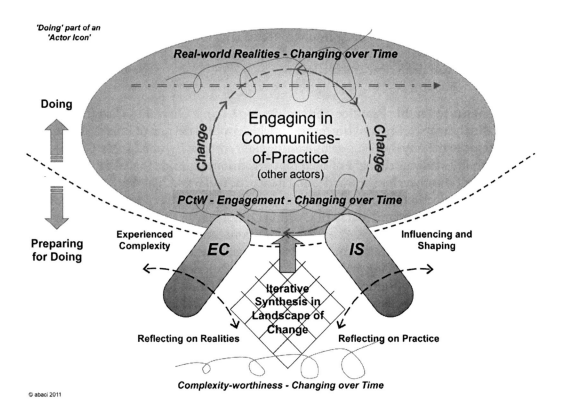

Figure 6 – A Focus on the Dynamics of Practice.

A. **Element 'IS': Dynamic Influencing and Shaping – Doing Things in the Community-of-Practice.** The IS Element has two sides to it – one has been described above in the deliberative mode, but it also has a role in the on-the-fly implementation of the options that have been selected through the 'Reflecting on Practice' loop. In this position, 'Dynamic IS' consists of a number of context-dependent activities concerned with informing and adjusting the things going on in practice. This is very much about 'on-the-surfboard' dynamics, yet it employs complexity science-inspired techniques such as those already mentioned for bringing about change. This enables practitioners to engage appropriately with, and to influence, the changing realities in context-relevant timescales. What practitioners get out of this, the 'real-time' end of the IS Element, is an increased likelihood that changes in the world that were anticipated will indeed fulfil the intent.

B. **Element 'EC': Reactive Experienced Complexity – Immediate Perceptions of Real-world Realities.** The EC Element also has two sides to it – one is in the deliberative role mentioned above and the other is in this role, supporting practice, where it is usually involved in the minute-by-minute sensing of complex phenomena, behaviours and changes. This 'Reactive EC' then provides a way of forming and sustaining immediate impressions of the situation, the actors, how they relate to each other and of apparently important or significant indicators. But, as indicated above, practitioners may also need to be asymmetric in time and space and so the ways that they use the Elements always depend very much on the circumstances. This is fully accommodated within our Approach by enabling Elements to be invoked and threaded together in different orders, and in ways that flow naturally in the circumstances.

Note the 'boundary' between doing and preparing for doing, which is both porous and mobile. For someone who is fully familiar with a context (e.g. in the case of a highly experienced surfer for whom the necessary competencies are innate and preparing for doing is instantaneous) then the boundary would move to the bottom of the diagram to indicate that the person operated almost entirely in the Practice domain. The converse would be true for an entity in a context which required the entity to do a great deal of reflecting and preparation before anything could be done – in which case the boundary would be above where it is shown in the Figure.

What we have done in the book so far is to examine three themes, set within a context: practitioners' experiences and needs that have to be met by the Framework; insights from complexity science that underpin the Framework; and the Framework itself. As a summary of this section, it can be seen that the Approach and Framework described here provide, potentially, full coverage of the issues raised by practitioners and incorporate the insights from complexity science underlying these issues. In addition, part of the eventual effectiveness of the way the Approach is employed depends on the actual capabilities that will be available at the time. Again, this can't be fully appreciated in advance by ourselves, the authors, but we allow for it in our Approach, as you'll see in the discussion of complexity-worthiness that follows.

CHAPTER 5:
HAVING COMPLEXITY-WORTHINESS

'The voyage of discovery lies not in finding new landscapes, but in having new eyes.'

Marcel Proust (1871-1922)

We have indicated that in order to put complexity to work successfully practitioners have to be able to integrate three aspects in a dynamic and concurrent way. This requires them to:

- use an appropriate approach for reasoning about change in the context and for developing and employing options for engagement (already discussed in the previous chapter),

- have the necessary capabilities available do things differently to bring about change – the topic of this chapter,

- engage with their context to bring about change in reality (how to do this will be discussed in Chapter 6 in detail).

Given the cross-over between all the related topics discussed previously we felt that it was important, in this chapter, to explain what it means to have 'the necessary capabilities available to do things differently'. We will characterise these capabilities, and explain how to judge appropriateness and how practitioners can assess complexity-worthiness.

Complexity-Worthiness

Part of the Approach for Putting Complexity to Work is to have suitable capabilities available to employ as required, and the ability to match them dynamically to context (using the complexity-worthiness loop). We use the term 'capabilities' to cover all types of resources, skills, knowledge, information, devices and techniques that could be required to 'Put Complexity to Work'. Obviously this includes people, but we mean anyone/anything, that might be involved in what is going on. Note that complexity-worthiness is an across-the-board enabler. One of the things that will be revealed when you reflect on your context, therefore, are the capabilities that can be accessed and which, depending on the nature of those capabilities, can be employed to enable complexity-worthiness:

A. **Why it is Needed – Drivers and Underpinning Principles.** We need to appreciate complexity-worthiness because, as has already been mentioned various times, appropriateness is everything. A key principle here is the requisite variety that we explained in Chapter 3. This means that to engage with or to affect something, abilities must match or exceed the nature of things being affected/engaged with. If you want to change the behaviour of a class of children and all you do is shout at them then you are not going to get far; it needs a larger repertoire to engage effectively with the children. In everyday terms people would say 'You don't need a hammer to crack a nut', or 'If you give someone a hammer they will make every problem look like a nail'. In other words, without understanding the significance of complexity-worthiness you might not be able to achieve much – indeed you may cause damage by blundering about 'like a mechanistic elephant in the complex realities of a porcelain shop'. So complexity-worthiness is more than just matching your capabilities to the current context and much more than just 'responding' – it is about appreciating what the context *could be* and being able to influence it through having the necessary capabilities available.

B. **The Role of Complexity-Worthiness in Putting Complexity to Work.** Complexity-worthiness is to do with whether one is open to the possibility of change, whether one can detect change and, if so, whether one can then reason about it, formulate intent and develop appropriate options. It is also to do with whether one has the necessary appreciation of the real-world dynamics and the capabilities, possibilities and the will to do anything about the changing situation, and so on. And it is about being able to estimate the ongoing degree of complexity-worthiness and then, depending on the nature and extent of any 'mismatch' with the context, working out what needs to adapt, change and even be transformed to achieve the appropriate degree of complexity-worthiness.

C. **What it Produces – Its Utility to Practitioners.** Having complexity-worthiness is a state-of-being not a specific tool itself. Hence what it produces for practitioners is the 'ability to do things differently'. It tells us all about the degree to which the capabilities available (from ourselves, through the community or from the environment) can support practice in different types of context – it is about being able to judge and adjust, dynamically and appropriately, the viability and feasibility of using various capabilities, independent of whether they exist, are available or need to be acquired.

CHARACTERISTICS OF COMPLEXITY-WORTHINESS

So, (at last!) we'll explain complexity-worthiness in detail, based on the comparison of closed and open thinking shown in Table 2. The characteristics we have assembled in the Table are the hook for us to describe the state of 'being complexity-worthy' and of discussing the corresponding capabilities needed to enable it. The comparison in the Table below provides us with a more detailed understanding of the differences between reductionist and complexity-aware approaches, not just in the thinking but more so in the actual doing and gives, therefore, an indication of the sorts of capabilities which might be relevant in each case. While reading the entries in the table, for a closed situation think of the type of car-manufacturing methods[59] that Ford created in 1914, and for an open situation think of one typical of dynamically-changing real-world challenges such as nature conservation or community health.

'Closed' Reductionist Ways-of-Working	'Open' Complexity-Aware Ways-of-Working
Relies on order – if necessary imposes it	Embraces disorder of complex phenomena
Is based on objective, proven and normative analysis	Trusts the value of subjective appreciations
Seeks to work with single, rational view of the 'truth' – categorises against a fixed taxonomy	Adopts contradictory viewpoints deliberately and works with diverse and changing meaning
Directs – fixes purpose/assumptions, constrains	Encourages initiative, diversity, degrees of freedom
Fixes boundaries, structures and 'frames of reference'	Engages in open negotiation and collaboration
Expects to predict through probabilities	Accepts unpredictability, considers possibilities
Solves puzzles – extrapolates trends from the known as 'linear' steps	Explores mysteries – imagines 'illogical' hypotheses and competes them to gain insights
Wants certainty and repeatability at the entity level, robust averages are not 'good enough'	Accepts individual uncertainty, but knows that patterns at collective level are reliable, repeatable

---

59   Called Fordism: 'The eponymous manufacturing system designed to spew out standardized, low-cost goods and afford its workers decent enough wages to buy them'.

'Closed' Reductionist Ways-of-Working	'Open' Complexity-Aware Ways-of-Working
Specifies ways-of-working/proscribes top-down formal processes	Enjoys versatility, novelty and inventiveness – engages in informal collaboration
Decomposes problems	Employs holistic understanding
Wants advocacy, authority and power	Promotes enquiry and freedom, facilitates
Centralises decision-making	People take responsibility and ownership
Expects people to be process-followers	Assumes people will explore, discover, challenge
Blames based on notions of defining 'right thing, right place, right time' in advance – punishes accordingly	Judges based on context, sees failure as inevitable, a way of learning/improving – self-aware
Measures outcomes against plans, goals, end-states and 'arbitrary', project-centric timelines	Evaluates through experience, keeps in mind timelines which are realistic given nature of change
Implements solutions using own means	Works with those best placed to change
Presumes the 'system of interest' is owned, territorial	Knows situations are open and unbounded
Risk averse, unlikely to act without the right information. Managers do things right	Takes risks despite uncertainty, accepts that there is no right answer. Leaders do the right things[60]

Table 2 – Comparison of Closed and Open Ways-of-Working

The complexity-aware approach in the table above might appear to some readers a bit too philosophical, even impractical. Reality implies that, based on the open mindset required for complex situations, the characteristics of doing things practically arise largely from ourselves, our own thinking, our own capabilities – and from other entities and structures, such as an enterprise, institution or community – as well as from the context.

So why then is complexity-worthiness relevant? Well, the Elements of our Framework are in themselves not able to 'put complexity to work'. Effective practice in changing circumstances relies on appropriate complexity-worthy thinking and the corresponding capabilities being accessible and employable. But

---

60   This row in the table is based on a quote by Warren G. Bennis (born 1925), a Leadership professional.

it is not enough just to have these capabilities; they too must be put to work – it is from their interactions that complexity-worthiness arises in a particular context. Complexity-worthiness depicts a way-of-working, of switching the Elements of the Framework on, of keeping them in motion and supporting practice. In short: a way-of-working that cannot be bought off-the-shelf in a box. Rather, it is a mix of capabilities able to morph with the changing context in a dynamic looping way. As we have said, complexity-worthiness is emergent in a context and cannot be tied to a particular instance of practice, rather it winds itself through all aspects of putting complexity to work and requires capabilities as follows. We'll group them under the 'axioms of complexity' headings as before:

A. **Complexity-Worthiness Aspects of Capabilities Available and Accessible in the Environment.** People tend to take for granted the capabilities that are native to the environment in which they work – the resources of all types that are available in all sorts of ways and that people use because they are there. These resources range from basic things such as rain, sun and wind, through to the energy we can all extract from gravity (falling water) etc. and the plants and animals that we all eat and herbs that a healer might need. The changes intended will depend on these capabilities to some degree, where Zero-Sum games may come in to play, and the limitations on the straightforward accessibility of these capabilities may be factors (there may be issues of ownership or religious sensitivity, for example). Capabilities in the context not only include what one could broadly call natural resources, but also infrastructure and technology resources as well. Our Environment will also be influenced by rules, regulations, policies and the political situation such as when governments change and new directives are issued. Capabilities available and accessible in the environment are also human resources. Practitioners need to work with those in the environment who are able to bring about change, such as people who already have the necessary skills, or access to people (such as village leaders) and/or permissions or recognition. Working in a federated community, and drawing on a wide range of contributions from those best placed to make them, requires practitioners to have a high degree of complexity-worthiness because a variety of interfaces between many players will have to be accommodated. As Don Tapscott and Anthony Williams say in *Wikinomics*:

> 'Whenever a shift occurs there are always realignments of competitive advantage and new measures of success and value. To succeed in this new world [of Internet-mediated activity], it will not be enough – indeed, it will be counterproductive – simply to intensify current policies, management strategies and curricular approaches. Remaining innovative requires us all to understand

both the shifts and the new strategy agenda that follows. We must collaborate or perish – across borders, cultures, disciplines and firms, and increasingly with masses of people at one time.' (p33)

B. **Complexity-Worthiness Aspects of Dynamic Change**. The changes that might need to be brought about are not necessarily of one type or driven by one set of imperatives, and so the capabilities used will need to be adjusted appropriately. This is especially challenging if, as part of doing things differently, the change desired requires the transformation of the entity itself. The degree to which an entity is set up for dynamic change falls into a set of categories: Type A, welcome change; Type B, would find themselves forced to change because of the way they are set up and Type C, would be indifferent to change. These categories can be further refined as follows:

- [A1] People change all the time (it is just what they do naturally and voluntarily and they are fully set up to engage, shape, influence, etc.).

- [A2] People want to change and may be able work out what their options are (but don't know how or in which ways to change).

- [B1] People have to change in a way that is determined and a manner that is imposed (because they are told top-down).

- [B2] People are forced to change in ways they have not considered/foreseen (but have to because the circumstances force it).

- [C1] People don't see the need for change, or only consider it if it is change on their terms (because they are indifferent to change or can't see it/wouldn't know how to see it).

- [C2] People don't need to change as they think their environment is, for all intents and purposes, static (so, other than refreshing what they do, they carry on as they are until they are forced into being Type B).

As a consequence of these various types of dynamic change the requisite variety we have talked about comes into play. As Figure 7 shows, the complexity-worthiness competencies that define a Type A category are different from those you would need for Type B and are probably absent in Type C. So, a Type A person, community or enterprise would be well equipped for dynamic change. The Figure shows the three main aspects of complexity-worthiness: being open to change; able to reason about it and able to do something about it and illustrates how variations in these aspects affects practice (adapted from Lorraine Dodd, Gwyn Prins and Gillian Stamp's paper *'Going from closed to open: how may we help to make it bearable?'*). Though using caricatures as examples, the Figure shows how important the aspects are in terms of outcome, and especially that all three are needed for effective practice. A key part of complexity-worthiness regards the ability to learn, adapt and apply the learning quickly in dynamic situations across all these aspects. As a consequence, there are various degrees of complexity-worthiness required for different types of dynamic change.

Aspects of Real-world Complexity-worthiness

Example Caricatures	Open to change - appreciates what to sense	Can reason about change - has will to act appropriately	Can engage, influence and learn by doing	Ability to PCtW	Consequences in Real-World Terms
A1: Effective practice	Yes	Yes	Yes	Well-placed	
A2: Inhibited practice	Yes	Yes, but not how	No, so ineffective	Aware, well meaning, but inhibited	
BI / 2: Directed practice	Yes, but forced to	No, 'empty-headed'	Yes, possibly inappropriate	Outside Intent provided. 'Dysfunctional'	
Watcher / 'lurker'	Yes, 'voyeur'	No	No	Aware, not interested in opportunity	
C1: Ill-informed volunteer	No, so 'blind'	Yes, based on own doing	Yes, but ill-informed	Could do it, can't detect what or when	
'Arm-chair' volunteer	No	Yes, hypothetically	No	Has visions, dreams about change	
Interfering volunteer	No	No	Yes, impulsively	'Loose-cannon' capability - miss-aligned	
C2: Entrenched institution	No	No, in 'world of their own'	No	Detached, indifferent	

© abaci 2011   NB: Assume the natural complexity is a similar for all cases

Figure 7 – Aspects of Complexity-Worthiness and their Effects on Practice.

Note that, in our Approach, the three essential aspects of complexity-worthiness at the top of the Figure are dealt with as follows: appreciating what to sense is provided by Reflecting on Realities/Symptom Sorting; reasoning about change is dealt with by the 'Reflecting on Practice' using the Trade-off Space; and engaging and influencing in practice is supported by the use of the Landscape of Change.

C. **Complexity-Worthiness Aspects of Personality and Intent**. Practitioners fully understand the extent to which outcomes can be affected by people with different types of personal competencies and individual capabilities. In Chapter 2 we have already mentioned the importance of people having appropriate mindsets, attitudes, ethos, values and skills. But complexity-worthiness also draws on people's personality, on their courage, motivation and determination – attributes that are not always on the tick-list of your Human Resources department! As Smuts (1926) says 'The essence of Personality is creative freedom in respect of its own conditions of experience and development; as an initiator, metaboliser and assimilator it has practical self-determination. Again, as a selector and coordinator of the features in the situation that confront it [Personality], it also has practical freedom. Its very nature as a Whole confers freedom upon it.' (p291) It is these practical and pragmatic qualities, being self-critical and self-aware, that are, apparently, in short supply, along with culturally-aware and empathetic people who are at home with almost anyone. Competent use of these skills will enable initiative and the confident exploration of diversity and 'degrees of freedom' for doing. The challenge, as it is felt among practitioners, is to make people feel comfortable going into and working in open-ended situations.

D. **Properties of Entities as part of CW.** Some of the practitioners' observations under this heading included: how do you select for and judge fit for purpose; how do you foster and sustain learning by individuals and groups; how do you nurture initiative, robustness, resilience and the self-organisation we have learned about in Chapter 3? They ask how you should prepare for complex situations so as not to be faced with the condition described by Peter Drucker (1909-2005): 'So much of what we call management consists in making it difficult for people to work.' The properties of entities defines the repertoire of possible behaviours that they can express, employ and/or display in practice and, hence, contributes to the degrees of freedom/wiggle-room that the communities-of-practice have overall. These properties and behaviours, such as the degree of 'interoperability' of mindsets, also determine the types of interactions and relationships that entities can form and sustain, as well as affecting how they see the world. Associated organisational capabilities required include: adopting contradictory viewpoints deliberately to consider possibilities; fostering versatility, novelty and inventiveness; enabling people to take responsibility and ownership.

JUDGING APPROPRIATENESS

Complexity-worthiness, therefore, is largely about being able to match capabilities to the nature of things being affected – about judging 'appropriateness'. Whether or not you use this Approach or another one you'll still need to select the 'right capabilities for the job'. The tricky thing is working out what 'right' means, especially in dynamic complex situations where 'rightness' is not a fixed quality. That is why we realised that, for our Approach to work effectively, we had to address this rightness issue here. We also realised that the kinds of artefacts and representations/visualisations generated needed to be appropriate too. The word 'appropriate' is so important (and we have used it so often) because it gets to the essence of putting complexity to work – that because you can never[61] be sure, definitively, unambiguously and with certainty about what is right or correct in any complex situation – you cannot follow predetermined 'if-then' rules. Being successful is then about being able to continually judge, match and adjust appropriateness of engagement and intervention with the realities of context and capability and sustaining that over time. This appropriateness has more than one face to it; it is necessary for all of the following:

- Practice itself – the **Doing** – engaging in the communities-of-practice and doing the iterative engagement, contributing and influencing; and

- Adjusting Conditions for Practice – the **Shaping** – affecting the conditions of practice depending on what can be changed in the context; and

- Reflecting on Realities/Practice – the **Being** – reflecting on the factors for matching capabilities/contributions to conditions in the community-of-practice; and

- Preparing for Practice/adapting complexity-worthiness – the **Having** – setting up, across the context, to do all of the above – the necessary ways-of-working, competencies, flexibility and so on.

We will now look at this topic in more detail under the headings of appropriate capabilities and appropriate artefacts.

---

61   And we really do mean never! Complexity science and common sense confirm this – as we discussed in Chapter 3. Obviously, prior experience helps you make a judgement about the right tool in familiar circumstances.

A. **Appropriateness – Matching Capability to Context Dynamically**. This part of the Framework is for matching available capability to shape possible situations and is, in a way, the main supporter of all the loops. This is all about increasing confidence, scoping tasks and being able to 'defend' decisions about why particular approaches and toolsets have been selected. Practitioners need to be able to make judgements about appropriateness for the following reasons:

1. **Why it is Needed – Drivers and Underpinning Principles**. The ability to judge appropriateness is needed not just because practitioners have asked for it, but also because it supplies a rational basis for doing the matching, which is critically important in real-world terms. A principle from complexity science is that complexity manifests itself in different situations through different types of phenomena and that these affect people in different ways. If you think about the open/closed situation discussions in Chapter 1 and previously in this chapter, and the Hurricane Katrina experience, it is apparent that we are not always good at matching approach to context for the given situations – even when it seems obvious. This is further complicated by the ways that practitioners perceive the contextual complexity in the area where they work – experienced people will use different techniques to novices – and again by the diversity of capabilities available.

2. **What it Does – Why it Works**. Judging appropriateness is actually a 'tool for thought' in its own right and provides a systematic way of mapping a number of relevant factors against dimensions of contextual and experienced complexity. This mapping reveals the classes of ways-of-working (i.e. of toolsets etc.) that would therefore be appropriate to use in different 'types' of context. The types of context shown in Figure 8 are examples that range from the 'routine' (where change will be self-evident arising largely from what can be thought of as simple, 'mechanistic' interactions) to the 'crisis' (where phenomena are turbulent and unconstrained and where change is so fast, transitory and unexpected that practitioners would struggle to engage with the underlying 'regularities'). Complexity-worthiness matching works because it largely uses common-sense indicators and everyday language rather than a model that would require weeks or months of data collection before it could work – if indeed the necessary data could be collected at all. Figure 8 summarises these factors, and appropriate ways-of-working are characterised as follows:

	Nature of Context (Symptoms)			Appropriate Iterative Ways-of-working		
Example 'Type'	Phenomena	Structures		Strategies	Information	Influence
Crisis	Unordered, apparently random, no recognisable relationships	Fleeting transient opportunistic ('rhizomic' / swarms)		ENACTING Imagine-Probe-Compete Hypotheses-Seed	Possible futures / potentially significant indicators - hypothesise	Susceptible to bottom-up influences - usually indirect
Challeng-ing	Ever-changing novel emergent patterns - only coherent in retrospect	Shaped on-the-fly by events. Identifiable leaders (franchise)		EXPLORING Engage-Perceive-Adapt-Learn Influence	Equivocal indicators with many potential meanings - judgement	All ways of influencing are potentially relevant
'Predict-able'	Complicated but deducible varying in time, space and mode	Shaped by process and formal organisational 'templates'		DISCOVERING Sense-Analyse-Plan-Respond	Probabilistic factors induct / hedge / deduct procedurally - gap filling	Susceptible to top-down influences - via processes, templates and assumptions
'Routine'	Simple, familiar phenomena, perceivable, repeatable and self-evident	Determined by history and imposed / embedded institutions / instructions		'VIEWING' Sense-Recognise-Act / React (repeating the known)	Data are observable facts - categorise knowns	Change the rules / constraints / structures and procedures

Increasingly Hyper-dimensional Stressing Ambiguous

'Stable' Understandable Tractable

© abaci 2011

Figure 8 – Appropriate Ways-of-working for a Range of Types of Context.

a. *Crisis – Enacting: conceive futures, probe, hypothesise, seed in crisis, shock contexts (such as in an emergency response situation after an earthquake).* The aim here is to focus on the impossible and unpredictable, to generate possible futures. Approach: develop competing hypotheses and identify potential indicators that could be significant (including the possibility that there may be a lack of indicators). Example: identify 'seeding' options to increase likelihood of preferred phenomena arising or enact 'shake the tree' to probe and flush out patterns.

b. *Challenging – Exploring: engage, perceive, adapt, influence in challenging contexts (such as the kindergarten and surfing example).* The aim here is to focus on the possibilities – to avoid being surprised. Approach: engage with and examine viewpoints within a variety of interdependent perspectives and explore/test (iterate) alternative hypotheses. Example: continually adaptive 'what-if'ing' or participatory narratives. This provides sense-making for those dealing with more ordered phenomena, indicating items of possible significance or to influence existing patterns and features in the context in order to stabilise or de-stabilise as required.

c. *Predictable – Discovering: sense, analyse, plan, respond in 'predictable' contexts (such as being the logistics planners supporting the practitioners in a refugee camp).* The aim here is to focus on probabilities – to hedge bets and balance options. Approaches include systematic analysis based on what can be known from directed sensing supported by conventional tools and models (trying to detect common indicators). Example: tasks are context-specific, such as identifying missing information, and then collecting, processing and exploiting resulting insights in accordance with set procedures. This can give sense to things for those dealing with disordered phenomena but may lead to simplistic cause-effect responses.

d. *Routine – Viewing: sense, recognise, react in routine contexts (such as in supermarket chains).* Here the focus is on the manipulation of 'facts', developing orders/tasks with predictable outcomes and processing reports about known events. Approach: set procedures will be followed for the development of formal artefacts (orders/reports/databases). Example: tasks tend to be context independent (the activity is 'the same' regardless) – categorise/recognise, monitor and respond – and follow pre-canned/'rote' procedures ('we always do this – it's best practice').

3. **What it Produces – Its Utility to Practitioners.** This ability to adjust ways-of-working dynamically with changing contexts means that outputs, in terms of 'toolset selection', support the ongoing activities of practitioners. A basic principle is that the use of plug-and-play capabilities provides the sort of requisite variety that is needed for complexity-worthiness. For example, when reflecting on what action or information is needed for engaging effectively with the dynamics of the context, capability selection works if the techniques etc. have been catalogued and marked up using the kind of complexity-worthiness criteria that are relevant to putting complexity to work, rather than using other criteria from management, system engineering or even complexity science. Note that it is beyond the scope of this book to provide a full analysis of appropriate toolsets and so instead, throughout the Guide, we have introduced a few relevant examples.

B. **Artefacts – their Importance and Relevance.** If artefacts are to be used to capture the results of reflecting or as products from the Elements of the Framework, it is important that they are able to represent the issue at hand in a way that does not impoverish the issue itself, its meaning and/or its significance. The principle here is that, as we know, even an object can affect outcomes in complex situations and if artefacts, in their role as components of complexity, do not represent the world adequately then they change meaning, and this will change outcomes. Artefacts, of various sorts, are generated as part of using the Putting Complexity to Work Approach. They are not usually tangible and formal but are rather as follows:

1. **Why the Artefacts are Needed – Drivers and Underpinning Principles.** We have discussed appropriateness above and it applies as much to the artefacts produced as it does to everything else involved in putting complexity to work. In Chapter 3 we contrasted the difference between the kind of information needed for solving puzzles from that required for dealing with mysteries. Given the range of factors needed to express the different contexts during Symptom Sorting, an appreciation is needed of which types of artefacts fit with which types of situation. Figure 9 characterises these differences in a set of (somewhat idealistic but based on hard-won experience) 'Information Levels'.

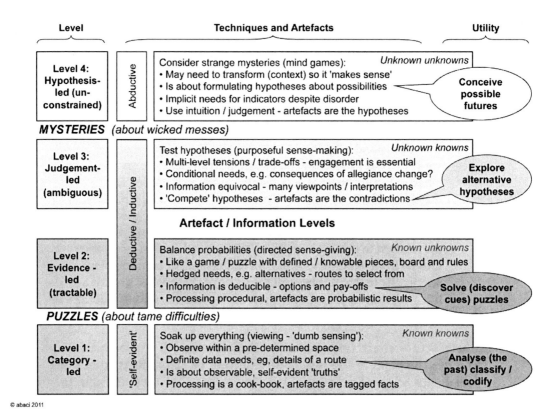

© abaci 2011

Figure 9 – A Range of Artefacts Suitable for Use in Different Types of Contexts.

2. **What they do – Why they Work**. This range of artefacts supports practice across a variety of contexts by enabling information appropriate to the contexts to be captured, stored, manipulated, transformed and employed as necessary. The characteristics of the artefacts in the different Information Levels are described below:

a. *Level 4 Information*: Supports user-led intuition and brain storming about possible futures. It involves considering intangibles, such as people's intentions, which are, largely, mysteries. Considering them is not a formal 'process' – it involves creativity and wacky thinking. There is, as the circumstances are ever-evolving, no 'final, correct' answer. Thinking starts with little or no knowledge of the nature or extent of the context and builds hypotheses or fantasies of what might be going on and projects these ideas into the future and 'competes' them.[62] Here, it may not even be possible to adequately determine what needs to be decided upon, nor even how it can be acquired or visualised – it often has to be imagined. In many situations, even the absence of information can be very significant. Most of this kind of 'information' (e.g. concerning the mind-games being played by other actors) will be in peoples' heads as mental maps and so is not be able to be stored directly elsewhere (especially not in machines). These abstractions include those required to support so-called 'red teaming' and to capture judgements about deception and/or malicious or dysfunctional behaviour. For the foreseeable future, machines will not be able to participate in dialogues[63] about these issues – and the consequences of this must be fully acknowledged.

b. *Level 3 Information*: Supports user-led exploration, problem-framing and probability evaluation where the analysis requires creativity and insight (as the levels of significance are low and hard to determine). Thinking considers potential indicators/weights of evidence that might exist (the significance of which depends on the likely perspectives and viewpoints being adopted) or be required to support or refute hypotheses and looks to see if they exist in the 'real'/perceived world or in cyberspace. This looking is purposefully directed sensing – it is not 'dumb' looking and then 'sense-making' afterwards as is often suggested. Different time-horizons must be considered and sequences and patterns over potentially long periods of time noted. The artefacts are so-called abstract information – not static facts but 'morphable ontologies'. These have dynamically adapting networks of linkages (some of which may be historical, predictive, contradictory, duplicate, hypothetical or unknown) that arise from the subjective interpretation of evidence from different perspectives and viewpoints and over different timelines. They are given different connotations depending which competing hypotheses are being examined.

---

62 The hypotheses definitely need to be competed using human judgement – they cannot, by definition, be computed owing to Gödel's Incompleteness Theorem as previously discussed in Chapter 3. By competing we mean comparing relative merits.

63 This is a subtle and *critically important point*. It is one thing to write down ideas in a text document and store it electronically – it is another thing entirely for the machine to *understand the meaning and significance* of what has been written in human/operational terms. Current software cannot do the latter. The degree to which computers are capable of forming *'human-machine teams'* with people is discussed in Patrick's poster entitled 'Putting Complexity to Work – achieving effective Human-machine Teaming'.

The linkages themselves have very significant meaning and are made between items such as indicators, assessments and judgements (e.g. about significance, provenance, normality and confidence). Alternative meanings must be allowed to co-exist and not be 'normalised' into a single truth or a common view of the world. It should be noted that current computers cannot support human-machine dialogue about matters at this Level of information.[64]

c. *Level 2 and Level 1 Information*: Practitioners need artefacts with the following features to support them in solving puzzles: The puzzler knows in advance what the puzzle is and so can bound the context. When something is missing, it is easy to classify the missing item(s), describe it in fact-like terms (a red piece with a face on it) and then search for or collect the missing item(s). Once candidate pieces have been found, it is possible to compare them (because prior models exist) and match an item as being the missing one. It is then possible to fit the new fact into the puzzle (as the puzzle is static) and confirm it is the 'right' piece. The consequences of finding the piece can be understood because the relationships between the new and existing items make sense within the puzzler's own experience and world view. The assumption is that the puzzle can be solved – that there is only one solution. Level 1 and 2 artefacts support Puzzling. Level 2 Information are deducible facts about a known situation or about previous events. Here we are dealing with artefacts which can be identified, matched, labelled and stored, for example, in a relational database and explored and manipulated using a conventional computer. Level 1 Information includes the givens/universal facts which support simple analysis of familiar environments. They can be tagged and can easily be stored, for example, in conventional flat file databases.

3. **What they Produce – Their Utility to Practitioners.** As such, artefacts do not produce outputs – their utility is in assisting with expressing, generating and maintaining an appreciation of the changing context, and in providing evidence of that understanding. Note a very important point here: the artefacts themselves are not the understanding; they are merely

---

64   The reasons for this are authoritatively discussed by W. Daniel (Danny) Hillis in Chapter 9 of his book *The Pattern On The Stone: The Simple Ideas That Make Computers Work.*

mediators of it. Think of a brainstorming session that produces some wonderful flipcharts covered in writing at the end of it. They are a very effective reminder to those who took part in the understanding that was achieved, but they are almost unintelligible to anyone else – even, and even more so, when turned into PowerPoint! The artefacts play different roles in the Approach as follows:

a.   *There are those which are internal to the Approach – in that they support specific Elements by doing things such as:* providing the basis on which tools are selected for use; or being the 'stores' needed for capturing material for each of the Elements – for example, for noting the understanding of contextual and experienced complexity.

b.   *There are also those which are internal to the Approach – but are required for employing the overall journey, such as:* keeping track of where one started in the dynamic loops and how one has stepped through them; or helping to identify mismatches/synergies between views of contextual and experienced complexity.

c.   *Some artefacts are 'external' to the Approach and Framework in that they are visible to others and part of engagement/ influencing, such as:* helping to identify and make explicit the different actor's roles/capabilities in the context of interest as the basis for collaboration; or helping to identify/ make explicit the options for change – a basis for trade-off discussions. A trivial example is captured in the cliché, 'A picture paints a thousand words' – yet if your reader is blind, the picture is useless without the spoken word – so these artefacts are very contextually dependent. The caricature in Figure 10 (overleaf) graphically expresses this in the way in which a request for a child's swing to be hung from the branch of a tree might become misinterpreted along the way and the 'message' morph as it was re-interpreted by the different artefacts used by the various agencies involved in the supply-chain.

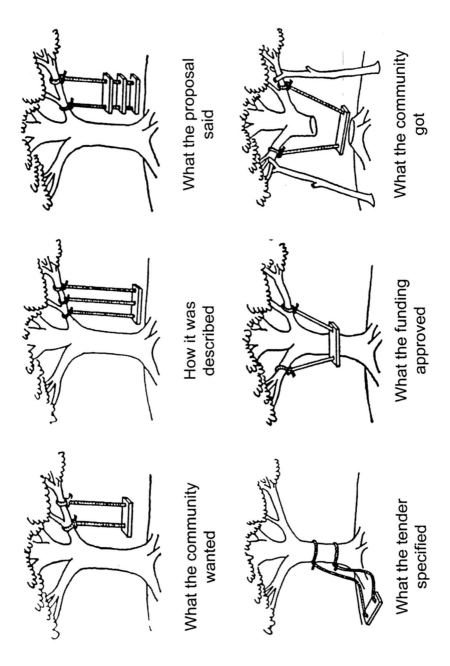

What the proposal said

What the community got

How it was described

What the funding approved

What the community wanted

What the tender specified

© abaci 2011

Figure 10 – How Artefacts Can Change Meaning and Outcomes.

INDICATORS OF COMPLEXITY-WORTHINESS

So, how does one go about assessing complexity-worthiness of individuals or organisations i.e. their capacity to engage and influence appropriately with a changing context? Table 3 provides 'pen-picture' indicators of complexity-worthiness grouped by capability criteria. These can be used to assess the extent of ongoing mismatch between current capabilities and those required in the context.

Criteria	Context-independent Indicators of Complexity-Worthiness
Governance	Able to change policies, adapt structures and adjust authorisations, obligations and permissions in near real-time.
Environment/Scope/Scale	Able to adjust 'upward' and 'downward' dependencies and interactions, work without predefined boundaries in multi-stakeholder and multidisciplinary communities and scale up/down dynamically.
Operational Dynamics	Able to form federations, agile groupings and communities-of-interest using flexible sets of procedures that can be 'morphed' as required.
Requirements assessment	Comfortable with continually changing stakeholder values, needs, interests and viewpoints manifested as user-centred services.
Risk	Open to change. Can trade-off risk and opportunity, accepts that there is no 'right' answer and embraces learning-by-doing – resilient.
Training	Learns from experience and insights; is able to integrate what has been learned seamlessly, aims at non-process-following capabilities.
Equipment	Supports human-machine teaming – active, informal decision-making activities – is 'process neutral' and fundamentally user-configurable.
Tools and Techniques	Employs participatory techniques; is demand-driven and flexible in changing the employment of suitable approaches on-the-fly.

Criteria	Context-independent Indicators of Complexity-Worthiness
'Process'	Able to carry out informal sense-making in the face of uncertainty and change, collaborates, generates transparency, builds trust, creates ownership, promotes the emergence of creativity, discovers, iterates.
Personnel	Seeks out and enjoys working with confident, courageous people with open mindset and informal competencies; introduces diversity, promotes initiative and innovation.
Information	Collects information and indicators from a variety of sources; weighs up hypotheses; uses contradictory, equivocal information.
Doctrine and Concepts	Goes for agility from outset that creates options and wiggle-room. Seeks out degrees of freedom; transdisciplinarity; is integrative.
Organisational Setup	Shows flexibility; takes adaptive stance; seeds space-of-possibilities.
Infrastructure	Designed to be flexible; adaptable 'come-as-you-are'.
Logistics	Able to deal with on-demand requests; change nature of service provision between *ad hoc* and predefined.
Interoperability	Able to re-configure as circumstance/expediency requires to enable accessibility.
'System' Architecture	Able to be part of and adapt to federations with no single owner on-demand and as required.
System Engineering	Provides elements which can be adapted/configured, on-the-fly at 'run-time'. Uses dynamic discovery, resource aware adaptation.
Monitoring	Adjusts ongoing activities to circumstances; is flexible when unexpected events take place.
Evaluation	Involves evaluators right from the beginning, captures actual change, queries whether a difference has been made, questions whether the appropriate thing has been done, deduces learning benefits.

Table 3 – Indicators for the Assessment of Complexity-Worthiness.

DEGREES OF COMPLEXITY-WORTHINESS

As we mentioned earlier in the Guide in our surfing example, part of having this complexity-worthiness is being able to transition from the static state of observing to the dynamic experience of doing. In practice, one also needs to be able to adapt complexity-worthiness appropriately and continuously in an event-driving/event-driven way with the changing circumstances over time.

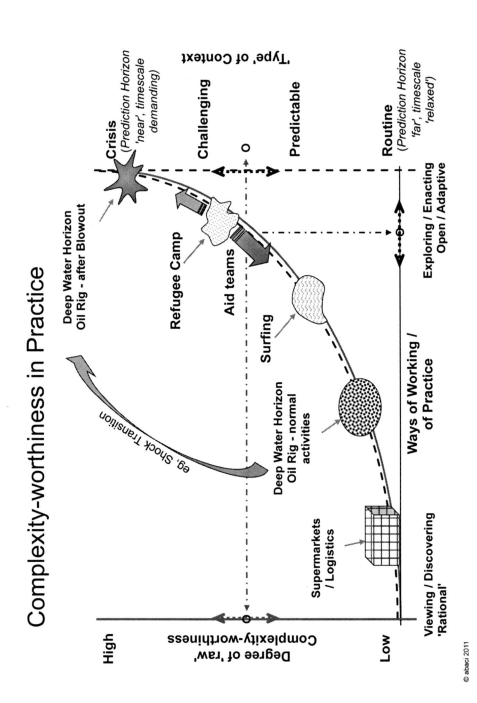

Figure 11 – The Dynamics of Complexity-worthiness in Practice.

Figure 11 shows these dynamics in a schematic way where, at any time, there is an interplay between the three axes that affects the dynamics of practice and of all the entities in the context. To the right are the 'types' of context described above, to the left the degree of raw complexity-worthiness and along the bottom the various ways-of-working that might be appropriate. Many of the tensions of practice come from the mismatches between the capabilities and ways-of-working of those involved in a situation. Assessing complexity-worthiness can really only be done in relation to a context – it is not an abstract quality. Some examples of different degrees of complexity-worthiness follow:

A. Supermarket logistics are, at the macro-level, relatively 'routine' – they have the initiative and can take their time with planning and deployment, major transitions are unlikely and so procedural ways-of-working are appropriate and complexity-worthiness can be low.

B. The day-to-day operation of the Deep Water Horizon oil rig in Florida in 2010 was largely predictable and 'relaxed' with procedural ways-of-working. To cover accidents, the companies involved wrote instructions to deal with every contingency – they had 'complexity' mastered it seemed.

C. Surfing is relatively predictable, yet the immediacy of the environment, i.e. the continuous wave formation means that people cannot have the initiative. Previous training and experience provides the complexity-worthiness 'templates' that are applied during practice.

D. Consider life in a refugee camp. Agencies need to, and need to be seen to act and react decisively and are forced into time-critical activity. The wiggle-room required is higher in order to maintain enough agility and to keep 'degrees of freedom' as open as possible.

E. In the Deep Water Horizon blowout, a shock transition occurred. People had zero initiative and time and so it was inevitable that change would be disruptive. A sudden transition to high complexity-worthiness would have been required (as the Figure shows) but, as we all now know, it wasn't available in this particular case. What should have happened is that intervention (enacting), firstly *ad hoc* (by people with natural leadership) and later by institutionalised response teams, changed phenomena such that the context became more predictable, and eventually returned to 'routine'. What seems to have happened is that staff were mandated to follow procedures that were an appropriate way of working for a crisis in theory but not for the reality of one. We will look at this crisis situation in more detail through a case study example in Chapter 7.

Hence it can be seen that there may need to be purposeful effort to transform from non-complexity-aware capabilities to being appropriately complexity-worthy – it cannot happen by chance. For example, the technology that was used to make steam engines and bicycles can't be used to make iPods and enable Facebook social networking. The possibilities offered by iPods and Facebook are completely different from those available with steam engines and bicycles and can only be achieved by transformation. More importantly for practice, steam engineers (in a Facebook world) would have no way of understanding what was going on in a modern context. Indeed, the consequence of this for practice goes further than just individual capabilities. If you specify and evaluate projects and people in steam-engineering terms, you are only going to get more steam engineers and steam engines. Complexity-worthiness as a mindset, has to extend end-to-end across and beyond enterprises for its benefits to be fully realised.

Transitions Because of Changing Contexts. How do the various types of transitions that can occur affect complexity-worthiness? In theory, almost any set of transitions[65] are possible. Some *are* more likely and so can be 'planned for', some just happen regardless, a lot are opportunities. In addition, some transitions in the context may be smooth, others a step-change, whilst others may jerk suddenly or oscillate. Note that in any context there are always background transitions to work with: one transition drifts day-to-day towards stagnation; there is an opposite one, caused by innovation and 'the unexpected', which continually generates change and inherent instability. In reality, these two tendencies oscillate about the 'edge of chaos', such that complexity-worthiness is always necessary regardless of any other transitions that may be introduced. To examine the complexity-worthiness consequences of a couple of these let's look at an example context. Think of a refugee camp in a country ravaged by drought and civil war where aid agencies are working to support people right now as well as assisting their return to their homelands. The situation is ongoing over months or even years and is relentless – ever-changing as the civil war ebbs and flows, and extremely uncertain.

---

65   Transitions are often seen as potentially damaging or requiring existing structures to be thrown away. But this only true if the organisation is 'brittle' and not agile enough to adapt.

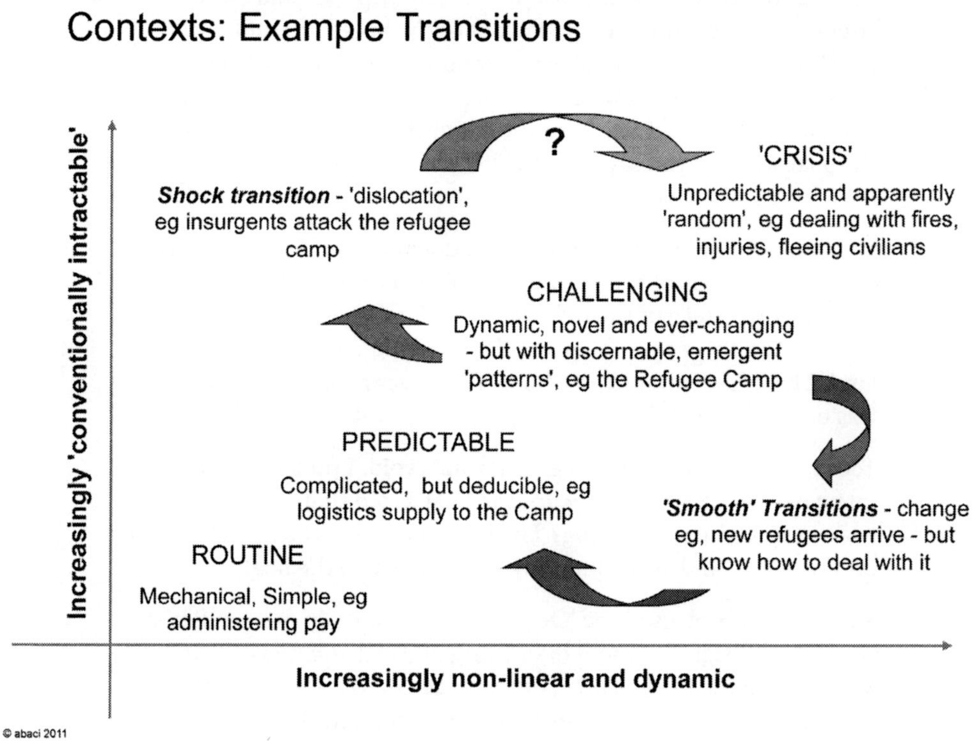

Contexts: Example Transitions

Figure showing a diagram with the vertical axis labelled "Increasingly 'conventionally intractable'" and horizontal axis labelled "Increasingly non-linear and dynamic".

Shock transition - 'dislocation', eg insurgents attack the refugee camp

'CRISIS'
Unpredictable and apparently 'random', eg dealing with fires, injuries, fleeing civilians

CHALLENGING
Dynamic, novel and ever-changing - but with discernable, emergent 'patterns', eg the Refugee Camp

PREDICTABLE
Complicated, but deducible, eg logistics supply to the Camp

'Smooth' Transitions - change eg, new refugees arrive - but know how to deal with it

ROUTINE
Mechanical, Simple, eg administering pay

© abaci 2011

Figure 12 – Example Transitions Between Contexts.

Figure 12 shows two of the main types of transitions that might occur:

> **Smooth Transition**. The first transition is shown in the bottom-right-hand corner of the Figure. A sudden change or novelty (e.g. a new wave of refugees arriving) is dealt with by falling back on 'behavioural templates' that have been developed based on experience and that enable a transition through a predictable space back to 'activities as usual'.

> **Shock.** Another type of transition is shown in the top-left-hand corner of the Figure. Here, a shock transition (e.g. a sudden attack on the camp) means that recovery can probably only go via the crisis space (as all normal assumptions are invalidated). Shock transitions are a 'dislocation' that are, at first, almost impossible to make sense of because the frame of reference, the contextual complexity, disappears in a moment. This is nicely described in Rosamund Stone Zander and Benjamin Zander's book *The Art of Possibility* (p5) as follows:

'I signed up for my first white-water rafting trip and paid close attention to the guide. "If you fall out of the boat," she said, "it is very important that you pull your feet up so that you don't get a foot caught in the rocks below. Think 'toes to nose'," she stressed, "then look for the boat and reach for the oar or the rope. "If you fall out of the boat what do you say to yourself?" she said. "Toes to nose, and look for the boat," we chimed.

We climbed into the boat and started downstream. Surging into the only class 5 rapids of the journey, I vanished into a wall of water that rose up at the stern of the raft, as into a black hole. Rolling about underwater, there was no up and down, neither water nor air nor land. There had never been a boat. There was no anywhere, there was nothing at all.

Toes to nose ... the words emerged from a void. I pulled together into a ball. Air. Sounds. Look for the boat ... did that come from my head or was someone calling? The boat appeared, and an oar. Reach for the oar ... I did, and found myself back inside the boat.

Since then, I have used the 'Out of the boat' story in many different situations. It signifies more than being off track – it means you don't know where the track is. 'Out of the boat' could refer to something as simple forgetting a familiar task, or to floundering in the wake of a management shake-up. When you are 'Out of the boat', *you cannot think your way back;* you have no point of reference. You must either call on some possibility you have considered before – like 'toes to nose' – or seize whatever opportunities present themselves by chance.'

The ability to transition appropriately through a repertoire of behaviours is a key part of the capabilities required to put complexity to work in real-world practice. Some other common transitions that practitioners might face or initiate, and their complexity-worthiness consequences, include the following:

A. **Pattern Breaking (Collapse[66]).** *Routine straight to crisis and stay there.* This is a complete breakdown with no guarantee of any particular type of order re-appearing. Extreme disaster scenarios fall into these categories such as the crisis in Japan in March 2011 following the largest earthquake and tsunami in Japan's history. The consequences of the damage to the Fukushima nuclear reactor on the east coast of Japan are still being played out at the time of writing. Of course, if control

---

66   For more about collapse in its different and more extreme forms, see the book *Collapse* by Jared Diamond or *A Choice of Catastrophes* by Isaac Asimov .

isn't restored then the context becomes 'unordered' – a situation that probably no degree of complexity-worthiness can deal with.

B. **Pattern Breaking (Contrived).** *Oscillations between crisis and predictable or between challenging and routine.* This type of pattern breaking is sometimes used during training exercises to encourage people to consider novel options or to 'teach lessons' and give permission to explore their complexity-worthiness'. Here the exercise controllers and 'Red Team' are manipulating various aspects of complexity to release different phenomena that the players then have to deal with by being flexible and adaptable. Being an exercise controller is a great way to learn about practice in complex environments.

C. **Pattern Exploration (Liberation).** *Routine to challenging then predictable and back to new routines.* Here circumstances (or general agreement) result in a 'letting go' of the routine and an acceptance of the freedom and possibilities of new patterns. Alternative patterns are explored (not usually systematically) and preferred ones selected and 'stabilised' as predictable features, which may in time become routine. The social, economic, feminist and political changes of the 1970s and 80s are of this type as is the 'steam engines to iPods' transformation previously mentioned. This may mean that capabilities need to be fundamentally reinvented before complexity-worthiness that is appropriate to the changed context can be regained.

D. **Pattern Imposition (Lock-down).** *A forced change from crisis to routine.* This may be a brutal military coup, or something milder such as dispersing or containing a mob – as in the policy for the so-called 'kettling' (corralling) of protesters by UK police. In complexity-worthiness terms, this is about recognising latent phenomena already in place in the context that can be exploited as a capability by those doing the imposing. A failed coup may result in a liberating transition – as was seen in the change of governments in Tunisia and Egypt in February 2011.

E. **Pattern Imposition (Crisis-management).** *An opportunistic change from crisis directly to predictable and back to a previous routine.* Following a shock or sudden novelty (as previously discussed), this transition relies upon there having been some previous consideration of possibilities – being robust and resilient. In complexity-worthiness terms, 'spontaneous order' can be created using behavioural templates such as fire drills or 'toes to nose' behaviours.

F. **Pattern Disruption (Novelty/Creativity).** An oscillation between crisis and challenging where so-called disruptive opportunities arise. This type of transitions is actually a continual creation of novelty for which the complexity-worthiness of 'supermarket-chain' enterprises are often ill-prepared. One extreme of such an opportunistic context, perhaps surprisingly, is the space where, among others, terrorists also sit. In one of our case studies we'll examine public protest against the Government of the UK (over rising fuel prices) and how the potential opportunities were handled by those concerned.

SUMMARY OF COMPLEXITY-WORTHINESS

In this chapter we indicated that certain capabilities are needed to put complexity to work. We have characterised those capabilities as 'complexity-worthiness' and have shown that it can be assessed in a systematic way. To some extent, the whole book is about complexity-worthiness, about adjusting capabilities and conditions for practice with the context as required so that they are applied in ways that make the most of the dynamics of the situation. Achieving this is as much about mindsets and ways-of-working as it is about capabilities – i.e. to be able to bring together and energise the various diverse mixes of capabilities needed to put complexity to work in any situation. Which means we're ready for the last section of the Guide, where we show how to make the Approach work in practice!

> 'Out of clutter, find simplicity. From discord, find harmony. In the middle of difficulty lies opportunity.'
> *Albert Einstein's '3 Rules of Work'.*

PART TWO – Using the Approach in Practice and Case Studies

'The earth is like a spaceship that didn't come
with an operating manual.'
R. Buckminster Fuller (1895-1983)

CHAPTER 6: USING THE APPROACH IN PRACTICE

We have now arrived at the second part of the Guide where we will explain how to use the Approach and Framework to do things differently in practice. This is where we get to the heart of the main story we have been developing which, in a nutshell, is this – that, because of the way that change comes about in the world, complexity can be comprehended and influenced in a purposeful way as part of successful, everyday practice. And, practitioners need to be able to do this all in the kind of integrative, dynamic way we have been discussing in the Guide. We'll begin this chapter by comparing conventional ways-of-working with our Approach and, hence why practitioners might use the Framework presented in this Guide and how they might get started. We will then, in three sections under the headings below, explain how to work with and between the main loops of the Approach (remember that these are not ordered in a 'process') which are:

- **Engaging with communities-of-practice and using the Landscape of Change** to dynamically and continuously shape, contribute and influence in a context (i.e. practice – in the on the surf-board sense);

- **Reasoning and reflecting about practice** and setting the 'conditions for doing' by examining mismatches, tensions and drivers of change in the Trade-off Space (i.e. preparing for practice in the 'on-the-beach' sense of assessing wave conditions vs capabilities and so on);

- **Appreciating and reflecting about the realities** of the context using Symptom Sorting to iteratively gather, express and explore the features (i.e. in the way a surfer might find out about different beaches, the type of surf to be found there, facilities, social-life and other relevant items).

As we mention in Chapter 4, where we discussed the dynamics of the loops of the Approach in practice, the degree to which any of this 'looping' would be done innately and reactively by an individual entity as part of practice (as opposed to being done deliberatively in a collaborative manner with others on the beach to prepare for practice) depends on the skill and experience of the entity and their familiarity with the context and, of course, on the dynamics active in that context.

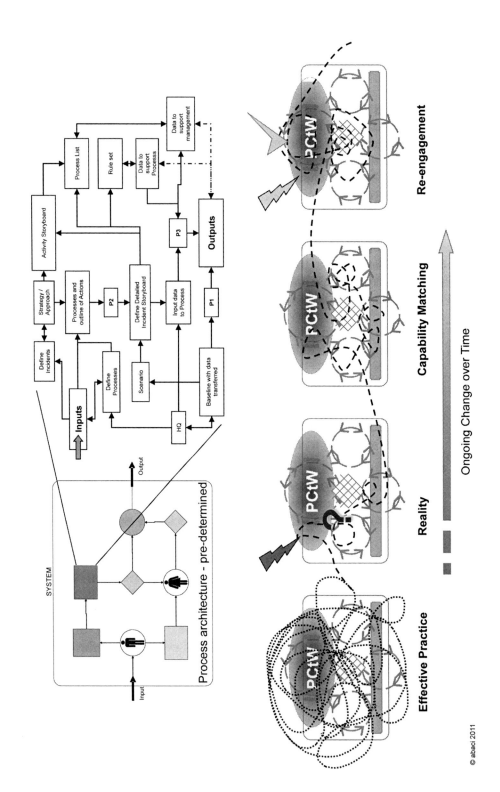

Figure 13 - The Integrative Dynamic Loops of PCtW in Practice.

So, when fully applied in practice the Approach synthesises activities across the dynamic loops shown at the bottom part of Figure 13. But how does this contrast with how things are done conventionally? The diagrams in the top row of the Figure are a flow-chart process and an example from an architecture framework showing information exchange requirements and links[67] between processes. These are fully defined in advance of practice and imply that you need to know what has happened, is happening or might happen and populate the boxes with data before starting. When an unexpected 'stress' occurs, such as a strike by airport staff, unless specifically foreseen (and contingencies included) the system will almost certainly behave in a 'brittle' way and fail to adjust because all components are rigidly linked and will struggle with the unexpected knock-on effects.

The bottom row of diagrams in Figure 13, in contrast, illustrates the context-driven/context-driving/learning-by-doing journey of putting complexity to work where, at any moment in time and given the circumstances, people work with the factors that matter to practice. The bottom-left diagram attempts to show the flow of practice. It looks, at first sight, like an incoherent mess because the flow has been unnaturally compressed into one chart. However, when you spread out the flow of the journey over time to expose the iterations (as we have done along the bottom of the Figure), then the rational nature of how one activity triggers another by circumstance becomes apparent – as does the robust and defendable nature of the practitioners' 'dance' that our Approach supports. Hence, it is possible to generate the kind of audit trail needed for accountability purposes – even though the artefacts produced would be rather different from the kind of tick-box checking that conventionally would be used in the process in the top part of the diagram.

So, in the dynamic looping in the bottom half of the Figure, an event (shown by the lightning symbol) introduces stress into the context and changes the contextual complexity that triggers a period of reflection (indicated by the ?-symbol), adjustment/matching of capabilities and then successful re-engagement with the community in the context despite the ongoing stress. Note that putting complexity to work is not just about 'living in the now'; there is nothing to say that this reflection has to be 'real-time' or that long-timescale deliberations can't be included. Indeed, this is where the formulation of possible futures through competing hypotheses, previously discussed in Chapter 5, come into play and it

---

67 If you are presented with one of these 'architecture'/process diagrams try asking a simple question, 'What do the links mean?' After the decode has been provided from the legend, ask again 'But what do they *mean*? What causes the links to come about? How do they change, to what degree, in which ways?' When you get blank looks, it is time to worry about the real-world relevance, validity and use of the legend and the process/information/architecture model.

is perfectly possible to have a number of strands of practice concurrently active at various levels and across different scales. These would not necessarily be coordinated as a single unit – instead, potential touch points and opportunities for 'rendezvous' would be used – all part of monitoring the overall energy, flow and dynamics of practice. In other words, the Approach can be used equally well by one person on the fly as by a team of 'x' people working across a diverse federation where, given this variety of circumstances, loops may last seconds, hours, days, or even longer – it all depends.

WHERE TO 'START' WITH THE APPROACH

So, why might people decide to use the Approach, and how would they determine where to start and where to 'go' next on their Putting Complexity to Work journey? We, the authors, can't recommend *a priori* 'Start your journey here', or tell you where to go next because that depends on the issues and dynamics of your context. Only you have knowledge of that context and, over time, more will become apparent to you (though of course the dynamics have already been active for some time before you came along and so have a certain 'history' of their own). However, there are a number of potential starting points leading to very different journeys and threads of activity (to use the cliché 'Success is not getting to the destination, it's the journey'[68]). We have picked out a few typical situations that give some idea of the reasons why people might use the Approach, for example when:

A. There is a desire for change (e.g. one wants to change, has decided to change) and one wants to work with the changing context and make the best of the opportunities;

B. There is a need to change (e.g. one is being told to change or forced to change by circumstances, or current approaches are 'failing') and one wants to compare options;

C. There is a need to scale-up and scale-down activities as the dynamics of the context change so one needs to use an approach that is scale- and domain-independent i.e. not fixed to certain types of context;

D. More appropriate monitoring and evaluation has developed new understanding the consequences of which require that the degree of matching of capabilities to context be adjusted to correspond to the nature of the mismatches and tensions of change now exposed;

---

68   If you like this, try reading the poem '*Road to Ithaca*' by Constantine P. Cavafy. Here's an extract: 'When you start on your journey to Ithaca, then pray that the road is long, full of adventure, full of knowledge.'

E. There has been some kind of unexpected event or crisis that is beyond the range, spectrum and/or capability of current approaches – so fundamentally different alternatives must be considered;

F. Going into a new situation where there is a need to develop an appreciative understanding of the wider context, its possibilities and of the roles that the various actors play in it;

G. There is a recognition that one is not dealing with a supermarket-chain situation and that instead a complexity-ready approach is needed that can reveal any possible opportunities but one doesn't know how to change or what the costs, risks or benefits might be;

H. Practitioners feel an integrative approach is needed because they purposefully want to do things differently or to look at new capabilities;

I. An integrative approach is required to employ complexity science insights that otherwise might remain separate, single-domain solutions.

The first three examples above are about the dynamics of real-world change that would be dealt with, as it happens, whilst engaging in the communities-of-practice (CoP) – so practitioners would use the Landscape of Change to adjust practice (explained in the first section of this chapter). In examples D. and E., as there is already an appreciation of the drivers of change, practitioners would probably start in the Reflecting on Practice loop where the focus is on reasoning about the drivers of change and identifying trade-offs for setting the conditions for practice (the Trade-off Space is explained in the second section of this chapter). Examples F. and G. would start in the Reflecting on Realities loop, and particularly make use of the Symptom Sorter to develop and update the necessary understanding of the context (Symptom Sorting is explained in the third section of this chapter). The last two examples (H. and I.) start in the complexity-worthiness loop as they are about adjusting capability – through looking at alternative ways-of-working and by bringing in new techniques respectively (as complexity-worthiness is covered in detail in Chapter 5, it is, as such, not elaborated further here). Where practitioners might then 'go' next would, of course, depend on the circumstances and on the insights that the iterative revisiting and comparing of mismatches, tensions and drivers expose. If you are not sure where to start then we would recommend you answer the questions that are part of the Purpose and Intent Element listed in Chapter 4 to set you on your journey.

The rest of this chapter explains, in three sections, how to work with the dynamics, drivers and characteristics of contexts in practice.

Dynamics – Engaging with Communities-of-Practice – Landscape of Change

So, in this 'engaging with communities-of-practice' section practitioners are working with the dynamics of practice in a context-driving/context-driven way. Here the Approach offers a complexity-inspired Landscape of Change to provide a structured way for practitioners[69] to integrate, given certain opportunities, some of the dynamic influences so that they can be put to work in practice (within the limits we have already discussed).

Using the Landscape of Change. The Landscape is a rich expression of the dynamics of ongoing or potential changes. A way to use it is to plot into it the changes going on in the context so it can be seen who/what may be causing them to come about and how/when/where they might be able to influenced. For example, this may include noticing: the behaviour of key actors involved in change; whether some changes are out of the scope of the time-frame of this context and so cannot be influenced; the natural dynamics of the environment such as weather and so on. As we explained in Chapter 3, there are at least four main avenues available, in principle, for influencing all types of everyday emergence, adaptation and evolution and, consequently, for bringing about change in practice over time. Note that, as phenomena in cyberspace can also be affected[70] using the same environment (infrastructure) top-down, bottom-up and self-organising strategies as those discussed above its dynamics should also be included. The Landscape of Change, Figure 14, links these avenues of influence to context in a way that enables practitioners to work with the dynamics of practice.

The information to go into (and between) the cells, if not already known by the practitioners concerned, comes from a synthesis of two sources. These are, firstly, the context for doing, based on the 'axioms of complexity' (shown along the top-left axis of Figure 14) that provide a way of linking to the appreciation of context gained from Symptom Sorting. And, secondly, the ways in which change can be influenced in practice (shown along the right-hand axis of the Landscape) that are the link to the 'change issues' examined in the Trade-off Space. Both the Trade-off Space and Symptom Sorting are discussed later in this chapter.

69　This does not mean that the intervening actor has already been prejudged here. As we have mentioned, often the people best placed to bring about change are not those charged with the responsibility for doing it.

70　The Internet's self-repairing capabilities are already actively influenced by policy makers and system administrators. These are called autonomic, defined as: systems which self-adapt, repair and self-regulate with the minimum of human intervention. The term derives from the human autonomic nervous system, which controls key functions such as respiration, heart rate without conscious involvement. See IBM's *Autonomic Computing* website.

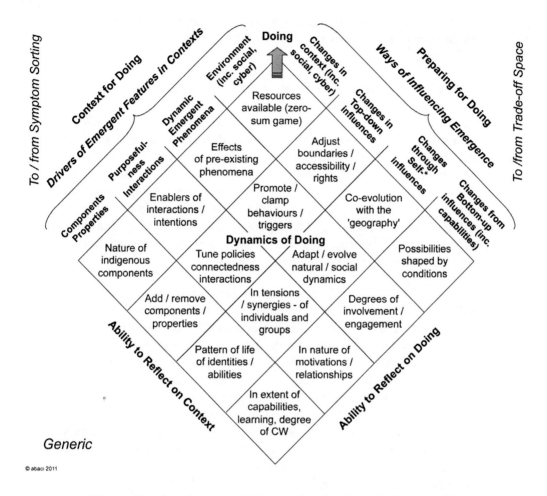

Figure 14 – Landscape of Change for Real-world Contexts[71].

Figure 14 has been populated with some general examples of the kinds of changes that could be made as follows:

A. **Making Changes in the Context/Environment.** These cells represent the environmental dimensions of change where practitioners would make adjustments depending on the amount of natural resources available, the nature of the 'background' phenomena that are active, the degree to which the environment is enabling or inhibiting interactions and intentions (e.g. conditions stable enough over time to achieve a specific aim), and changes of indigenous components (the people, organisations

---

71   A copy of Figure 14 is available on p257 to cut out and use while reading the Guide.

etc.). Depending on the time-horizon, greater or lesser efforts may be made to change the environment so that it becomes more suitable to the tasks at hand.

B. **Changing the Nature of Top-down Influences.** This row represents the top-down influences that are active in the context, such incentives, rules and permissions. This includes the ways that accessibility rights or 'boundaries' might be changed (say, in permissions to use land), or that behaviours might be encouraged or clamped (e.g. by offering or withdrawing rewards), or that policies, connectedness and interactions might be tuned (for example, through imposing safety rules or providing funding incentives to groups that agree to collaborate), or by adding or removing components or changing their properties (such as suggesting that certain actors should be included or setting minimum standards of competence).

C. **Changes Through Self-organisation/Self-regulation.** Changes in this part of the Landscape of Change come about of their own accord as a result of the ongoing interactions in the context. The sort of changes that may occur include those as a result of co-evolution with the environment (such as the livelihood of a settlement depending on how people care for it), or where social or natural dynamics transition in the ways already discussed in Chapter 5 (and so certain modes of behaviour become more or less acceptable). In some situations, tensions and synergies between groups may change the dynamics (e.g. local residents may object to commercial development or they may partner with the developers to help conserve the surroundings), or between and among individuals which might lead people to emulate 'iconic' behaviour as part of their pattern of life.

D. **Changing the Nature of Bottom-up Influences.** This row of cells on the Landscape of Change represent the dynamics which are driven bottom-up by individuals or by the underlying complexities that impact change. The environment cell in this row is where changes in water-table levels, for example following an earthquake, would make its impact on people's water supplies. Or, in the social environment, where small scale industries set up by women have been enabled by capacity-building activities. Note that certain phenomena are enablers for change at 'higher' levels and so have a bottom-up influence e.g. waves enable surfing, which enables people to have fun – these sort of 'cascades' of emergence will, of course, change depending on the degree of involvement or engagement of the phenomena concerned (a simple example would be changing the shape of the surfboard so that it rides the wave in a different way). Finally in this row, the very nature, in terms of their complexity-worthiness or innate properties, of all the components is a fundamental bottom-up driver of change which can be influenced (say through training and exercising to develop a surfer's fitness and agility).

E. **By 'doing nothing'.** There are, naturally, do-nothing options in all the cells and across the Landscape of Change, which may involve active disengagement or people just letting things follow their course. Actively doing nothing is a kind of doing something that is often not considered!

Degrees of Freedom between Public, Private and Community Influences. Of course each cell is not considered in isolation, there are influences between them which are considered as and when necessary. For example, at the 'Top-down'/Dynamic Emergent Phenomena cross-over one has the option to promote desired behaviours or clamp unwanted ones (as we saw in the kindergarten example) although this risks inhibiting the phenomena arising from people's degree of involvement and engagement where they have the option to change from the bottom-up – and so on. Hence practice needs to consider the overlaps, contradictions and opportunities available between achievable actions[72] of individuals, teams, organisations, tasks and the features of the context. As private individuals, we make these kind of adjustments every day without giving it much thought but, for practitioners who are dealing with change in their day-to-day work, these differences *are* the source of the 'complex realities' that they described in Chapter 2. As a result, they need to be able to consider the 'space-of-possibilities' for practice in a through way and we next describe an extension to the Landscape of Change, shown in Figure 15, which covers the interplay between public (top-down), community (self-*) and individual (bottom-up) influences as they interact in a way that can enhance or inhibit wiggle-room. For doing so we have adapted the work of the Florida Institute of Human and Machine Cognition (IHMC), specifically that of Jeff Bradshaw *et al* in their paper on collective behaviour and adjustable autonomy *'Making Agents Acceptable to People'*. The Figure shows five zones, labelled (a) to (e), with dotted boundaries representing five types of spaces of possibilities. By plotting them for a context and then comparing them (looking for intersections, disjoint areas, omissions, conflicts and so on), practitioners can identify the actual degrees of freedom and wiggle-room available to enable or inhibit change, given the possibilities in practice. Note that the sizes and dimensions of these zones can change dynamically too, enabling the wiggle-room to be 'wiggled'. The Figure also shows some practical examples of this numbered (1) to (7). We will first look at the zones and their overlaps:

---

72   We are defining 'action' as any kind of behaviour, task, influence etc. which any kind of entity or group can do in any way at any time – this is just pragmatic as defining a full, tight taxonomy of actions would be impossible anyway.

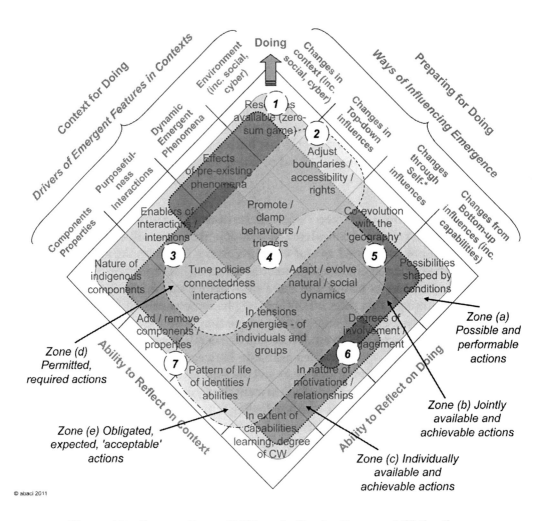

Figures in the diagram:

Context for Doing

Drivers of Emergent Features in Contexts

Doing

Environment (inc. social, cyber)

Changes in context (inc. social, cyber)

Ways of Influencing Emergence

Preparing for Doing

Dynamic Emergent Phenomena

Purposeful-ness Interactions

Components Properties

Changes in Top-down influences

Changes through Self.*

influences

Changes from Bottom-up influences (inc. capabilities)

Resources available (zero-sum game) **1**

Effects of pre-existing phenomena

Adjust boundaries / accessibility / rights **2**

Enablers of interactions / intentions

Promote / clamp behaviours / triggers

Co-evolution with the 'geography'

Nature of indigenous components **3**

Tune policies connectedness interactions

Adapt / evolve natural / social dynamics **5**

Possibilities shaped by conditions

Add / remove components / properties **7**

In tensions / synergies - of individuals and groups

Degrees of involvement / engagement **6**

Pattern of life of identities / abilities

In nature of motivations / relationships

In extent of capabilities, learning, degree of CW

Ability to Reflect on Context

Ability to Reflect on Doing

Zone (a) Possible and performable actions

Zone (b) Jointly available and achievable actions

Zone (c) Individually available and achievable actions

Zone (d) Permitted, required actions

Zone (e) Obligated, expected, 'acceptable' actions

© abaci 2011

Figure 15 – Space-of-possibilities, Authorisations and Obligations.

Zone (a) In any context the space of possible actions that are performable by entities is represented by this background zone – this expresses their total wiggle-room and degrees of freedom that could exist in an unconstrained context. Of course there is not a single Zone (a); the space-of-possibilities in regard to finance, may be different from agriculture and so on – and they can be shown separately or aggregated.

Zone (b) Represents actions which are actually only achievable jointly by groups of entities working bottom-up and based on their willingness and ability to collaborate. Zone (b) is a subset of Zone (a).

Zone (c) This is the space of actions which are available to and achievable by entities working alone, based on their individual complexity-worthiness. There is some overlap with Zone (b) – the overlap indicates actions that a very capable individual could do alone or that could be done by two or more less capable entities working together. Zone (c) is also, by definition, a subset of Zone (a).

Zone (d) Represents the space-of-possibilities that may be permitted to, required of, or imposed upon entities. This Zone would originate from the top-down influences of, say, institutions or governments putting in place safety regulations or codes-of-conduct. For example, this might mean noting that people would be more involved in their local communities if some of the rules were relaxed. The intersection of this Zone with Zones (b) and (c) constrains some of the available actions, though not all (there are some things you just can't legislate about – happiness, for example).

Zone (e) This Zone covers actions that entities are either obliged to do or which they would be expected to do as part of the social norms and acceptable actions arising from, say, membership of religious or ethnic communities. The intersection of Zone (e) with Zones (b) and (c) constrains other types of available actions – usually in moral, cultural or ethical spaces – through, say, developing a sense of shame or honour. It is possible, for example, for there to be a clash between family honour and what the law allows people to do (indicated by the overlap with Zone (d)).

Note that Zones (d) and (e) have small sections that extend outside Zone (a), the space of possible and performable actions. These represent things that entities may be permitted, or even required or obliged to do, but which they cannot do because they are not capable.

'**Wiggling the Wiggle-Room**'. This extended version of the Landscape of Change enables practitioners to carry out the type of synthesis of multiple influences so necessary for putting complexity to work, if feasible, realisable changes are to be brought about. In practice it can be seen that the institutional and contractual constraints and influences operate largely top-down, the social and cultural influences/constraints generally self-organise, and the individual drivers mostly work bottom-up. Some practical examples of how the position, shape and overlap of the Zones might change and how the resulting interactions and influences might play out are shown on the Figure at (1) to (7), and imply:

(1) **Increasing the Possibilities.** Here, the underlying aspects of the context are changed to increase the range of what is possible – Zone (a) gets bigger.

(2) **Preventing 'Dangerous' Actions.** This would be about forbidding entities from attempting the impossible, unachieveable or undesirable (from the point of view of those in authority) by legislating against attempts to operate outside Zone (a) – this may require Zone (d) to be extended to legislate against theoretically possible, but not yet achieved, behaviours (as the UK's Human Fertilisation and Embryology Authority had to do to prohibit attempts at human reproductive cloning – see the *Human Reproductive Cloning Act 2001*, UK Government).

(3) **Adapting to New Realities.** This is the corollary of (2), that is increasing permissions to accommodate new capabilities. In this case, the extension of Zone (d) might be in response to changes in laws to cover the advent of new technology.

(4) **Untangling Conflict and Contradictions.** An example here that would be very typical of real-world practice is a project requiring open federated collaboration amongst all concerned, which tries to respect the diversity and sensitivity of viewpoints but which then falls foul of administrative and legislative realities on the ground. Such a situation may require a careful adjustment of Zones, especially of Zones (d) and (e), to enable an uneasy group consensus to form in fundamentally non-interoperable contexts.

(5) **Making Progress – New Ways.** Zone (e) may grow because there is an emergence of novel group behaviour, e.g. Internet online social networking, which extends social norms of acceptable, so-called 'netiquette', behaviour into areas of people's personal, formerly private, lives.

(6) **Taking the Initiative.** Changes in the shape and size of Zones (b) and (c) reflect unilateral initiatives or actions taken by those independent of constraints or obligations. Note that there will be some things that can be achieved together that can't be achieved individually, as this overlap indicates. For example, this might represent 'free-thinkers' or inventors independently dreaming up capabilities in their back yard or even criminal elements, outside the law, making their plans.

(7) **Avoiding Unrealistic Expectations.** This example is where Zone (e) is reduced, to decrease the range of obligated constraints, so preventing obligations from exceeding the scope of permissions and possibilities. Of course, the range of possible actions in Zone (a) could be increased as well – it depends.

Using the Landscape of Change – An Example. We'll illustrate the use of the Landscape further with a practical example. Consider a feeding station of a refugee camp in a country ravaged by drought and civil war where aid agencies are working to support hungry people right now, as well as assisting their return to their homelands when possible. The situation is ongoing over weeks and is relentless – ever-changing as the civil war ebbs and flows – and extremely uncertain. The variety of communities, religions, cultures, institutions and agencies involved creates massive diversity and the range of perspectives, viewpoints, values, concerns and power-structures means that no single group can be 'in charge'. Authority, initiative and influence flow dynamically from one group to another as the circumstances change. Aid agencies must work with these social and cultural dynamics where, for example, they may have to counter rumours that their supplies are part of a conspiracy or deal with people staying away because of intimidation. They must also adapt to the realities of climate and weather, to intermittent supplies, political interference and the inclinations and moods of those donating to their charities who tire of 'yet another crisis'. Some of the dynamics of change revealed by the Landscape include:

A. **Making Changes in the Context/Environment.** In this example, growing vegetables or raising animals *en masse* and *ad hoc* to increase the space-of-possibilities is obviously out of the question in the timeline of this context. So, bringing in food from outside, which is not available in the local environment, is one possibility and also the most likely one. There are also many legacy issues in the context that reflect the history leading up to the formation of the refugee camp. That means that some potential degrees of freedom are locked by their history – e.g. the civil war is a given, as much as people might wish it were not so, it just is (for now anyway, until someone starts working on that purpose and intent issue). As to the components in the context, until the civil war is over, attacks by so-called militias will continue to be a factor in the work of the aid agencies.

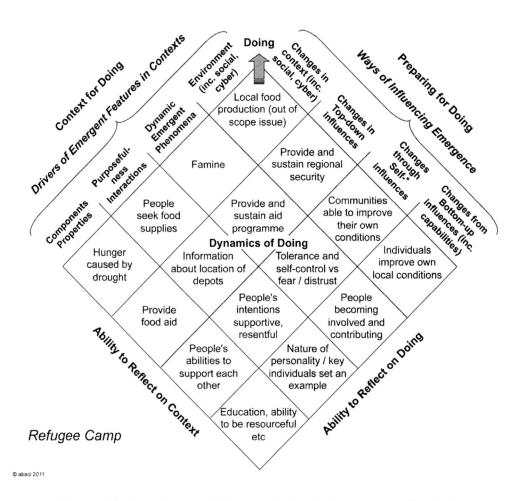

Figure 16 – Landscape of Change for the Refugee-camp Context.

B. **Changing the Nature of Top-down Influences**. Top-down, UN
resolutions may be able to change local politics and help set more
favourable conditions for change by providing and sustaining an
aid programme. However, there may be a tension with the local
government's view of how to provide regional security where the
degree of fear or distrust of the local government may be decisive.
The UN may authorise aid workers to do things that the government
won't permit, leading to contradictory tensions within Zone (d).
There are behaviours that the aid agencies might be able to encourage
e.g. by offering support to those who volunteer to return to their
villages. In terms of adding or removing components or changing their
properties agencies can, over time, augment/substitute for their own
hard-pressed staff by training-up suitably competent refugees.

C. **Changes Through Self-organisation/Self-regulation.** Here, cultural, ethnic, tribal and religious influences will be very important modifiers of behaviour. Aid agencies need to work with and within local sensitivities and identify key nodes – the well-connected influential people who can help shift opinions and set an example. Of course these are not just the people with the obvious labels of leader. Someone who is respected and revered can have disproportionate and decisive influence (say in the way that Mahatma Ghandi of India did) and can 'flip' community behaviour. The aim here is to foster an atmosphere of trust and tolerance that will increase the likelihood that communities can begin to improve their own conditions. In transition terms there is a threshold here where change can only occur when the underlying conditions for doing achieve a favourable critical mass, a tipping point. The Landscape can help practitioners identify and track the indicators of those underlying factors – though it is the people themselves who will make the transition; it cannot be done for them nor can the time of its occurrence be predicted.

D. **Changing the Nature of Bottom-up Influences.** An obvious reality here is that people, because of their circumstances, may not be able to help themselves much at first when they arrive at the camp. In Landscape of Change terms their Zone (a), space of possible and performable actions, will be minimal. The agencies are obviously compensating for this by providing food and shelter. However, the more people can take responsibility/acquire the capabilities/change local conditions and, in time, feed themselves, the easier will be the transition back to ordinary life and dependency on aid agencies will be reduced. In addition, through education and through mutual support, previously disenfranchised people may begin to make their voices heard. Overall then, where in earlier times actions weren't available they may now not only be a possibility for individuals but also, with the help of the UN's top-down influences for example, achievable.

E. **By Doing Nothing.** In this aid agency example, the 'do-nothing' option may be adopted by warlords or political figures who will bide their time till the UN and the aid agencies have gone and then carry on as before. Worse still are those who promise to help and then just quietly, through inaction, let the opportunities pass. As a result, practitioners may need to use assertive cunning.

May we suggest, as an exercise, that readers plot and annotate the various Zones on a blank version[73] of Figure 16 and experiment with some of the degrees of freedom and potential interactions to expose alternative spaces of possibilities for each of the actors associated with this context.

Working with Multiple Viewpoints. In situations like the refugee camp, which are typical of practice, the notions of 'understanding the problem first', 'implementing the plan', 'defining end-states' and so on, which are normally associated with projects and management, are largely meaningless. Obviously, behind-the-scenes and back at headquarters in a comfy office somewhere, careful planning and logistics are underway – but these activities support practice, they are not practice itself and this can create tensions between those in the field and those in the office. Why is this? Well, because the planners and practitioners have very different viewpoints and experiences of practice in the context. The planners, usually for accountability purposes, demand data from the practitioners that they simply cannot supply as it is just not observable or collectable. For example the planners may, understandably, want to ask: 'How many doses of milk-feed Type ZZ1 were stolen? Who took them and where are they now?' or 'What are your forecasts for antibiotic usage next month?' or even 'Why has the uptake of high-energy biscuits from Country-X suddenly dropped off, what do you think are the causes? What are your proposals for turning the situation round as Country-X is offended?' Clearly, those in the field and those in the office have different ideas about 'causality,' about the nature of dynamic phenomena in the context, and how they manifest themselves and the degree to which they can be understood and influenced in reality. Practitioners are greatly helped if their office colleagues appreciate the touch points between the real-world context and their administrative accountability context. We suggest that developing multiple versions of Landscapes of Change separately, and then comparing them together, will help expose these differences and promote complementary, but not unified, understanding. So, as practitioners and planners use the Landscape, Trade-off Space and do Symptom Sorting collaboratively for the real-world context and as change is considered, they will, in effect, be describing alternative journeys that they can take 'together'. These routes/threads will develop over time – which is no problem as our Approach can perform the integrative functions necessary to enable complexity to be put to work. For example, at any point one might divert off to consider trade-offs or to spend time studying the context more closely, to understand new aspects of its features and dynamics, and then come back to practice – and when and whether you do that... depends.

---

73   Blank PDF versions of the Landscape of Change, Trade-off Space and Symptom Sorting
      diagrams are available on the Triarchy Press website at:
      www.triarchypress.com/ComplexityDemystified/diagrams

DRIVERS – REASONING AND REFLECTING ABOUT PRACTICE – TRADE-OFF SPACE

In this section you might want to re-examine some of the drivers of change in your context or, having gained an appreciation of the context, you wish to consider some of the trade-offs you may need to make. Fundamentally, what drives the dynamics of practice are mismatches, tensions, potential contributions, discomforts and 'deltas' – i.e. differences, gaps, opportunities and gradients of one sort or another. Given what has been learned from complexity science, it would make no sense in the Guide to enumerate these and to try to link each driver to 'appropriate action' in a predetermined cause-and-effect way. However, it is possible to pick out some of these drivers and tensions and identify the sorts of dynamic changes that they generate (that would be modifiers of context) so that they can be 'traded-off' one against another in order to compare their influences. So, how would this be done as part of reflecting on practice? We offer a simple tool that can be used to plot some of the modifiers and tensions – the Trade-off Space diagram[74] is shown in Figure 17. This is a tool for thought that is designed to help the reasoning necessary to surface issues and enable reflection about some of the consequences for practice. The outputs from the Trade-off Space are candidate 'change issues' which, in terms of our Approach, correspond to the ways of influencing the context shown on the top-right axis of the Landscape of Change.

---

[74]   Please note that this is *not* a so-called Ishikawa 'fish-bone' diagram (which is based on too simplistic a model of cause and effect and on unrealistic assumptions about 'knowns' for it to be reliable in practice in complex contexts).

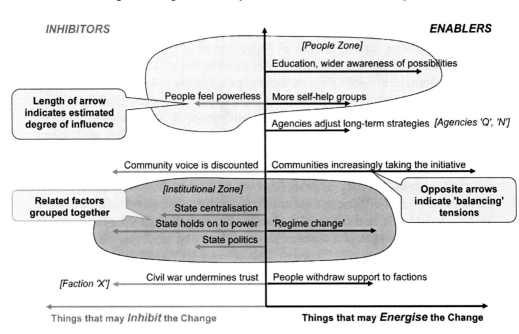

Change issue, eg: "*Community becomes less Reliant on Aid Agencies*"

Figure 17 – Tensions and Modifiers of a Context Shown on the 'Trade-off Space' Diagram.[75]

Using the Trade-off Space. Depending on the change issue selected, the diagram would be populated with tensions and modifiers (which we list and discuss below). It is unlikely that one would try to plot all the tensions in a context on a single diagram – one would select, using judgement, those which are relevant to the change issue and must include the givens and realities. The Figure shows a generic example. At the top the change issue under consideration has been stated – in this case that the 'community in question becomes less reliant on aid agencies'. So the diagram represents understanding about the trade-offs which might have to be made/to be taken between the tensions and/or modifier factors in this context. Factors nearer the top are considered to be more important, those further down, less so. Arrows going to the left indicate things that may inhibit/impede the change and those to the right indicate factors that may enable/promote change. The longer the arrow the more significant the estimated/judged potential effect. Arrows are grouped around related/interdependent factors.

---

75   A copy of Figure 17 is available on p258 to cut out and use while reading the Guide.

Balancing factors are shown by opposite arrows. Where it is possible to identify key actors or other 'agents' associated with unblocking or facilitating something then arrows are annotated accordingly (e.g. in the Figure the activities of 'Faction X' are undermining trust, so 'Faction X' might be a key player and agencies 'Q' and 'N' are those who might need to adjust their strategies). To populate the diagram, either individually, or in groups, people might propose change issues and 'compete'[76] them, identify candidate modifiers and tensions and add them to Trade-off Space diagrams. It is important that these factors are not just what is known and familiar – possibilities (however unlikely) should be considered and imaginative insight encouraged. Trading-off is probably best done as open discourse, as most of the value of this activity is in the dialogue that takes place and the narratives that develop – the diagram is merely a shared artefact from those discussions. The idea is to identify the relationships and interdependencies between different combinations of these tensions and modifiers to explore the space-of-possibilities around the change issue. The aim is not to 'solve' the change issue or to build a plan or develop the 'steps leading up to the end-state', but to appreciate the different ways in which practice might flow around and through the change issue. A very important insight for practitioners is that the transition from now to some desired future cannot be a single step – the journey may have what seem to be setbacks at the time – but these often set the enabling conditions[77] for later success. Again, this trading-off is more than just cause-and-effect 'what-if-ing' – it is about getting a feel for the ways that the dynamic changes may influence each other – directly, indirectly and in the other ways we will discuss in Chapter 7. The types of tensions and modifiers include the following special cases (the list is not exhaustive):

A. **Blockers/Fundamentals**. These include factors which could hold up everything else if not removed (such as the 'State holds on to power' in the Figure) or those fundamentals on which opportunities seem to depend. It is especially important to consider who or what is in the best position to change these should that be necessary.

B. **Contradictions/Paralysers**. Of course, there are some tensions and mismatches that just seem downright contradictory e.g. 'You can't have endless growth and a sustainable future – can you?' That seems a

---

76 'Competing' change issues sounds competitive and confrontational but, depending on the community involved, it may be the best way of surfacing and challenging some of the hidden assumptions and ingrained thinking to develop a really practical sense of contextual complexity from a diverse set of experiences.

77 At the time, it may not even be apparent that what happened was an enabler and so it is unwise to close down or exclude activities which, in the current frame of reference, seem to 'make no sense'. They probably will with hindsight!

contradiction but do these two *have* to be in opposition and mutually exclusive? What does 'growth' mean in the planetary ecosystem sense? There has been 'endless growth' of biomass on Earth for some 3 billion years. And then there are 'paralysers', tensions which are apparently locked in some mutually self-defeating way that holds up everything else, such as, in the example, the way that people feeling powerless undermines the formation of self-help groups.

C. **'Gate-keepers' / Enablers / Energisers / Intermediates.**
Gate-keepers are mediating tensions in a position to free-up some dynamic indirectly. Examples include: a person who acts as an intermediary, or a set of negotiations that, as long as they continue, provide the goodwill for other activities. In terms of the enablers (setting the conditions for change which may occur some time in the future), energisers and the intermediate influences, these may be very non-linear and disproportionate – something that seems very insignificant at the time may have global impact later.[78] For example, in the way that education, especially of women, has brought about social change.

D. **Unknowns / Unknowables / Hypotheticals.** Practitioners should think about factors which, if they did exist or could happen, might totally change practice – and what sorts of indicators of their presence could be expected to be detected. For example, considering the 'vulnerabilities' inherent in the purpose or intent that has been formulated may lead to identification of 'countermeasures' that people might employ to undermine desired change. In the Figure, both the state and the factions in the civil war may wish to frustrate the efforts of the aid agencies. Positioning such things on the Trade-off Space at least puts down a marker that these items should not be discarded.

There is plenty of scope for extending the Trade-off Space diagram as seems fit. Regions (shapes) could be placed to show where there is, for example, a shortfall in capability or to group items that involve mostly top-down, self-* or bottom-up influences, or to indicate particular types of communities-of-practice and so on as shown. Colours can be used to emphasise other dimensions of influence that are considered significant – it is all up to the people concerned and what makes sense to them. A standardised scheme could be counter-productive as it may end up limiting the meaning that can be represented on the diagram. The Trade-off Space could certainly be used and adapted as a shared artefact where

---

78   An everyday example is when people say 'We've looked at the statistics and have filtered out the things that don't happen very often and the marginal opinions' – the, unwise, assumption being that obvious things are the most significant indicators of change – which of course they often are not.

groups have differing perceptions about the issues. There may be multiple Trade-off Spaces being used at once (to represent the viewpoints of different actors for example) and they can be printed on transparent material, overlain one on top of another and compared visually if necessary. They may be iteratively revisited as change occurs, they may become a significant shared artefact or just an idea in someone's head. As change issues are suggested/dealt with the looping may take the practitioner onto the Landscape of Change for implementation or back to Symptom Sorting if further information is needed – it all depends.

Modifiers of and Tensions/Opportunities in Contexts. We now present some of the modifiers and tensions that we consider to be significant to practitioners, along with a description and an indication of what their potential influences might be as part of putting complexity to work in practice. We have arranged them in an approximate order with items concerning individuals first, then those relating to communities and then on to tensions and modifiers of context:

A. **Emotion, Passion, Arousal, Anger, Empathy and Apathy.** Human emotions are significant drivers and modifiers of change and are certainly far too transient to be factored into practice individually. However, *en masse,* it is surprisingly easy to estimate what people are likely to do – though not what the outcomes might be. The use of emotion to generate 'creative tension' from the bottom-up and a drive for change in practice is a good thing – but may need the presence of a facilitator. Practitioners who are culturally-aware will recognise triggers for emotion and the scope for *faux pas* in negotiations if inter-personal signs and signals are misinterpreted. In these situations the role of a 'local expert' can make all the difference to appreciating the real issues in a context as a route to achieving self-sustaining change.

B. **Expertise, Repertoires, Capabilities and Complexity-Worthiness.** Clearly, mismatches in complexity-worthiness capabilities are a driver of tensions and opportunities. Expertise cannot be 'handed out'; it is something that people generate for themselves bottom-up – though enabling conditions can be provided. Actors with a limited or inflexible 'repertoire' of behaviours, once identified, can be accommodated, educated or bypassed. Practitioners need to be able to assess complexity-worthiness in a way that enables them to see when a mismatch, or lack of it, is holding up or deflecting change. If this lack is in their tasking agencies or donors then this may be tricky to deal with unless the consequences to the project and to real-world change can be clearly demonstrated.

C. **People's Will – Intents, Motivations, Fears, Hopes and Needs.** These tensions, which also include levels of trust, have a negative impact if motivation clashes, or will and motivation of actors and/or institutions in the context are an undermining influence in the context or even stifling the dynamic. Consequently, such states of mind need to be noted, motivations and concerns understood, which often requires, yet again, good facilitation skills and/or local expertise to obtain insights. Change may be seen by some people as being competitive, creating anxiety. The context presents opportunities and potential benefits for some and, for others, 'disadvantages' (or perceived disadvantages) – in terms of land, wealth, access to services, rights, cultural goods etc. Practitioners have to take account of this potential divergence within and among (groups of) people holding an interest. These features are deeply held internally and expressed individually, socially and 'politically' through personal choices, allegiances (unity or fickleness) and so on.

D. **People's Personal Qualities of Experience, Worldliness and Maturity.** People's experiences and maturity are important resources that can be drawn upon by others or contributed through collaboration. They affect the formation of opinions and shape the way people relate to the world, to groups they belong to etc. based on how they interpret events, relationships, news, political moves and other influences. In practice, there may be large differences between the levels of experience, worldliness and maturity of groups and entities in a context. Because these qualities can't usually be changed quickly e.g. education may be required or social conditions changed, this means that practitioners need to be open, patient and have the willingness, space and ability to foster teaching, learning, personal development, and to help build (community) capacity.

E. **Money, Wealth, Possessions and Access to Resources (inc. Land) and Status.** This modifier creates strong dynamics that drive change. Manipulating the asymmetries in real or perceived amounts of possessions is, and always has been, fertile ground in human endeavours. Practitioners often have to deal with the consequences of differences in (physical) ownership. These may manifest themselves in conflicts, for example when (non) possession threatens livelihood, when stifling and limiting dependencies or seemingly insurmountable (and illegal) power 'structures' have been created through wealth and possession of a few individuals or of a strata in society. Or it may simply be about finding equitable ways to use money that is available. This may require compromise in negotiations, where ethics allows, and being pragmatic about tolerating some inequalities even though idealism would be preferred in getting 'fair shares for all' regardless.

F. **Viability and Vitality of Livelihood – Self-Worth and a Sense of Purpose.** This modifier is a major one in many contexts. Viability and vitality of livelihood is not something you can give people *per se*, it is a feeling that emerges bottom-up from having opportunities and the possibility and ability to be able to realise them. Internal tensions can arise where someone aspires to 'better' themselves but is blocked in some way and feels upset about it – or external tensions come about where someone is seen to have an 'unfair' advantage, which might in reality only be there for the short term. Interventions that appear to affect only some livelihoods, or some more than others, are sure to trigger a strong response, not necessarily of competition, but also in terms of self-initiative, positive motivation and energy. The inequality of and variability in access to creating viability of livelihood is present in any practitioner's context. Practitioners can have a role in exposing opportunities with the actors, and of acknowledging and facilitating agility and capacity creation, even in institutions, as a route to change.

G. **Types of Viewpoints and Perceptions Held.** In real-world, multi-stakeholder situations the context is shaped, often unexpectedly, by the multitude of viewpoints and perceptions held, and by the extent to which they may or may not be significant in relation to particular types of change. Practically, viewpoints need to be elicited, considered and compared, often in a variety of ways, using different techniques that practitioners judge to be appropriate. Many views are unspoken yet they affect private and public motivations and intentions in a way that sets agendas in a context. Perspectives are facets of contexts, such as economic, social etc.

H. **Degree of Understanding and Appreciation of Context.** Flowing from the variations in people's viewpoints, perceptions, experiences and worldliness are the differences in experienced complexity i.e. the degree to which people appreciate the realities of the contextual complexity. These tensions can be a source of dispute that can be inhibiting, but they can also provide alternative insights that explain the context in a way that wouldn't have been possible or wouldn't have occurred otherwise. Some may be able to sense a change that others cannot; some may consider it tractable and others be defeated by it.

The degree of understanding can be manipulated by providing or withholding information, through people agreeing to collaborate more openly or by individuals being prepared to reveal previously hidden insights, that did not seem to matter before, for the benefit of the group.

I. **Consent, Involvement, Detachment, Indifference and Contentment.** These tensions and modifiers of context are positive if they are supportive of change, if there is enthusiasm and people get engaged because they can see the benefit for themselves, or when new ideas can be realised. Bottom-up enthusiasm can then be turned to advantage in a way that becomes infectious and self-generating, by supporting relationships and influences that seem to be 'going the right way'. Enthusiasm can lead to self-organisation as a driver of change, if appropriate wiggle-room is enabled by practitioners or the people themselves.

    Quite often, when contentment is prevailing, little can be achieved, people cannot be mobilised, and the situation is static. As participation of the ones who will bring about change is indispensable, practitioners cannot take for granted that all those involved in a context will agree equally. Tensions arise from the degree to which people 'buy-in' to an idea or on how confident or vulnerable they feel in declaring their support. There is a kind of flocking behaviour here – if people see others withdrawing, they too may decide to detach. Strong incentives/peer pressure that reinforce people's inclinations may tip the balance. Practitioners may need to set the conditions for engagement by fostering or even providing an appropriately nurturing atmosphere for bringing people together and making them think it is their change. Changing involvement means being realistic about the kind of negative or supportive influences of all types going on behind the scenes, which may not be able to be fully appreciated or influenced directly.

J. **Culture and Cultural Tendencies, Beliefs and Attitudes.** Contexts can be influenced by a vast range of, often subtle, cultural and belief issues and their manifestations, such as religious holidays and traditions, eating habits etc. Culture and belief will also influence human behaviour and attitudes through taboos, superstition, and social control. Practitioners might find that these factors play a dominating role in their context – especially when novelty and opportunity arise in a form of change that would question, ignore or inhibit the predominant beliefs (whether actually or by implication).

K. **Relationships, Interdependencies and Connectedness.** The types of relationships and interdependencies that modify interactions, and hence dynamic phenomena in the context form a pattern. These 'degrees of connectedness' are: independent, interdependent, co- dependent and assimilated. Groupings with different qualities of (internal) connectedness work in dissimilar ways and they may find cross-group working hard and that tensions arise as each group has 'incompatible' degrees of freedom. These differences are reflected in the variety of ways that collaboration can be organised: separate, in federations, shared or 'unified'. The degrees of connectedness can be directly and indirectly modified by changing rules, incentives and amounts of initiative, and so on.

L. **(Openness To) Collaborate, Share and Interoperate.** When there are differences between how open people are, this can undermine confidence and trust and slow down collaboration and progress generally. Differences in the willingness to 'interoperate' can be misinterpreted – for example, if people hold back because of a lack of ability rather than caution or protectionism. Effective collaboration is emergent but can be influenced by leaders setting good examples, by bringing people together through effective procedures/training being in place to make it easier, and through a strong, reinforcing sense of reward/group achievement. Also, practitioners can bridge across diverse groups as a way of achieving a degree of interoperability.

M. **Presence or Otherwise of Leaders, Heroes, 'Icons', Gurus and Villains.** Practitioners recognise that such individuals or, in some cases, fashions, are important drivers of a context. Understanding their impact and mental and political power in the informal sphere, and the corresponding motivations of 'followers' is essential in any context. These are not constituted in rational', graspable structures – instead, intuition and common sense are required to make sense of them and their influence and significance in the context. These kinds of leaders can act as proxies, through a social contract, for those who lack individual power in their own right. Practitioners will have to engage with them as drivers of change even though their, mostly transient, manifestations of referent power, whilst influential, are hard to alter in conventional ways because it mostly exist in people's minds.

N. **Societal Norms, Morals, Ethics, Values and 'Democracy'.** These are modifiers of the self-organising, self-adjusting and 'self-healing' phenomena of societies that emerge from the continual interactions between people, their context, the various societal groupings previously referred to and the coercive and/or regulatory structures that are in place. When these norms persist over time they can become institutionalised in various ways, sometimes being enforced even when they are out of date or irrelevant in a manner that can be very constraining. However, if they evolve too quickly, then society may become too permissive ('anything goes') or, in a positive sense, very agile and adaptive to changing opportunities/imperatives. In most contexts practitioners can take these modifiers as givens about which little can be done in short timescales – unless it is a part of some transition that generates wiggle-room.

O. **Types of Symptoms, Indications, Indicators, Measurements and Goals**. Symptoms give strong indications of what is going on in a context and are expressed in diverse ways – such as, 'a dilapidated, degraded environment' or 'a buzz among-the-people' or 'last month's trading statistics'. They cover a wide mix of qualitative observations and impressions that practitioners will come across. Because of the nature of practice the indicators are usually not quantitative and not expressed in terms of goals or end-states. For example, risk assessments take the probability and frequency of occurrence of an event, the degree of impact and cost of mitigation and multiply them to produce a risk factor; practitioners might take the possibility of a change and consider its potential in terms of the extent and nature its influence and its feasibility in practice as a measure of opportunity. This means that practitioners need to identify those features or phenomena in a context that could be used as appropriate indicators of instances of change in the context – note that these are, once again, often detected or observed through third parties who are better placed and/or connected to sense the necessary phenomena.

P. **Significance, Meaning, Interpretation (Evidence, Outcomes) and 'Truth'**. This leads on to a related modifier concerning the meaning or significance that is attached to features and phenomena in a context. To use a geographical analogy: on a map, whose legend is used to interpret the symbols on the map? In supermarket-chain types of situations these kinds of things can be mandated. In practice, items that might be significant to a government, such as administrative boundaries, might not even be recognised by local people as being relevant to their lives. Also, evidence which is acceptable to the community may not be seen as valid by the state – and vice versa – and notions of the nature of 'truth' can differ greatly depending on degrees of trust. Hence, to align, but not necessarily standardise, the meaning and interpretation applied top-down with that understood bottom-up may require practitioners to be involved in a collaborative activity to explore cross-over items of significance to all concerned.

Q. **Structures, Collaboration Patterns, Organisational Forms and Federations.** In each context, a variety of organisational structures and forms of social organisation and informal collaboration are present. Contexts can be characterised by the presence or absence of these different forms and the resulting classes of interaction and the degree of 'interoperability' that emerges, which can itself become a driver of change. Practitioners, therefore, will not only need to be able to recognise the structural forms adopted by the entities they are dealing with. Also, they have to be able to understand the consequences in terms of the types of collaborative discourse that the entities are likely to use and relationships they may build as a result, as described by Etienne Wenger in his book *Communities of Practice*. Practitioners should be able to judge which types of organisational forms are needed in particular circumstances and set them up and evaluate their utility, directly or indirectly.

R. **Natures of Social, Institutional, Religious or Cultural Groupings/ Communities-of-interest (CoIs).** These forms manifest themselves in practitioners' contexts as different types of groupings and their potential interdependencies are an important feature. Groupings follow their own interests and societal engagement in professional or voluntary ways and, to a greater or lesser extent, have certain reputations, associated structures and statutes. Individual groups each have their own type of impact on context, such as the degree of disagreement or collaboration between two or more of them or the nature of their dislike of other groups. Set types of 'communities-of-practice' always co-evolve in any society (and in some form in most ecosystems) with identifiable characteristics (discussed further below). In all circumstances, what is relevant to practitioners is the way in which one can engage with such groups as partners and identify the role they might play as modifiers of change in practice.

S. **Types of Power-structures and How Power is Exerted/Manipulated.** Types of power and the structures they generate can have a strong impact on a context and also establish the criteria affecting which options are possible. These structures can be engaged and worked with, but sometimes one has to work around them. Power-structures are present at all levels, but often do not reveal themselves in a tractable manner. For example, having positional power doesn't necessarily mean you have influence. As a given, power dynamics can inhibit change, but can also be a vehicle for 'empowerment' when constraints are released. Practitioners will always be part of the power tensions and trade-offs that can be used to modify organisational and social structures.

T. **Ways-of-Working.** Ways-of-working are about more than just differences in administrative procedures. Overall, some people may work in flexible ways whereas others need to get approval for everything they do. The variations in ways-of-working emerge from intersections between power, organisational forms, permissions and obligations, moods and habits and even cultural and religious sensitivities and other degrees of freedom. For practitioners this means being prepared to adapt to, and employ, very different ways-of-working – even in different parts of the same context.

U. **Compliance, Justice, Punishment, Legal Codes and Political Order.** One cannot legislate top-down for everything that happens (and there will always be novelty), and regional, social and cultural differences will create tensions that prevent compliance being identical everywhere. Also, what would be seen as a serious punishment in one situation may be laughed at in another (They exclude you from the tribe? So what, we don't have tribes!). It requires good understanding of the justice system and legal codes applicable in a context, as these shape peoples' expectations, desires, their wiggle-room, and status, capacity and capability for engagement. Many practitioners are already aware of the possibilities and constraints that the intersections and differences between regulatory approaches offer in their option space – such as moving people or tasks to where regimes are more appropriate or, as already discussed, changing the 'shape' of the codes. Options include altering the regulations, working with the dynamics they create or, from the bottom, working round them.

V. **Scale, Scope and Boundaries (Open, Closed, Hidden).** In any real-world context there are many levels of existence (from the sub-bacterial to supra-cultural phenomena and everything in-between), so there will be many different actors and entities working at different scales and within different scopes at different levels. The scale issue is relevant to practitioners who, with change propagating through levels, might need to consider a broader set of actors, and who or what in the context is best placed to bring about change that is effective at multiple levels.

This can cause tensions, potential misunderstandings and even total disconnects, but also enriching insights and influences. In practice mandating a unified view concerning levels and boundaries negates the benefits of diversity. Where common ground is needed, it will have to be discovered and described appropriately – and adapted over time through learning.

W. **Time-Horizon, Tempo, Timeliness, Rates of Change.** We can consider time as a modifier of context and a source of tension in four ways: how it is absolutely, how it is in relative terms, how rate of change is perceived and in terms of time-horizons for issues of interest. For practitioners, time as an absolute is an environmental given, but it is one that will be relative to the viewpoint of the multitude of (key) actors, each working with different time-horizons in their viewpoint of the context. In terms of how rate of change is perceived then, for example, small, quick-witted creatures will notice events that larger ones won't register – in practice we could liken this to comparing an individual's perception of events on the ground with those of an institution. The timescale for both making sense of significant events and/or engaging with them appropriately – *relative to the challenge* – is a significant driver. Note: too short *doesn't necessarily mean you only have seconds* – it may mean that you can't intervene or influence 'in time' to have any effect within the dynamics of the current circumstances. In terms of a time-horizon therefore, practitioners may be required to work to a project life cycle containing milestone deadlines, when in reality the dynamics and rate of change cannot be fixed by arbitrary dates that might put practitioners out of touch with the 'long-wave' cycles of a real-world context.

X. **Accuracy, Precision, Certainty and Predictability.** In practice, mismatches in meaning and usage of precision, accuracy and certainty can create tensions in expectation, accountability and measurement of outcomes. For example, one may be very precise about something inaccurate such as 'we are 23.965 miles from home' when in fact it is nearly 26 miles away. Practitioners need to be prepared for this, in cross-cultural situations where the formal language of commerce, say, is at odds with colloquial usage or the received wisdom of the streets, but where information communicated in 'imprecise' terms can be crucial for a context. Practitioners also need to apply judgement when the dynamics in a context seem, to stakeholders, to be predictable and describable with a certain precision as a basis for working, which in reality, and for practitioners, is not applicable.

CONTEXT – APPRECIATING AND REFLECTING ABOUT REALITIES – SYMPTOM SORTING

This section is for practitioners who need to develop or update their appreciation of a situation by reflecting on realities. This Symptom Sorting, as part of our Approach, picks out the features[79] of contexts and the related issues that shape their characteristics, regardless of their origin or type. Given the nature of the endeavours with which practitioners are involved, however, the examples below are mostly framed in terms related to people's lives and to practice.

So, how does one go about doing Symptom Sorting? Well, it just so happens that the way that practitioners' issues were grouped, at the end of Chapter 2, relates strongly to the way that complexity science explains how complex phenomena emerge. Symptom Sorting investigates the cross-over between the two and so the matrix in Figure 18 can be used to represent what is known and might be found out about a context. On reflection, the utility of this cross-over isn't surprising at all. Complexity science has indicated that these phenomena arise in an environment where entities, especially purposeful ones, interact. In a similar way, practice is about influencing the phenomena that are apparent in a real-world (complex) context and practitioners are concerned largely with relationships and with social, purposeful behaviour among people (entities). This means that mapping one against the other captures a rich description/appreciation of contexts. Of course Symptom Sorting can't just be a snapshot in time – there has to be iterative revisiting and review as circumstances change and novelties arise.

In this section we will first look at the Symptom Sorting matrix and how to populate it. We'll explain how to capture and represent the main characteristics of contexts: the types of communities-of-practice that may be present and then the perspectives that would have to be considered.

---

79   We're using the term 'feature' in the same way as described in Chapter 3, to mean objects, emergent phenomena or persistent patterns which are tangible to an actor in a context.

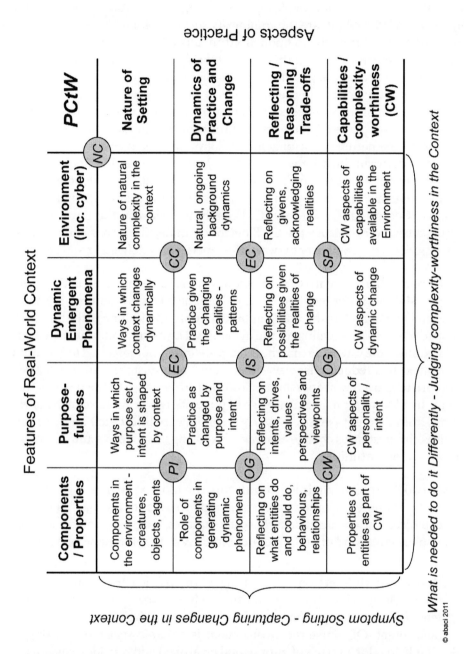

Figure 18 – Symptom Sorting – Capturing Context and Appreciating the Differences[80].

---

80   A copy of Figure 18 is available on p259 to cut out and use while reading the Guide.

So what is the idea behind the Symptom Sorting matrix? Along the top of the Figure, from left to right, are the complexity science axioms that we first heard about in Chapter 1, from the components through to the phenomena that emerge in a complex environment. At the right-hand side are the real world issues, the aspects of practice, as the practitioners see them, extending from the enabling capabilities at the bottom to the dynamics of practice occurring in a setting at the top. In each of the squares is a statement of what the cross-over signifies to practice in terms of the characteristics of the context. For example, judgements concerning the nature of the ongoing background dynamics are placed at the cross-over between Environment and the Dynamics of Practice. Regarding the Elements of our Approach, on Figure 18 we have indicated where, roughly, the various Elements[81] introduced in Chapter 4 are on the grid of the matrix. For example, Contextual Complexity (CC) clearly sits between the Environment/Setting cross-over (because the CC Element examines the givens and realities) and Experienced Complexity between the Practice and Reflecting and so on.

The Symptom Sorting matrix does not always have to be fully and methodically completed if this is not required – once a baseline has been captured it is more beneficial to either learn-by-doing in practice or to spend time with the Trade-off Space developing a feeling for the dynamics. The matrix can be revisited and updated along the way. Note that the cells are definitely *not* intended to 'partition' the context in a reductionist way – that would be a mistake – so it is entirely appropriate to overlay shapes and regions that make sense to the users as they see fit. In addition, it may make sense to populate two or more versions of the matrix from different perspectives (e.g. economic, political etc.) and compare them as circumstances change as a way of exposing unspoken assumptions and overlooked opportunities.

How to do Symptom Sorting – Populating the Matrix. We'll now go through the cells in the order that they appear from right to left and starting in the upper row to indicate the characteristics that each captures, but please don't take it that this implies some kind of preferred order in the way that the Approach is used.

A. **Nature of the Setting.** The setting is the particular circumstances in which practitioners may find themselves working. It includes the environment, its dynamics, the entities in it and their purposefulness and intent. Of course the environment is a shared space for working and living (for all types of entities and creatures) and provides, sustains or inhibits different conditions affecting the use of resources. The state

---

81   Key to names of Elements: EC Experienced Complexity; CC Contextual Complexity; PI Purpose and Intent; SP Strategies and Possibilities; OG Option Generation; IS Influencing and Shaping. NC stands for Natural Complexity.

of the environment and competition for use of resources generates tensions that affect practice. The environment cannot be thought of as a single feature – the variety of level, scale, use, detail and the time-horizon of many of its processes can be influential in different ways even in the same setting. Let's examine these issues:

1. **Nature of Natural Complexity in the Context.** A particular mix of natural and/or social features in a context may pose specific challenges and/or offer opportunities. Hence, these features, their occurrence and composition, should be captured – such as types of settlement or the political situation. An example of something that would matter to practice is the 'Zero-Sum Game' factors – finding out which types of critical resources are significant in this context. The Contextual Complexity Element would be used to expose these issues and the relevant factors that might be modifiers of the context or be the basis of tensions.

2. **Ways in which Context Changes Dynamically.** When practitioners asked us, 'How does change happen, where is the theory of change?' they were in one breath apparently wanting to understand all the laws of nature – life, the universe and everything – whilst also asking, 'Why is this change occurring?' These are actually two different questions. The first has been dealt with in Chapter 3 in the discussions on givens and realities – natural complexity is as it is. The second question, 'There is a specific change happening – why is it occurring (as this matters to me)?', is a practitioner-centric one. The answer will be different from one practitioner to another. That is why it is important here to characterise the types of dynamic change faced, including those depending on the context, those which extend into and through cyberspace, and the degree to which these dynamics depend on/affect givens in the setting. The Contextual Complexity and Experienced Complexity Elements are designed to capture these factors. It is because 'effect' isn't localised in time and space that, in the Approach, we emphasise the importance of iteration over timescales that may extend way beyond those of an initiating project to pick up long-wave dynamics.

3. **Ways in which Purpose is Set and Intent is Shaped by Context.** It is difficult, without the sort of robust evidence that Symptom Sorting generates, to challenge the mindset of someone who doesn't understand realities such as: change doesn't happen in isolation, or there are co-evolutionary aspects, or the 'boundaries' of a project do not delineate the limits of effects. The insights

gathered in this cell express the implications of the realities of the setting in a way that supports the formulation and adjustment of purpose and intent. We accommodate this in the Framework by ensuring that, in the Purpose and Intent Element and in the Reflecting on Realities loop, the unavoidable issues, even if they seem to be hindering certain endeavours, are explicitly identified, acknowledged and factored into the ongoing work in the community-of-practice.

4. **Components in the Environment – Creatures, Objects, Agents.** One of the things that practitioners can do little about is the actual people, communities and institutions they find themselves (working) with in a setting. Who these are will present either a significant opportunity or constraint depending on what they are like. In practitioners' terms, as well as objects such as buildings, creatures in the world and digital agents on the Internet for example, people, institutions, etc. are also 'components' and it may be necessary to affect their properties, and those of the 'human ecologies' to which they belong, through education, empowerment, funding, coercion and so on, to achieve the changes required. This cell of the matrix is where practitioners gain an appreciation of which entities are involved in the setting, which ones have to be involved in the context and which ones could be left out without consequence, and to what degree the practitioner's involvement has, of itself, shifted the dynamic. Whilst such things cannot be predicted with certainty, they definitely need to be considered – and this is part of the task of the Purpose and Intent and Contextual Complexity Elements.

B. **Issues Related to the Dynamics of Practice.** The 'cells' of the matrix in Figure 18 are not neatly and discretely bounded units with no connection to each other. They are more like overlapping regions, and this is very apparent in this next row. Here, we are concerned with the space of practice and of experiences of bringing about change – i.e. capturing those insights gained by being 'on the water' before we return to the beach and contemplate ways to improve our surfing. This is why on the matrix the Experienced Complexity Element is in more than one place – to pick up on experiences of practice and of the realities. All the cells in this whole row are about characterising different aspects of one and the same thing – what practice is like in this context:

1. Natural, Ongoing Background Dynamics – Givens. It might seem from Chapter 3 that there is little that can be done about the dynamics of natural complexity in an environment, but of course

this is not true. Humanity has the ability to reshape landscape and change ecologies fundamentally – for example, and all too often, through wholesale 'commercial development' of farmland or by vast new building programmes for residential housing, such as those going on in China, that disturb the natural dynamics. In this cell practitioners need to characterise ongoing change, possibly using a version of the routine, predictable, challenging, crisis 'symptoms' introduced in Chapter 5. Noting these things is part of the role of the Contextual Complexity and Experienced Complexity Elements.

2. **Practice given the Changing Realities – Patterns.** We could write a whole book about this one cell as it encompasses so much: about the types of complex patterns, how to recognise them, about their transience or otherwise, etc. and how they affect us all and we all affect them. Set types of communities-of-practice always co-evolve in any society (and in some form in most ecosystems) with identifiable characteristics (discussed further below). In all circumstances, what is relevant to practitioners is the way in which one can engage with such groups as partners and identify the role they might play as modifiers of change in practice. Again, the trick here is not to get caught by the idea that you have first to identify and represent (say on a network or system dynamics diagram) the specific[82] patterns of interactions that are active in your context. This is not recommended, both because you won't manage it with any degree of certainty or reliability anyway, and also because you will expend a great deal of nugatory effort trying to do it. Instead, either through learning-by-doing or from shared experience, one has to identify the kinds of general dynamic patterns that occur in the context. As this cell is the 'gateway to practice', its outputs inform the Influence and Shaping Element as the basis for understanding how to work with the dynamics to change outcomes (using the Trade-off Space and/or Landscape of Change).

3. **Practice as Changed by Purpose and Intent.** Some of the potentially complementary and contradictory factors in a context, in real-time, are driven by the actions of everyone involved in a situation. In other words, in this cell practitioners need to identify how the dynamics might change based on how people might adjust their intentions. However, for the deliberative aspects of

---

82   Imagine if our surfer tried to do this before surfing by, for example, trying to map the hydrodynamics of a particular wave. However, understanding wave phenomena in general is very useful as it could form the basis for strategy.

purpose and intent the tensions between Experienced Complexity, Purpose and Intent, Options Generation and Influencing and Shaping Elements have to be considered. Concerning cyberspace, let us not forget that the software agents and devices (such as those in so-called 'ambient intelligence' buildings) have a degree of intent, too, which may, increasingly, be a factor that practitioners have to consider – obviously in some contexts more than in others. As an example, it is well-documented that the so-called 'Black Monday Crash' of the Stock Market in 1987 was caused by the 'program trader' computers (software agents that perform rapid stock executions based on external inputs) entering a self-reinforcing downward spiral. Human traders saw the apparent fall in the Market, and their perceptions led to panic selling – actions which appeared to 'validate' the computers' deductions, and which then triggered another round of selling.

4. **Role of Components in Generating Dynamic Phenomena.** Structures, communities-of-interest, collaboration patterns, organisational forms, and federations can also be considered to be 'components'. The aspects of the components that affect dynamic change, even when the entities involved are not human, need to be captured as part of the Purpose and Intent Element. For practitioners, the key point here is being open to the range of things that might be significant 'game changers' in their area of concern. For example, a swarm of locusts can generate a political and economic impact far outside the area in which they have devastated crops – though obviously they didn't 'intend' to do it, their need to eat created these wider impacts. Something as simple as varying the diversity of the components involved in a task changes team dynamics – add computers and people stare at the screens rather than at each other (the computers are a kind of primitive, and possibly inhibiting, team player)! Insights from this cell inform the Option Generation Element as do any complexity-worthiness factors noted concerning the components.

C. **Issues Related to Reflecting and Deciding.** As we mentioned in Chapter 2, across the various domains in which practitioners work they had similar kinds of experiences of complexity and of trying to 'do things differently', and so they raised many common issues. This was true even when practitioners worked in completely separate situations on different types of tasks. Inevitably though, for some, certain issues were high on the agenda that in other domains were not there at all. The reasons for this are apparent when we look at this next row where, though the ways in which the reflecting is done are similar, the context is the major driver of what matters and what does not. It is for this reason that, as far as possible, in this row, as far as possible, practitioners should examine how reflecting should be done and what to tease out in this context in order to find, for example, potential change issues for the Trade-off Space or patterns or dynamics to add to the Landscape of Change:

1. **Reflecting on Givens and Acknowledging (Past) Realities.** Here practitioners have to take a deep breath, note the realities and givens and face up to the consequences of these – and this, of course, includes being open to the unexpected opportunities that might reveal themselves. In the Framework, the way that practitioners would do this would be to use the Contextual Complexity Element to expose the realities and then, by comparing them with their experienced complexity, practitioners have the basis for considering the consequences in terms of the feasibility of what can be done (Strategies and Possibilities) in the context and take this into the Trade-off Space. Other givens in the environment might include regulations, laws and policies, issues of environmental awareness, political situations and morals, cultural and ethical issues. This 'environment', as it is now, owes its current form to things that have happened in the past. Therefore, reflecting needs to consider more than just the 'now'. As a result, people may find that when they look into the past there was an opportunity that was missed or, on a positive note, that past events have laid the groundwork for possibilities that they can take advantage of in the future.

2. **Reflecting on Possibilities Given the Realities of Change (Now).** The type of insights from this cell tend to concern the more proactive/immediate/reactive issues, driven by dynamic change, where people are adjusting what they are doing as a result of what is happening right now. This can be done as part of practice itself – supported by what goes on in the Influencing and Shaping and Experienced Complexity Elements. It is in this space that issues of power come into play strongly and where finding uncontested spaces can provide a way of making a breakthrough. In this cell practitioners should look for the types of transitions discussed in Chapter 5, whether triggered deliberately as part of enactment or learning, or arising unexpectedly as a result of changes over different scales, levels or time-horizons. These changes and transitions may be undetectable (directly) by humans but might be evidenced by surges of precursor activity, possibly in cyberspace.

3. **Reflecting on Intents, Drives, Values – Perspectives and Viewpoints (Futures).** This cell is at the heart of practitioners' concerns about what to do differently when, given the changing realities that are detected, considerations about purpose and intent may need to be re-formulated. Some of the drivers that result in things altering purpose and intent come from answering questions such as: Which cultures are present and active in the context and what are the 'norms' to take note of, what is "the other" to me, how well do people understand each other, do they have enough common ground? Also, people may ask: What is implicit in my intent, in the way others are viewed, and when considering what part 'they' may have in what is to be achieved? How are people working together, in what sort of structures, federations or alliances, and what challenges and opportunities does that present? As our partner Merfyn Lloyd says, 'It's mostly common sense to work this out – but whose common sense?' So the reflection in this cell is informed in a number of ways including looking at the potential differences between the Option Generation Element and complexity-worthiness balanced with the successes or otherwise of actual practice.

4. **Reflecting on what Entities do and could do, Behaviours, Relationships and Interactions (Preparing Options).** Under this heading practitioners need to consider the types of people recruited for different types of situations, how they should be trained, whether they needed different kinds of skills and how this might affect what could or couldn't be done. They should also think about whether access to different types of tools and facilities could affect options for practice. Practitioners should use common sense to consider the effects of changing the properties of components such as people's sense of initiative. As an example, initiative will be suppressed where there is an 'ethos' of blame and punishment and the consequences of that, in changing how people interact, is that they will become cautious and seek to work only within the rules. The Option Generation Element provides a way of identifying some of the tensions between intent, possibility, capability (complexity-worthiness) and practice and, in doing so, supports the use of the Trade-off Space.

D. **Issues Related to Available Capabilities/Complexity-Worthiness.** This row is where practitioners assess which capabilities are available in the context that may affect the complexity-worthiness of actors/entities and how differences in levels or degrees of complexity-worthiness may create tensions and opportunities for practice. This is partly about employing the assessment criteria we discussed in Chapter 5 but is also about capturing any factors that may change the conditions needed to be complexity-worthy (such as the constraints that we have discussed – that may deny an entity the use of capabilities which would otherwise be available). Therefore, in this row, practitioners should identify complexity-worthiness factors for use in the Trade-off Space or patterns or dynamics that depend on it that may modify the dynamics in the Landscape of Change:

Symptom Sorting – Representing Communities-of-Practice in the Context. We have heard in this chapter about many of the features and tensions of a context – some occur at the environmental level, some are between individuals, others between groupings, and many are just variations in the overall nature of the dynamics of a context across all of these aspects. There is a larger-scale pattern to the way these features and tensions manifest themselves because of the way human beings 'just are'. In this section of the chapter we examine how these patterns – that one might call the 'social dynamics of practice' – can be put to work. But are these groupings distinct and separate, or interdependent in some way? What are their characteristics, and do they form a pattern? Indeed, they do form a pattern and we use the term communities-of-practice for these clusters of human activity. The intersections between these characteristics, which would be plotted on the Symptom Sorting matrix as regions/shapes, determine how the identity of specific clusters are defined through:

- their dynamics and 'purpose' – which can be expressed as lifecycles which include how:

  - they form (why and where do they come about and for what purpose) and how they sustain themselves (the nature of internal and external linkages and interdependencies);

  - their cohesion and persistence is sustained (what keeps them together, what kinds of shared values etc. drive the dynamics) and which interdependencies they have with other communities-of-practice and the patterns of connectedness between them;

  - they transition (change structures, scale up and down) and under which kinds of circumstances particular instances of clusters may dissolve.

- their behaviours arising from their organisational/structural forms – practitioners would plot out the characteristics of real-world instances of clusters and how they function in practice such as:

- the types of power that drive them and how it is used;

- the nature of and degrees of coupling/clamping between their components and the resulting extent of wiggle-room, degrees of freedom and innate resistance/openness to change (leading to phenomena such as flexibility, robustness, agility etc.);

- their control mechanisms – how accountability, authority, archiving, repudiation, security (where boundaries are set and which transgressions occur) and risk are handled.

These clusters are not distinct and independent and people do not 'join' one cluster to the exclusion of the others – there is a rich interplay of forms driving society. We heard a little about these forms in Chapter 3 where Thompson (2008) identified four general classes of what he called 'solidarities' in human society based on their organisational characteristics, their relationship with each other and with the environment. Depending on what people are doing at any one time, they are aligned with or give allegiance to, concurrently, one or more of them.

In practice, the four solidarities alone are not enough to 'explain' or express the rich variety of specific behaviours seen in and between communities-of-practice. For example, as a private individual someone may be a father, whilst at the same time being a public employee, a community leader and part of a religious group. Also, the clusters are mutually co-dependent and co-evolve in various ways: the 'silent majority', generally, look to the public institutions to make and enforce laws that 'keep them safe'; commerce needs the silent majority (and others) to be their consumers; criminals need people to prey on and so on. As an example, in their book *Freakonomics*, Steven D. Levitt and Stephen J. Dubner point out that the organisational detail, incentive structures and economic distribution of wages within drug dealing matches that of many burger companies. Despite the fact that these two examples of different communities-of-practice are organised in very similar ways, other than at a theoretical level, one would not say they were equivalent in terms of their respective impacts on society at large. Recognising and dealing with these types of inter-dependent factors is the bread-and-butter for practitioners that this Guide supports.

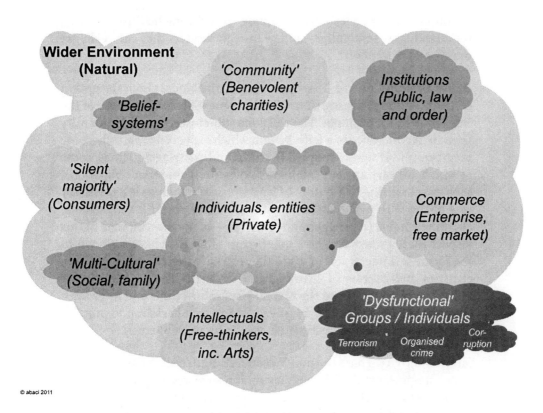

Wider Environment (Natural)

'Community' (Benevolent charities)

Institutions (Public, law and order)

'Belief-systems'

'Silent majority' (Consumers)

Individuals, entities (Private)

Commerce (Enterprise, free market)

'Multi-Cultural' (Social, family)

Intellectuals (Free-thinkers, inc. Arts)

'Dysfunctional' Groups / Individuals

Terrorism   Organised crime   Cor-ruption

© abaci 2011

Figure 19 – A Range of Communities-of-Practice.

The Communities-of-Practice. Let's look, in clockwise order, at the communities-of-practice in Figure 19 in more detail to identify how their features, modifiers, mismatches, tensions and interdependencies may help practitioners to put complexity to work in reality. We'll pick out a few of the practical characteristics of each community, beyond their organisational forms, below:

A. **Intellectuals.** This cluster of clusters includes academics, artists and those outside the mainstream of society in the sense that they wish to maintain an independence of viewpoint. Their power largely comes from their expertise and they are organised bottom-up and often informally in open, fluid and lightly connected ways. Though the academics depend on institutions like universities to provide them with the infrastructure and administrative support they need, they would claim the right to academic freedom of expression and dissent from anyone and everyone if they see fit. People we might call 'hermits' can be found in this cluster – free-thinking 'gurus' detached from society, yet often highly influential – and as thought leaders they can really set the agenda in a context.

B. **Belief-System Centric.** This cluster has distinct ideas about the notion of 'truth' – though arising from very different sources from those of the Intellectuals, for example. The religious sub-clusters get their identity from their adherence to a faith system which expects people to become members and is tightly coupled to truths and doctrines/dogmas, some of which are very ancient. Membership can impose strict obligations, such as submitting to a system of laws whose observance is a necessary part of the faith – where the ultimate source of power is unassailable and unreachable (directly) by any believer – or any practitioner! In this respect these groups can be a microcosm of all the clusters shown in the Figure in a fractal sort of way – they too have their own institutions, charities and centres of learning and so forth. The multiplicity of influences of all types and the vast range of inter-ethnic and inter-faith tensions and opportunities usually provide a rich backdrop to practice that should not be underestimated, even after years of study.

C. **Silent Majority.** That's the public manifestation of all of us – the source of people-power and of the public opinion so feared by politicians and of the fads and fashions that is the concern of commerce. This cluster is so open and free it can become anything it likes and can indirectly exert a lot of power. If, *en masse*, it is influenced by single events, peer pressure and the actions of (sometimes previously insignificant) individuals this can be a catalyst of sudden and disorientating change (think of the worldwide reaction to assassination of the US President John F Kennedy in 1963 in Dallas, Texas). The Silent Majority can have a slightly fatalistic attitude to any turn of events – in the modern idiom they would say 'Whatever' and carry on with their lives. Every community-of-practice depends on the Silent Majority and they, in turn, on the other communities.

D. **'Multi-cultural' (Ethnic, Social/family-centric, Tribes/Clans).** These clusters get their proud identity from an inward-looking attention to, usually, family-based allegiances many of which go back tens of generations, but also from traditions and common roots. In this way the group provides a mutual support structure for its members which is self-sustaining – all for one and one for all – the focus is on survival by reinforcing 'cultural operating codes' such as patronage, honour etc. The size of such groups tends to be limited by the span of control of family influence. Important types of sub-cluster co-exist here, for example gender-based/cross-family groupings. Of course, when a social group such as a tribe or clan develops territorial and linguistic features it would have an ethnic identity. When a group grows large enough and takes on formal institutions then it would be called a nation. The diversity of form and details of rituals in these groups is immense, and practitioners usually work with a representative in their dealings with them. Ethnic groupings, tribes and clans can be quite self-contained and independent of some of the other communities-of-practice and can be unwilling to be involved without a clear incentive that makes sense on their own terms – as even that supremely confident negotiator Gertrude Bell learned in her dealings with the people of Persia and the Middle East in the early 1900s (described by Janet Wallach in her book *Desert Queen*).

E. **Community Groups.** These include charities, voluntary community groups, aid agencies and other 'egalitarians' whose identities are defined by their views about caring, sharing and equality and the need to take a nurturing attitude to the environment. Such groups form around common interests, shared values and, often unspoken but assumed, aligned intent. As such, their memberships can be fluid and organisational structures 'weak'. Power is a mixture of expert and referent power with often an uneasy tension between positional power and the need, or otherwise, for leaders in such groups. They require flexibility and agility in form and function to work effectively among-the-people to meet their practical aspirations, yet also have to have more formal structures as part of accountability.

These internal tensions can be creative, but sometimes result in a group being burst apart for a time by the contradictions. Notable examples being the reinvention/reforming of some of the Green parties in the last thirty years. In many ways, these egalitarian groups are highly dependent on the other communities-of-practice – as a source for their members (Silent Majority), to implement statutes (Institution), to contribute funding and patronage (Commerce/Arts) and even, in some extreme cases, protection provided by the Dysfunctional (underworld) elements so that the egalitarians can continue to support disadvantaged people in that very underworld.

F. **Institutions.** These groupings would include governments (nations) and government departments of all sorts and institutions with a largely 'paternal'/philanthropic role in society (such as many of the bodies which accredit, monitor and regulate professional life). The common view here is that humanity needs the firm, authoritative influence of long-lived institutions with a proud history for there to be order, accountability, control on excess and good governance of society – that without their control 'there would be chaos'. The cohesiveness of these institutions often depends upon shared history and is reinforced by rules, detailed processes, rituals and the so-called 'old-boy network – it's not what you know it's who you know' way-of-working. This tight internal connectedness and monumental strength means that they are long-lived and hard to change – there is an inbuilt inertia, a kind of immune system that filters and spits out novelty as if it never existed. As a result, institutions can be very ponderous and inflexible, and therefore find it hard to adjust or adapt their capabilities of ways-of-working. Because they are lightly connected to the outside world they find it difficult to engage with and/or influence the realities of the wider environment or of the other communities-of-practice. This is largely the reason why their dominant mode is to use top-down power and reward and punishment to bring about control and forced change on their terms.

Practitioners should accept these realities as givens in their dealings with institutions and, where possible, work with them rather than attack head-on – unless they can acquire equivalent power or find a decisive asymmetry in tension or opportunity (e.g. become appointed to the governing body).

G. **Commerce**. This commercial cluster of clusters seeks advantage in a free-market atmosphere of unfettered competition with minimal accountability and maximum exploitation of resources. The view here is that commerce is the 'engine of society', providing opportunity, prosperity and the space for people to fulfil their potential. People are seen as rational and it is assumed that they will not do anything which is not in their best interests. Given the financial crises of the World in 2009 onwards, many of the basic assumptions about how finance, the markets and commerce function in relation to the wider society are under close and critical scrutiny. Power in these clusters is also usually positional and exerted top-down in an hierarchical structure – but managers are really enablers; they can't, in practice, mandate everything. As has been pointed out, commerce is fundamentally interdependent and reliant on the other communities-of-practice – for its workers and consumers, for government support when things go wrong (and the provision of national and international infrastructure when it's going right) and on the institutions that regulate its activities. It is true that commerce often supplies the means to enable community organisations and aid agencies to do their work, so practitioners must be competent in understanding the realities of economic life. Forming mutually beneficial win-win relationships where all involved can claim benefit and gain on their own terms is no mean task, but one that we all, as practitioners, should strive for.

H. **Dysfunctional Individuals/Groups**. These communities-of-practice could be labelled 'The Underworld', the underbelly of society where dysfunctional[83] variants of all the clusters previously discussed exist. For example, contrast commerce with organised crime or compare the organisation and motivations of tribes/clans with that of the Mafia. To what extent the good side of society needs the Underworld to co-exist for good to prevail is open to debate. Maybe some things can only occur if they go via the Underworld because there is no openly accepted route 'legally'. However, what practitioners do need to do is acknowledge the influence of and dynamic between so-called good and bad in practice. Really, it's a continuum between all of the clusters – as we all know – and so the dysfunctional side has to be, by definition, part of practice whether people like it or not.

Symptom Sorting – Capturing Perspectives. We have used the terms 'perspective' and 'viewpoint' extensively throughout the Guide and now wish to show the differences between them and the importance of examining context from various perspectives. Just to clarify the differences: viewpoints relate to the Experienced Complexity of individuals and/or entities of any type – 'How does the context seem to me/us from our viewpoint?' Perspectives are the various ways of looking at complex realities that would be needed as part of developing and sustaining an appreciation of Contextual Complexity. Perspectives have different types of degrees of freedom and so iterating through the relevant ones whilst Symptom Sorting improves the coverage of the context and the expression of factors. When put together with the communities-of-practice, when Symptom Sorting and when using the Trade-off Space, the synthesis across perspectives and viewpoints enables practitioners, individuals and entities to really work with the possibilities of a context over time. Some of the relevant types[84] of perspective include:

---

83   Actually, dysfunctional is a poor description. Most of the Underworld operates in a very ordered and calculating way – it would be a significant mistake to assume that everything that happens there is because of people who are 'crazies'.

84   There are of course many versions of this list that could be generated – and of course they overlap.

A. **Welfare, Medical.** Including hospital services, disease prevention and control, care-giving, epidemiology, mental health programmes.

B. **Scientific, Industrial, Technological (inc. cyber, infrastructure, mining, transport etc.).** Covering all technical and technological activities whether for profit or not.

C. **Economic, Commercial, Financial.** Includes financial models, stock markets, property, commodities, business activities, private and corporate investments, banking.

D. **Political, Legislative (policy, legal, regulatory).** All forms of 'codified' control, whether national/governmental or as part of professional institutions or other bodies.

E. **Military, Security, Police, Emergency, Insurance.** Covers regulation enforcement and control and 'contingency' activities to mitigate against the uncontrollable.

F. **Environmental, Ecological, Agricultural.** Very broad category based on concerns arising from sustaining the viability of the environment, the land, the seas and atmosphere.

G. **Cultural, Artistic, Expression, Recreation (inc. sport, hobbies).** All forms of human entertainment, expression and 'self-improvement'.

H. **Social, Family, Moral and Ethical.** Based on family and society, this perspective covers what is 'right and proper' for the ongoing cohesion of people's domestic lives.

As an example of how the use of these perspectives might add to practice, consider the prevalence of human trafficking and prostitution in Europe. Let us imagine the work of an NGO supporting vulnerable women, based at the border between three countries. One country has legalised prostitution and the women work openly in suitable facilities. In the second country, it is illegal, and the women are criminalised and are the assets of organised crime and the drugs trade. The third country is unofficially tolerant but, as a token of disapproval, has 'named and shamed' some of the men who 'kerb (curb)-crawl' after the women. How could comparing perspectives and viewpoints contribute to the work of the NGO? Well, let's take the commercial perspective – in the first country the women have chosen to do this work in a business-like way which adds to their independence, in the second they are little more than slave workers and in the third there will be a mix of circumstances. From the legal perspective, there are three different legislative frameworks which, taken together, are 'contradictory'. In terms of the welfare/medical issues – in the first country the NGO provides advice, in the second refuge and in the third its activities may not be welcome (in that it brings unwelcome attention to such sensitive issues). Importantly, there are cross-border opportunities to be exploited – lessons from one country can be helpful in another; criminal activity, which is no respecter of borders, can be identified in ways that might otherwise go unobserved and so on. In short, the wider perspective exposes more degrees of freedom and a bigger space-of-possibilities for the NGO than it would otherwise obtain from a single-issue focus.

In the next chapter we'll illustrate the ways in which the Approach might be used in action and indicate the specific value added to practice through examining a number of case studies.

CHAPTER 7: CASE STUDIES

'Results are obtained by exploiting opportunities, not by solving problems.'

Peter Drucker (1909-2005)

CASE STUDIES – BACKGROUND AND OVERVIEW

In this chapter we'll look at some case studies, provided by practitioners, that give examples of putting complexity to work in different ways and that examine the contributions that complexity-aware approaches did make – or could have made – to practice.

We have, as far as possible in this Guide, tried to develop a sense of discourse with you, the Reader, and we intend that this chapter will provide a more tangible basis for this virtual discussion.

We have selected case studies that cover different types of human endeavour in some of the communities-of-practice, previously discussed, with which practitioners are involved (shown in Figure 20). Our aim is to use the Approach to show what could, should, or might be done differently.

Please accept that we are not itemising a set method in this chapter but are, instead, describing some of the different types of journey that might be made when using the Approach in practice.

Practice in the context of the Case Studies

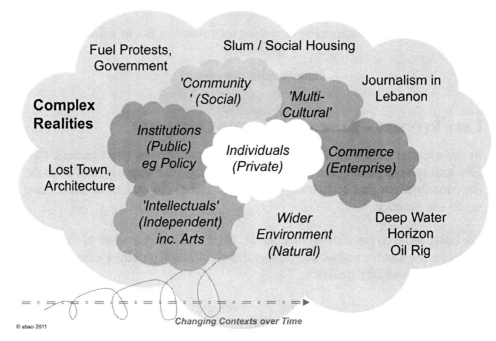

Figure 20 – Communities-of-Practice and Case Studies.

A short summary of each of the case studies is provided below (they are in the order shown on the Figure starting top-left):

A. **Fuel protests in the UK in 2000.** In 2000 there were protests over the rising price of fuel for vehicles. The most vocal protesters were the lorry (truck) drivers who blockaded city centres and oil depots, and caused traffic jams on motorways by driving very slowly. Fears of fuel shortage led to panic buying and petrol (gas) stations soon ran dry. The Government faced the prospect of losing control of the situation but the fuel protesters had no leadership and did not belong to an established group of any sort and the Government, initially, could not find a way of engaging with them or of exerting influence. As this case study reveals, the Government realised that their only option was to trigger a change such that the protesters transformed themselves into a cohesive group that could then be engaged with and made ineffective. The case study will examine how this change was brought about and will use the Approach to look at other options that were available to both 'sides' of this dispute.

B. **Upgrading Slum Housing.** The case study deals with a slum upgrading programme in Cameroon implemented by the Dutch NGO Intervolve. Their experience is that in such projects there can be a strong mismatch between expectations and values among the beneficiaries, those who have the political commitment to such programmes and the supporting financial institutions. The case study examines the issues involved in upgrading a slum neighbourhood in Cameroon, the various asymmetries, their consequences and how change is being brought about in such circumstances.

C. **Social Housing in Ludlow, UK.** This case study is about shaping public opinion concerning the provision of 'social housing' in small towns on the border between England and Wales in the UK. In late 2001, communities were considering how their local plans needed to be changed to accommodate new planning guidance. This activity involved individuals and a number of organisations and institutions who were each asked to submit their views. These views then had to be collated and, to some extent resolved, before submission to higher authorities. One of the organisations was the Civic Society, a voluntary, non-elected local decision-making body with over 500 members, whose focus was on the conservation of the historic fabric of the town and its sustainable future. This group became extremely divided and strongly polarised on the issue of the provision of social housing. The case study examines the use of a complexity-inspired approach, which enabled useful trends and indicators to become apparent. It was evident from feedback at the time that much more could have been done if a better and more developed approach had been available. We examine the potential contribution our Approach could have made.

D. **Journalism in Lebanon.** Robert Holloway, the Director of the *Agence France-Presse* (AFP) Foundation was asked by the UNDP to run a course on peace journalism in Lebanon. Robert says: 'It is an extremely complicated society with 17 officially recognised religious communities. The political structure, the State itself, is extremely weak. [...] The civil war resumed at a much lower level of intensity about three years ago. Society now is [...] precariously calm. The UN asked us to go in and do a 'peace journalism' training course. AFP said they'd do it but not under that title, which it was thought would be misunderstood. Instead it was called "Objectivity in covering conflict". We got together 24 journalists, ten from the Television Sector, ten from the written press and four from the radio. We had three trainers, all Arabic speaking. And that's how we did it.' This case study examines how group solidarity developed under such challenging circumstances.

E. **Deep Water Horizon – Crisis/Transition.** This case study into the Deep Water Horizon (DWH) oil rig disaster in the Gulf of Mexico explores sudden transitions of the type described in Chapter 5. This is about, literally, change 'under fire', and examines how the situation required people forced by the circumstances to flip from one type of complexity-worthiness to another – we analyse the issues (based on the official National Commission's report into the disaster) and recommendations.

F. **Lost Town, UK Development Agency.** The Lost Town is one of four winning projects in the Landmark East Competition, initiated and run by the East of England Development Agency (EEDA) in 2004. A feasibility study was undertaken, at Dunwich, for a highly innovative and creative sculpture of a church located at its original site in the sea off the East Coast. The idea for the Lost Town project came originally from the loss of Dunwich old town to coastal erosion. Owing to local opposition in Dunwich, an alternative site, at Walton-on-the-Naze was considered. A second feasibility study there secured strong support. EEDA funding was provided for the initial feasibility studies but the team was unsuccessful in obtaining funding from other sources to continue the project, and so Lost Town remains an, as yet, unfulfilled dream. The case study examines the range of aspects that were covered in the feasibility study and makes suggestions as to why the Project, other than because of the funding issue, has stalled – and what could occur to revitalise it.

The case studies will now be examined in detail. For each one we will set the scene – describing the context and showing the nature of the journey and its effects on those involved. We will then use the Approach to examine the dynamics, patterns and features of the context and, using techniques from Chapter 6 as appropriate, to identify what we think are the key aspects of practice in the case. Next, we will explain what actually happened and what the consequences were. Lastly we will see what deductions can be made and lessons drawn for practice – and comment on contributions that our Approach could have made.

FUEL PROTESTS IN THE UK IN 2000

In 2000 there were protests in the UK over the rising price of fuel for vehicles. The most vocal protesters were the lorry (truck) drivers who blockaded city centres, oil depots and caused traffic jams on motorways by driving very slowly. Fuel shortages led to panic buying, which had a knock-on effect for the UK Government who had, as part of cost-saving measures, abolished many of its own fuel storage facilities. This meant that emergency personnel, and some government workers, were also required to get their fuel from commercial petrol stations. As the supplies ran out the Government faced the prospect of losing control of the situation (when, for example, police cars ran out of petrol). The fuel protesters were individuals with a common interest to see tax on fuel reduced – they had no formal leadership and did not belong to an established group of any sort and this made it difficult for the Government to find a way of engaging with them or of exerting influence. An appeal on television to stop the protests by the then Prime Minister Tony Blair received a derisive response from the general public who were, generally, behind the protest for their own reasons. Mr Blair ordered the formation of a task force of oil executives and police officers to work out how to deal with future demonstrations. Home Secretary Jack Straw, who headed the group at that time, admitted that the government had not been fully prepared for the events. 'We were not caught on the hop about the concerns – it is certainly the case, however, that the scale and escalation of the protest was something which was unexpected', he said. [85] But one truck driver, encouraged by the widespread public support of this protest, promised more chaos if fuel prices did not fall. 'We could have brought this country down – we've got them on the rack, let's keep them on the rack.' he told colleagues. Given this setting, let us have a look, as dispassionate observers, at what could be done in practice in such a volatile and fast-changing situation. We'll be comparing the Government's use of the Approach with that of the protesters – in other words looking at two different ways in which the Approach might have been used and what the advantages might have been.

A. **Patterns, Features and Characteristics of this Context.** What were the characteristics of this real-world situation and how did they change as the protests got underway? The dominant feature is the protests themselves: they came about spontaneously in many places at once with little apparent evidence of overt coordination and their intensity grew quickly from being token protests to 'swarms' that brought the UK to a halt. For the Government, success would be achieving a rapid transition back to 'normality' – but could they work out what the appropriate requisite variety would need to be – in other words could they work out the contextual complexity and would they have the necessary means

---

85   See the BBC's website On this Day http://news.bbc.co.uk/onthisday/hi/dates/stories/september/15/newsid_2518000/2518707.stm

available to them to trigger the changes required? For the protesters, which included the people (i.e. the Silent Majority), success would be a fall in fuel taxes – their short-term achievements were evident, but how was longer-term purposefulness and intent to be sustained; indeed was it necessary? Transition and changes in structure then are the key characteristics in this context – transitions that had changed everyday behaviour into a different form, from benign, dispersed activity to challenging, purposeful *ad hoc* structures that, locally and nationally, overwhelmed Government capabilities. So, the case study focuses on timely transition and structural engagement and we'll look at which aspects of practice were key to how things turned out in the end – who brought about the changes that ended the protests and how it was achieved? Which routes for influence in the Landscape of Change were relevant? What happened afterwards is another story. Let's Reflect on the Realities as independent observers:

1. **There are some important givens in the contextual complexity that set the conditions for what happened.**
    One feature is the nature of oil itself – it is a liquid fuel that has to be transported by lorry from an oil refinery to stations where people can collect it (if the protests had been about gas the outcomes would have been different as it is not so easy to blockade a gas pipeline which is underground and which comes right to people's front doors). Other givens, such as the notions of money, capitalism, commerce and trade; the decline of the railways (increasing reliance on lorries for transport); and the demand for oil as an expression of personal freedoms, whilst relevant, we will put to one side for now.

2. **What about the actors and groupings – i.e. components, their properties, interactions, and the structures that arise?**
    Three types of 'component' and their experienced complexity are relevant in this context. The protesters had a certain demographic - yet the motivations, temperaments and personalities of key individuals were not apparent at first. The elements of UK society (and media) that became involved were from all types of social mixes and factions, and there were no obvious overlaps, relationships and exclusions – even to the people themselves. In a way, the 'simplicity' of the uniformity of all those involved in the protest made swarming in this way easy – underlying differences that might have been divisive were not manifested at the start of the protests. The usual leadership elements in society, whether formally appointed, informal

representatives or 'troublemakers' were not yet active. Despite the dispersed and diverse nature of the protests, the people involved found a sense of unity that was self-reinforcing – through their experienced complexity they had become a purposeful, self-organised entity of sorts and people sensed it and liked it.

3. **Concerning intent and purposefulness.** For the protesters their intent was simple – cheaper fuel – and their sense of purpose and their apparent success were being reflected/fed back to them through the media who were in a way, giving the swarm (The Fuel Protesters) an identity that 'it' didn't know it had and that didn't, other than in a virtual way, actually exist. For the Government and its institutions of law and order, the intent was equally clear – a return to the *status quo*. But, there were of course sub-agendas. It has been reported that oil suppliers wanted VAT to be reduced (and by siding with the Government they thought they could achieve this). In other words, though apparently a unified, single entity on the surface, historically, the Government and its departments and supporters have always been in an uneasy federation underneath.

What we can conclude is that there was clearly a profound structural mismatch on many levels here. The protesters were an undefined swarm of millions of people acting in unison and generating transient, yet nationally significant, effects by drawing on the innate 'simple' ability of large groups of people to coordinate their activities on a single issue across space, and then transition in a short time. The Government is a federation of institutions with identities, structures and capabilities formed over many centuries. This enables it to provide certainty and assurance over time as it has developed the internal procedures necessary to deal with a diverse range of issues. However, its stability denies agility. As we heard from Eileen Conn in Chapter 2, there is a mismatch between the Government's formal 'teeth' structures and the informal dynamics of community activity. In short, the protests and protesters existed almost exclusively in the community-of-practice dynamic – they were, to use our previous analogy, always surfing on the sea. The Government spent most of its time inland reflecting on its experienced complexity and sent the police to, certainly at the beginning, shout at the protesters (surfers) from the beach.

B. Dynamics and Tensions of Practice in this Context – Insights from the Approach. Let us now Reflect on Practice and consider some of the possibilities and options for the protesters and for the UK Government:

1. For the Government a lot is at stake here – they must bring about change before the country runs out of fuel, at which point both protests and public disorder will get worse, and they will have lost the ability to intervene (there will be no petrol for the police, etc.). Time is of the essence. What are some of the possibilities they would compare following Symptom Sorting? As part of Option Generation they could consider the environmental drivers: for example, long-term more oil reserves could be located which would bring the price down, but this is out of scope given the urgency of the situation. What about top-down intervention? Fuel tax policy could be changed as the protesters request and then raised again later. In economic terms fuel incentives and subsidies could be manipulated to benefit the lorry drivers so that they stop their protest and hope that the general public lose interest as a result. What about trying to influence the way people are self-organising? Through social pressure, preferably with a celebrity figure, try to demonise the protesters as a threat to security; or engage with protesters as 'partners' so that people defer to the Government. What about affecting the way the protests arise from the bottom up? Maybe appeal directly to people's sense of responsibility? In any case the Government would need to compete candidate options and interventions against each other in the Trade-off Space and consider issues such as: timeliness, ease, risk, cost (money, losing face, etc.), and review the practicality of candidate interventions – even develop potential 'influence networks' – though, as we have heard, this can take time and resources for potentially little gain.

2. For the protesters things are easier in a way. They don't have any formal structures to sustain, their intent and purpose are straightforward and there is, on the surface anyway, a common understanding of what should be done – protest! They are not really considering other possibilities and their options are concerned with variety in the form of their protests rather than dreaming up other forms of action. Anyway, the variations arise in an ad hoc, self-* manner determined by the circumstances in each case – this is also how their influencing and shaping is done. There

is a nucleus of lorry drivers acting as a catalyst but the way that the protests self-organise is informal and opportunistic – nothing is planned.

What, as detached observers, can we conclude from this in the light of what we have said about putting complexity to work in the first Part of the Guide? Well, one technique is to run the Approach twice, once for the Government and once for the Protesters, and by comparing the asymmetries that are revealed we can get usable insights. It is obvious that the protesters are vulnerable over time to a loss of interest and cohesion of their supporters – they have little or no permanence in anything they do, which is both an advantage and a vulnerability. For the Government, their challenge comes in two forms: either how to engage with the protesters on their own terms by directly intervening in the protests; or how to change the conditions of practice such that protesters are forced, or coerced, into engaging with the Government on its terms. How might it achieve this? As Figure 21 shows this might be easier than at first thought.

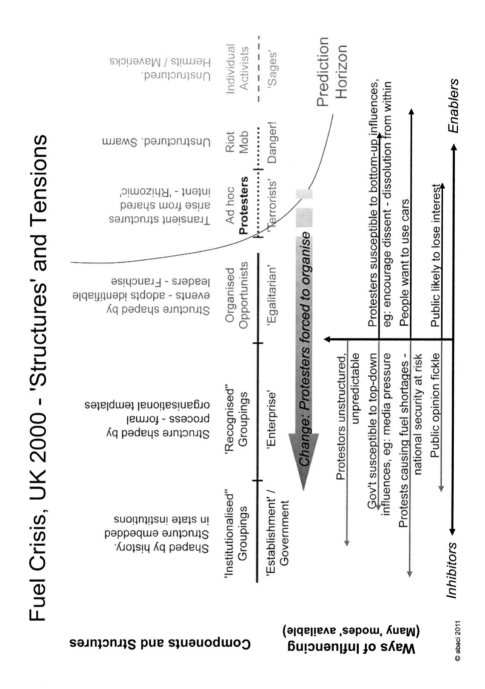

Figure 21 – Features and Dynamics of a Range of Organisational Structures.

The Figure illustrates a continuum of organisational forms, their origins and their dynamics with 'caricature' labels for the different forms, similar to those discussed in Chapter 6. To the right are where the protesters started out – as individual activists – to the left are institutional groupings. The Government obviously wants to avoid the 'Danger' regions when they are Influencing and Shaping and does this by triggering the fuel protesters to organise formally into some sort of recognised grouping with which it can engage. The Figure summarises the way that the change can be brought about. The upper part of the Figure shows a continuum of structural forms. The Government is an institutional grouping that cannot easily become 'unstructured'. Whereas, the fuel protesters are a type of unstructured swarm, and the properties of such swarms are, as we heard in Chapter 3, understood by complexity science. The tensions in the Trade-off Space at the bottom of the Figure indicate that, given the timescales and risks, the degrees of freedom that are available here are in the fluid nature of the protestors structure. We would recommend that the Government introduce a trigger that will cause the swarm to loose its dynamic, to 'crystallise out'. In other words, get the surfers onto the beach and so busy running their organisations that they have no time to surf (protest).

C. **What Actually Happened.** The initial catalysts for the fuel protests came from the French, traditionally more militant than the British, and their example became a behavioural template for protest in the UK, which quickly caught on. As this case study reveals, the Government realised that their 'only' option was to trigger a change such that the protesters transformed into a cohesive group. Such a group could then be engaged with and made ineffective through the usual methods of government control. After the failed televised celebrity appeal to the people by Tony Blair and with Britain at a standstill, as Paul Marston and George Jones describe it in their article from 14 September 2000 in *The Telegraph*, the Government agreed to negotiate with the protesters if they 'elected a representative'. The People's Fuel Lobby was formed and David Handley elected spokesman. However, other groups also became involved because of their interest in fuel issues. Tom Houghton was elected spokesman for Farmers for Action, and representatives from the Road Haulage Association (RHA) started to hold talks with the ministers. Barry Clement reports in *The Independent* on 22 September 2000 in his article 'Fuel lobby turns fire on Safeway for 5p petrol rise' that: 'Representatives from the Road Haulage Association (RHA), who have been in talks with the ministers all this week, yesterday held 'a meeting in Peterborough with 160 protesters. Eight farmers and hauliers were elected to join John Bridge, National Chairman of the RHA, and Roger King, its Chief Executive, in London for another meeting with ministers [today]'. The Government's strategy was working – formal structures were appearing and now divide-and-rule tactics could be employed. The general public lost interest at this point, fuel flows were restored and the issue faded from the headlines. *The Guardian* newspaper's Seumas Milne reported in the 26 of October 2000 edition in 'Demo leaders divided over tactics to force tax cuts' that: 'Leaders of the fuel tax protests have split into warring camps, accusing each other of hijacking the movement, while promoting rival direct action plans – including blockading supermarket food distribution centres – if Gordon Brown fails to meet their demands next month. At the centre of the in-fighting are two of the most prominent leaders of last month's fuel blockades, Brynle Williams, the 51-year-old Welsh smallholder, who kicked off the protests at Stanlow Refinery in Cheshire, and David Handley, Chairman of the People's Fuel Lobby, who has made the running since the blockades were called off. Mr Williams yesterday accused Mr Handley of 'running round the country setting up splinter groups.'. By November the Government had 'won'.

D. **Deductions and Lessons for Practice.** Could this happen again in the same way? Probably not. As we have indicated, sudden dynamic behaviour cannot arise out of thin air; there need to be certain underlying conditions, precursors and enablers in place first. In 2000, people were in the mood for protest, there was dissatisfaction and a certain militancy in the air ready to 'catch the wave'. Now, in 2011, people are all familiar with social networking and routinely set up flashmobs gatherings coordinated on-the-fly using their mobile phones – the threshold is lower and the following surge consequently smaller. Governments and individuals are all more familiar with people-power and its strengths and limitations and so when Reflecting on Realities they would consider different factors based on previous experience. Thanks to the Internet, the ability to organise planet-wide is now routine – cyberspace is now absolutely part of practice and of everyone's contextual complexity.[86] As of spring 2011 we have seen régime changes in Tunisia and Egypt fostered by this shared awareness. Wikileaks has blurred further the domains of public, private and secret – and all in just ten years. If the fuel protests were to happen again and the protesters used the Approach presented in this Guide, it would certainly help them be more savvy about how

---

86 Whereas, the surge in mobile phone SMS/text activity that preceded the petrol shortages in the UK in 2000 was a 'new and unexpected' phenomenon as people told each other which stations still had petrol.

to maximise the advantages of their structural and organisational asymmetry with respect to the lumbering institutions of Government. Specifically, it would have indicated the vulnerabilities of the protesters to just the kind of 'interference' that happened and the importance of maintaining the aim. Indeed, they could have 'brought down the country' and maybe, in the end, the prospect of more permanent damage to Britain is what led to loss of public support. And Government itself, when Reflecting on Practice, what could it do differently now that the realities have changed (options that were not available actions in 2000)? The Approach would indicate how to engage more effectively in the space-of-possibilities, which we discussed in Chapter 2, between community and institutions by forming partnerships with those who can exert the kind of influence that it cannot. Also, it does not have Internet-age complexity-worthiness – yet. However, politicians used social media to good effect in both the election of President Obama in the USA in 2009 and in the formation of the UK Coalition in 2010. The Framework certainly could be used by the Government to identify what needs to change in its structures and procedures to make the transformation to enable greater agility in practice.

This case study has examined a success in putting complexity to work. It was achieved when the UK Government employed a simple tactic to change *ad hoc* protests such that they became so burdened with the processes of collaborating in a structured way that the emergent dynamic collapsed. As we pointed out in Chapter 3, once this dynamic has dispersed and the energy has 'collapsed' to a lower-level state it takes special circumstances to restore it. Those special circumstances were beyond the requisite variety and complexity-worthiness of the 'Fuel Protest Lobby' – they had become, as people say 'history'. The capabilities they used, the general public, were no longer accessible to them and they had no power with which to coerce the public to change their minds and start protesting again. Despite subsequent attempts, the conditions were never appropriate in the same way.

UPGRADING SLUM HOUSING IN CAMEROON

In Cameroon, the NGO Intervolve, based in The Netherlands, together with a local organisation supports the redevelopment of the existing slum neighbourhood called Sopom on the banks of the river Mboppi in Douala as part of the Douala Neighbourhood Redevelopment Programme (DNRP). Slum upgrading programmes, in general, aim to improve the lives of the poorest urban dwellers, and hence to influence their daily activities and lives. Intervolve, for this programme, drew on experiences gained in another similar programme in Ethiopia where the aim had been *in situ* upgrading of dilapidated inner city housing areas with the intensive participation of the residents. Unfortunately, in that case, the national government regulations on housing and slum upgrading requested the construction of multi-storey condominium blocks that did not meet the economic (too expensive), social (not allowing traditional economic activities) and cultural (no space for group meetings) possibilities and demands of the residents. Under these circumstances, the slum upgrading programme did not come to pass in terms of actual housing improvement, but did come to pass in terms of economic and social strengthening – even though the residents are still living in the old slum housing. For the programme in Douala, these experiences were taken on board and contributed to both the formulation of components in the programme and the phases of implementation. The overall aims of the programme, which started in 2008 and is ongoing at the time of writing, are described on Intervolve's *DNRP fact sheet* as 'To improve living conditions in Sopom area through accessibility to credit, capacity building of the communities, improvement of housing conditions and access to basic social services'. Activities in which the NGO is involved in Sopom include the upgrading of the neighbourhood by offering the residents support in acquiring title deeds, as well as micro credits to improve their existing houses step-by-step and through shaping access to basic social services. In this case study, which was provided to us by Intervolve's project manager, Peter Gijs van Enk, we will look at the features of the specific context in Douala, the options that were identified for dealing with the tensions and engaging with the dynamics in the context, and finally, what the Approach could have contributed in this particular case.

A. **Patterns, Features and Characteristics of this Context.** The context in this case study is largely determined by the nature and state of the physical environment, the slum itself, in which certain dynamics and phenomena arise. The kind of changes that are possible in such an environment and the actual wiggle-room for carrying out a slum redevelopment programme, given the interests, intents and capabilities of the NGO, the residents of the slum and the authorities, will be synthesised after describing the realities in the context:

1. **One of the main characteristics in the contextual complexity** of the slum development case is the physical environment itself: unhealthy, cramped, living conditions, an unsafe environment, a lack of infrastructure, lack of access to basic services, lack of education facilities and of income generation possibilities. The limited infrastructure is vulnerable to seasonal weather impacts, such as heavy rainfall in the rainy season.

2. **The components, their properties and the interactions in the context are multiple.** First, there are the residents in the slums themselves, all affected by the poor conditions of their living environment to a greater or lesser extent. Apart from this unifying factor, the slum residents are a heterogeneous group, regarding issues such as: their status and responsibility within the community; the status of women; the participation of residents in income generation activities and the availability of means; their education, literacy and capabilities; their ethnic/tribal affiliations; the size of their family living with them; the ownership status of the land their dwelling is located on; the physical state of the dwelling itself; their health, and their interests, fears, expectations and motivations in changing the living conditions – to name some of them. A few of these can be appreciated easily, others are issues of experienced complexity, which need to be surfaced. Some of the inhabitants of the slum are organised in social or other interest groups, pursuing certain activities and interests within the slum area, others are not. The organised groups can be of a similar nature and can be rivals or in collaboration with others.

    Secondly, there is Intervolve itself, an NGO which works from its Headquarters in The Netherlands and also has permanent staff on the ground. The NGO has experience and draws on lessons learned from similar programmes in other African countries, which add to the exploration of the contextual complexity. It provides money for components of the slum upgrading programme and the facilitation capacity between slum residents, others involved, such as instructors, and the local authorities. Thirdly, there are the local authorities themselves, who have their say in the land titling issues and infrastructural aspects of slum redevelopment. Lastly, there is the Government who has made preparations to issue a social housing policy under which slum redevelopment falls.

3. **The intent and purposefulness of the beneficiaries** of the programme, the slum residents, are straightforward: a significantly better house with a plot of land, preferably at no or limited costs,

in the same location, where they feel at home, and the overall improvement of living conditions in the slum. In contrast, the Government expects a cost-effective and sustainable solution which is realised within the shortest possible time span and preferably at zero or limited costs – and this without providing clear guidance in their policy on housing or slum redevelopment. Intervolve's intent has been shaped and influenced by its previous experiences in the field in other countries. They want to support and implement a sustainable slum upgrading programme that brings about change by addressing the tensions that are a given for slum residents themselves and the possibilities arising from them.

B. **Dynamics and Tensions of Practice in this Context – Insights from the Approach.** Reflecting on Practice, some tensions became evident in the context and these influence the preparing for doing:

1. The value of safe and healthy living conditions for people in functioning communities is not promoted by a committed Government through a dedicated housing and slum redevelopment policy or funding. First, this raises the question of the size of wiggle-room that Intervolve has in working in a context where not having to conform to a policy creates more degrees of freedom on the one hand, but the potential for conflict on the other? Secondly, there is no/very limited funding support available on the part of the government, which might or might not be a factor in bringing about self-sustaining change. However, there has to be engagement with local authorities regarding the improvement of infrastructure in the slum and for the application and awarding of land titles for slum properties.

2. The residents of the slum area do not have a representation with a formal structure with whom they could engage in such issues with local authorities. No self-organisation to address the issues as a community or a representation thereof, with a sense of identity, seems to have taken place either. The driving factor for the do-nothing option for the people are financial issues – they do not see themselves capable of generating income for improving their living conditions, but expect support for free and without having to move from their current home, even though that might be necessary in the course of overall improvement of infrastructure and housing conditions.

3. Intervolve is faced with the constraints of taking ownership of and responsibility for the upgrading of houses by the residents themselves in the community, in order to bring about sustainable

change to a healthy and safe living environment with better quality housing in the slum. Such constraints are shaped by people's expectations towards slum upgrading, and their perception as a recipient rather than as somebody who can contribute actively to the improvement of conditions for their own good.

C. **What Actually Happened.** Learning from the experiences in Ethiopia described earlier, where residents' expectations on house construction were high from the start but, in the end, could not be met due to political, financial and cultural reasons, the slum upgrading programme in Cameroon was set up in a different way. In absence of a clearly defined housing and slum upgrading policy at the government level, the programme has been working with the following components:

1. Securing full community participation, formation of representative councils, technical capacity building and developing plans together with the community. This has been realised through involving the slum residents in exchanging ideas about housing improvements, educational activities and economic development on the one hand, and forming local, representative committees on the other.

2. Economic strengthening of the community and income-generation activities so that members of the community are enabled to contribute financially to upgrading their houses. This economic strengthening included income-generating activities such as skill development (in textile-dyeing or fish-drying) and training programmes on how to start small businesses, and in providing access to micro credits for entrepreneurs.

3. Community ownership of houses as this is now supported by robust land titles and incomes increased, the actual physical improvement of housing and the access to basic social services is addressed.

The implementation of these components was achieved by the residents of the slums themselves, and was done phase-wise, step by step, each within a reasonable time span and with achievable and affordable goals, but logically following each other. Implementation started with a phase in which a residents' committee was established, and micro credits were awarded to small entrepreneurs living in the slum. The phase also included negotiation by the NGO with governmental, local authorities and other partners on essential support that these could offer to the actual physical improvement of the living conditions in the neighbourhood. The second phase entailed the preparation of a local development plan through a participative approach and the training for building and infrastructure upgrading (individually and in small groups) and in the rights and obligations of land titles. The third phase will see the actual physical redevelopment on a larger scale.

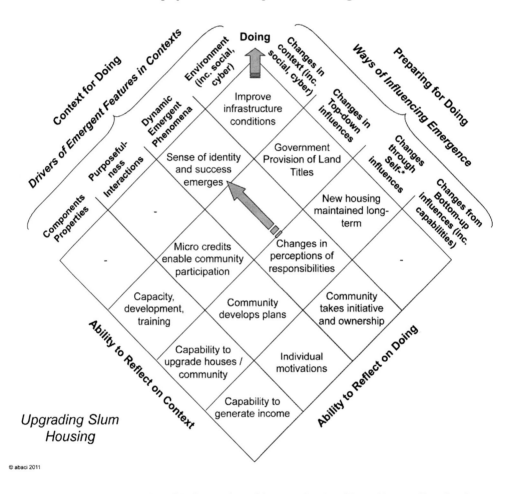

© abaci 2011

Figure 22 – Synthesis of Influencing Change in the Slum Upgrading in the Douala Neighbourhood Redevelopment Programme.

D. **Deductions and Lessons for Practice.** In this particular case, Intervolve carried out the Reflection on Realities including previous experiences and lessons learned in similar programmes for establishing the contextual context and the formulation of programme intent. The mismatch that emerged from these reflections, and which was crucial for the sustainability of the slum redevelopment, was in the perception and understanding of what makes people take ownership of and responsibility for their houses and what the reasoning by the residents meant for the success or failure of the programme. The Reflecting on Practice led to the formulation of a programme approach that embraced this issue. Its components envisaged that to bring about change, the slum residents would need to share responsibility in the financing of the projects; hence income-generating activities focused on the residents' capabilities in the local environment were initiated as a supportive measure. To enable residents to issue their wishes and expectations and to accept to what degree these could be included, and to be fully aware of their responsibilities, residents participated in the planning, decision-making and implementation of the programme from the beginning onwards.

The options that shape the 'doing' are synthesised in Figure 22. Implementing the components in phases, where one phase shapes the enabling conditions for the next phase, creates highly dynamic situations. For example, the participation of the residents or the negotiation with other stakeholders and authorities provides for ongoing changes in the context. Intervolve, in their programme planning, had allocated to each phase time-based boundaries whereas, in reality, the notion of start and end of phases respectively were often not as clear cut given the ongoing dynamics of engagement with the Community-of-Practice. The time-wise delineation of phases would also suggest that suitable indicators would be available to describe the success of each phase in these terms, which might not be possible if real-world changes invalidate initial assumptions.

In summary, such a complex interplay of ongoing and evolving tensions could not be dealt with by writing a fully-defined plan at that the start – adjustment and adaptation would always be inevitable along the way. The approach adopted by Intervolve, based on the lessons learned from the previous programme in Ethiopia, is a success story in the making. Our recommendation would be that the phase changes are not time-dependent but based on judging whether the appropriate conditions have been met, though this makes it harder to determine when the programme will become self-sustaining and hence when the NGO can complete its work. What can be concluded is that slum upgrading processes *should* be defined by local circumstances and movements, but that *in reality* the international donor is, in most cases, the organisation defining, through contract conditions and funding windows, how successful these type of processes can be. Unfortunately, very few donors are willing to support the integrated processes that Intervolve were trying to implement. The use of the Approach can address tensions such as these, between donor and implementor, through surfacing issues of joint interest in a defendable manner.

Social Housing in Ludlow, UK

This case study is about public opinion concerning the provision of social housing in small towns on the border between England and Wales in the UK as presented in our paper *'Complex Multi-modal Multi-level Influence Networks – Affordable Housing Case Study'*. In late 2001, communities were considering how their local plans needed to be changed to accommodate new planning guidance issued by the Department for Communities and Local Governments' *Planning Policy Guidance (PPG)* and *Planning Policy Statements (PPS)*. This activity involved individuals and a number of organisations and institutions who were each asked to submit their views. These views then had to be collated and, to some extent resolved, before submission to higher authorities. This case study focuses on one of the market towns in the area of the Welsh Borders, Ludlow, which has a population of around 11,000 people:

A. **Patterns, Features and Characteristics of this Context.** Ludlow has very diverse businesses ranging from traditional agriculture, light engineering and construction work through to so-called 'creative clusters' of artists, designers and cyber-technology startups (see the website *Facing the Challenges of the Creative Economy* by the Creative Clusters network for more information). Each of these have, for their viability, very different requirements in terms of infrastructure and facilities. Within the community, four main perspectives were considered to be important: geographical (i.e. agricultural factors), economic (i.e. low wages common), policy and government (i.e. the planning laws), and social and cultural (i.e. tourist and lifestyle). The local plans had to balance the following needs and factors: provision of social housing and town centre and retail developments; ensuring sustainable development in rural areas; carrying out transport planning; and conserving the historic environment. One of the organisations submitting their views on the plans in Ludlow was the local Civic Society, a voluntary, non-elected local decision-making body with over 500 members, whose focus was on the conservation of the historic fabric of their town and its sustainable future. This group became extremely divided and strongly polarised on the issue of the provision of social housing. Through community participation activities initiated by one of the authors, the then Chairman of the Civic Society, the group initially tried to identify a set of features and factors which were considered to be relevant.

B. **Key aspects of Practice – Dynamics and Tensions – Insights from the Approach**. An early version of a complexity-inspired approach using an 'influence diagram' was applied – see Figure 23. The diagrams produced enabled people to plot out the actors as 'nodes' and to indicate, by drawing lines between them, where they thought the influences were and to annotate their type (e.g. informal, contractual, friendships and so on). Though this analysis seemed helpful at first, it became apparent that it did not assist the Society in understanding how change in one factor affected another – indeed, everything seemed to effect everything else in a manner that led to impasse. This led to the insight that a number of complementary, yet distinct, perspectives had been mixed up together in the influence diagram and so the nodes were annotated accordingly to show to which of the perspectives were mostly relevant.

Next, the links/influences were examined from several representative viewpoints (such as single parent, pensioner, local policymakers, etc.) and were annotated with their significance as seen from each of these viewpoints. Even though these viewpoints were generalisations, useful trends and indicators became apparent. This technique, which is now part of our Approach, was partly adapted from Peter Bennett, Jim Bryant and Nigel Howard's paper '*Drama Theory and Confrontation Analysis*' and led to the Society working in new ways with individuals and organisations concerned to identify the blockers and enablers of change in relation to the needs for social housing. This activity included analysis and comparison of viewpoints in terms of 'what do I think' and 'what do I think they think' within and across perspectives to expose contradictions, alternatives, 'invisibles' etc.

The added value that the complexity-inspired approach provided was that, by examining a rich variety of levels and modalities, novel influences, effects and linkages were identified which would otherwise have gone unnoticed. Even in a basic form, this analysis proved to be a powerful technique for triggering insight, debate and action leading to successful outcomes.

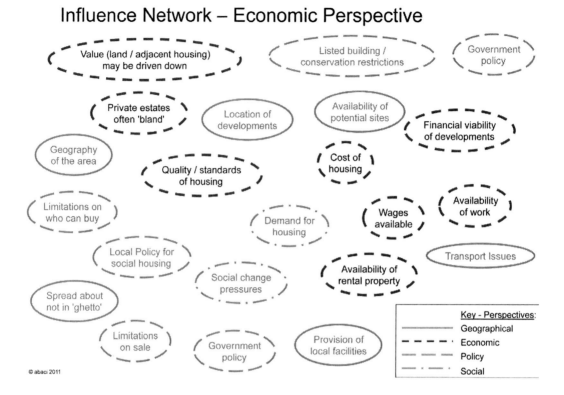

Figure 23 – Civic Society – Initial Influence Network Highlighting the Economic Perspective.

C. **What Actually Happened.** While the analysis of perspectives and engagement with other stakeholders was going on, a number of diagrams were produced for each of the four main perspectives considered important: geographical, economic, policy and government and social and cultural. Different modes of influence were highlighted both within each perspective and cross-perspectives on a selective basis. This clarification enabled different factors to be better understood in terms of the nature of their 'connectedness' and of the effects they generated. The result of this analysis was that the Society was able to develop a rich and defendable set of principles which they employed in their submission – a small selection of which follows:

- accept that this housing will be small, low cost and may be less profitable and that this may require pressure to encourage 'social responsibility' from developers, banks etc. and understand that housing associations often can't buy land as it is too expensive;

- understand the social mix that such housing will generate and encourage the design of affordable housing which is pleasing and not uniform;

- ensure that such housing is 'dotted about' and not in a 'ghetto', as social pressure from within 'ghettos' will increase social cost;

- try to provide housing where people work, to counteract environmental impacts and, in relation to policy, they noted that:

  - there are problems with the formula used for calculating district council funding;

  - local plans are often out of date – leading to ill-informed decisions;

  - they should lobby for the Government to encourage the use of the existing housing stock – reversing the migration away from/collapsing prices in certain areas;

  - the council tax banding/housing stock evaluation is very out of date and so they would challenge the figures about the demand for housing;

  - they should have a developed view on longer-term and wider implications – even if this means supporting apparent inconsistencies in short-term decisions, such as: restrictions on incomers, letting villages die.

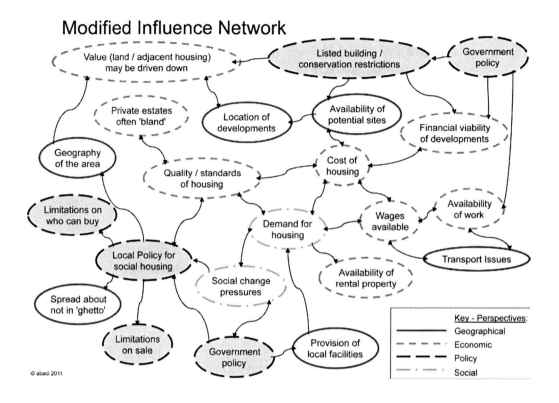

Figure 24 – Social Housing Factors by Perspectives – High-level Influence Network

The final high-level influence network diagram is shown in Figure 24 – note that, for clarity, the arrows are not annotated with their significance in terms of the nature, scale and timeline of influence. Also note that suggestions to turn the diagram into a system dynamic were actively rejected on the basis that the necessary social data could not be collected in a form that could reliably be represented in any model.

D. **Deductions and Lessons for Practice.** The Civic Society found that the use of techniques such as the influence network diagram had been very valuable in many ways – including helping to build bridges between parts of the community which had previously been in opposition. However, had the Landscape of Practice been employed in the Ludlow case, the options for influence potentially available could have been assessed – along with the degree to which they might have been able to be exploited in practice. To illustrate this, Figure 25 has been populated from the deductions below:

1. **Components and Properties**. Firstly, if the bottom-up components of the community are considered – e.g. the people – this involves looking at demographics, skill sets and even the temperaments and personalities of some of the key individuals. Potentially a very sensitive area, the Society dealt with it in an open manner by approaching some of the people concerned to seek their engagement. This in itself had a beneficial effect in fostering trust and openness (though this obviously may not work in all cases).

   Next the 'Configuration of the Community' was considered, its social mix, factions, groupings and institutions. This analysis mapped out the various groupings and their overlaps and exclusions and tried to see if there were any social groups who were being overlooked or which were having undue influence. Lastly, leadership roles within the community were examined to try and identify issues such as: nodes who were influential but who did not hold formal positions in the community or others who held positions but who did not really represent anyone. It turned out that some roles overlapped in the same person (e.g. the Mayor was very influential among those applying for social housing because she came from humble origins), and that some roles were quite isolated. This led alternative ways that the community could be linked up to enable new, beneficial, interactions.

2. **Interactions, Purpose and Intent**. Considering these issues enabled the Society to consider its own intent and that of all the other actors involved. As richer sets of viewpoints (related to these various actors) became apparent, there was a risk of the insights becoming unmanageable. This risk was mitigated by maintaining a clear focus on one viewpoint at a time. Mapping between viewpoints occurred subsequently – with viewpoints only being re-examined when it became apparent that key influences had been overlooked. This was one of the most useful activities and enabled the Society to identify their relationship to others in the community, such as: those with whom they could collaborate, those with whom they might form allegiances, those who seemed to be in opposition (but who should be approached). It also enabled the Society to consider issues such as relative degrees of power and influence and to identify vulnerable groups who would need support. Subsequently, it turned out that some of their earlier perceptions were wrong and this led them to make changes to the way they engaged, which allowed for more constructive progress than had been expected.

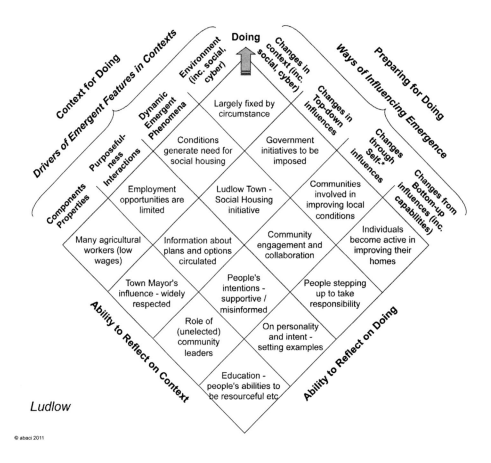

Ludlow

© abaci 2011

Figure 25 – Proposed Interventions for Ludlow Plotted on the Landscape of Practice.

3. **Dynamic Change.** The Society approached dynamic change by trying to identify the triggers of change and time-critical issues rather than trying to chase down every consequence (an impossible task in any case). They first looked at situations where influence could be applied from the top-down and then considered their position in relation to a number of options and identified which ones they would support/oppose. Next they considered influence through self-regulation and looked at the balancing, creative and negative mechanisms at work in the town and decided how they wished to engage with them and to what effect. Influence from the bottom-up was considered both in terms of what members could do individually and through social

networks in the community (which included through public opinion, i.e. influence those in the town who appeared to be just onlookers).

Next they considered the environment and discovered that a landowner near the town was considering building many inappropriate houses. The potential physical impact of this change was used to influence opinion. Lastly, the Society discussed their options in terms of how they might collaborate, compete, coerce or disrupt and used this to work out which indicators of change would be significant to them and how they could monitor the indicators over what, for some issues, could be many years.

It became evident that the social housing requirements were features which arose from the agricultural nature of employment in the area and the low wages associated with this work. In other words, some social housing was required because people were disadvantaged and some was required simply because of the economy of the area – things which could possibly be changed. This led the Society to develop the set of principles listed above on which they based their recommendations. As a side effect of the discussions, Ludlow became one of the first English towns to become a Slow Town and a thriving local Slow Food[87] group was established. In effect, what Ludlow had begun to do was to identify opportunities and possibilities afforded by the local circumstances, now a key component of the so-called Transition Model for Transition Towns. As a matter of fact, Rob Hopkins (founder of the Transition Network) in his book *The Transition Handbook: From oil dependency to local resilience,* picks up on many aspects similar to our Approach in the context of the sort of sustainable living in towns and cities that Ludlow is trying to achieve.

---

87   For more information on the Slow Food movement in the UK see: http://www.slowfood.org.uk/Cms/Page/home

Journalism in Lebanon

The next case study is based on material provided to us by Robert Holloway, the Director of the *Agence France-Presse (AFP) Foundation,* who spoke at our ECCS Workshop in 2009. Robert is a journalist with international standing who has reported from crisis situations all over the world. He spent five years in Lebanon and Egypt as correspondent for *The Times* and the *Irish Times* before joining the global news agency AFP in 1988. He has served as their chief correspondent in the South Pacific, as foreign editor, head of English language operations, United Nations correspondent in New York, and as AFP's editor in chief. Robert was asked by the UNDP to run a course on peace journalism in Lebanon and this case study examines how group solidarity was developed and effective progress achieved under such challenging circumstances.

A. **Characteristics of the Context: Patterns, Features and Tensions.**
   The best way to set the scene and the characteristics of the context is to let Robert tell the story in his own words. He clearly articulates the patterns, features and tensions of practice that he faced:

> 'I would like to recount to you the project that I am most proud of, which I think illustrates the theme of this [ECCS] workshop. We [AFP] were asked by the UNDP to run a course on peace journalism in Lebanon [...] It is an extremely complicated society. There are 17 officially recognised religious communities in Lebanon. The political structure, the State itself, is extremely weak. There are half a dozen families each of which is more powerful than the State. The only state institution which survived the Civil War [in the Lebanon] was the Central Bank – which says a great deal about Lebanese society. The way the state is structured is very, very complex indeed, with these different communities represented at different levels. The Civil War lasted for about ten years from the mid 70s to the mid 80s. There was then a reversion to a kind of stable society. The Civil War resumed at a much lower level of intensity about three years ago. Society now is [...] precariously calm.
>
> The UN asked us to go in and do a peace journalism training course. I said I'd do it but not under that title, which I thought would be misunderstood. I said I would call it "Objectivity in covering conflict". We got together 24 journalists, ten from the television sector, ten from the written press and four from the radio. We had three trainers, all Arabic speaking. I went along as a facilitator/coordinator. [...]

The UN said to me "You design the program, but what we want on the first day is – this being the UN – a high level, prominent speaker. At the closing ceremony we want a panel of big media owners in Lebanon and an international star journalist, that you will find, who will speak to the final session". And that's how we did it.

At the start of the course I made an introductory speech to these 24 journalists who were sitting on the table and they were [in the way they were sitting in the room] divided pretty much as the country is divided. The Shia Muslims sat here, the Sunni Muslims sat there and the Christians over there. After my introductory speech we then had a plenary session and we talked about objectivity. There was a lot of finger-pointing "We don't need to talk about objectivity, we know what it is, we're objective – he is not objective", and "We know what we are doing – its those people over there...", and the debate became extremely tense. At some point one of the UN people said to me "We've got to stop it". So I intervened and said "I expected a good interchange of views. This is quite passionate. This is good. Let's go and have lunch.".

We then did a couple of days of practical work. On the third day, we divided them into groups and took them out to do fieldwork in Beirut and its suburbs. I took a group of four people, three women and a man. One of the women was a television reporter for the Hezbollah Television. [...] The second was a Maronite Christian who worked for Lebanese Broadcasting Corporation. The third worked for a communist radio station. The man worked for one of Lebanon's most prominent mainstream newspapers, An-Nahar.

We went to two districts of Beirut. First of all we went to a district which was run by the Hezbollah, who were extremely uncooperative and told us "We weren't expecting you, we were expecting engineers. No, you can't film!" But we managed to get away from them and we went to a different part of that neighbourhood and we did film and we interviewed people on the street. And while we were doing that the woman from the Hezbollah Television said to me "I'm really very nervous about going to this other district", which was just literally across the boulevard, "because the people there are extremely aggressive and unpleasant". This district was run by the supporters of the assassinated Prime Minister Hariri. I said "We are all together, we're part of a team, we are protected by the UN, this is the whole point, that we do this together, so you're coming". We crossed the boulevard, she then did the interviews with people on the street and indeed, they were aggressive to her and said "What are you doing here" and so on. [When they were] asked "What do you think about the elections, would you be prepared to go across ... across the road over there?" [the people said things such as] "No, no – they eat babies over there, I am not crossing that road". This was the kind of talk we got.

But in the end, she [the woman from Hezbollah Television] and the Christian woman agreed to do a joint broadcast. They scripted it together, they edited it together and they then gave it to their television stations, which both broadcasted the same report.

I got a letter from the UN congratulating [us]. I really felt ten feet tall. [i.e. very good!]

On the last day – by this time a sense of solidarity had begun to develop amongst these journalists who on the first day had been... [extremely tense with each other]. On the last day we had the closing conference with the 'big bosses'. Only three of them deigned to turn up and turned a panel discussions into set speechmaking. The international star journalist whom I found from France and who came just sat there and said "Me, Me, Me". [...]

The unintended consequence of this was that it created a tremendous sense of group solidarity [among the course members]. There was a real fight between the journalists and the bosses. It turned into a slanging match "Why aren't we paid enough? Why aren't we given enough press freedom? Why are our editors always on our backs?"

And I recommended to the UN – if we ever do this again, we dispense with bigwigs. We just have a group like this and we work together. And we forget about the bosses. The UN were delighted. They asked me to come back in July this year [2009] and I did – and we did the same thing.

In the meantime, this group of journalists met five times. They went on picnics, they ran their own workshops. One of them was very severely beaten up by a bunch of Syrian Fascists [...] and they all went to see him in hospital.

We went back in July and we held the workshop again, but this time really focusing on the issue of what we call cross-community reporting, where you get people from different communities, sometimes hostile communities [...] you get them to work together on the issues which reveal the things they have in common rather than the things that divide them.'

B. **Deductions and Lessons for Practice – Insights from the Approach.**
This context was entirely in the space of doing, of practice. Preparing office-based plans, schedules or work-packages would have been inappropriate. What was evident, and what the Approach reinforces, is that this context was about bringing together a number of dynamic flows and then working with the resulting turbulence/opportunities as they became apparent. In this, the complexity-worthiness of all concerned, their ability to build trust, adapt, self-organise and go with the changing realities and givens, was to be crucial. Robert's role was partly to help facilitate that cohesion and partly to reflect back to the group of journalists their identity and achievements. In that sense he worked with the tensions and mismatches as they came along, turning them to advantage using his authority (respect from the group i.e. referent power) and experience (expert power).

An insight from the Approach is that a key intangible here was trust-building – which, once established, led to the group self-organising and gaining a strong identity. The role of the institutional bosses and 'bigwigs' is interesting. At one level they were easy to deal with – their behaviours were predictable and well understood. Yet, at the closing session when they tried to exert their positional power, they (unintentionally) triggered a transition in the journalists who became a strong entity of their own. They were then able to completely overwhelm the 'bosses' with their confidence, passion and determination. Whether the journalists appreciated it or not they drew their power from their solidarity, expertise, sense of 'rightness' and their connection with the flow of implicit support they received from the people on the streets – which they could tap into in a way that the 'bosses' could not. It is an interesting exercise to populate and compare a number of versions of the 'Landscape of Change' from the points of view of the various different actors to see what other options might have been available or outcomes arisen.

Deep Water Horizon (DWH) Oil Rig – Crisis Transition

This case study examines an example of the sorts of transition that were described in Chapter 5. It concerns the case of the Deep Water Horizon oil rig that exploded in the Gulf of Mexico in 2010 while it was drilling the Macondo well. According to the *Final Report* by the National Commission on the BP Deepwater Horizon Oil Spill and Offshore Drilling:

> 'Macondo was not the first well to earn that nickname ["the well from hell"]; like many deepwater wells, it had proved complicated and challenging. As they drilled, the engineers had to modify plans in response to their increasing knowledge of the precise features of the geologic formations thousands of feet below. Deepwater drilling is an unavoidably tough, demanding job, requiring tremendous engineering expertise.' (p2).

We understand, first-hand, from oil industry experts who work on rigs that each 12-hour shift period, therefore, starts with a review of proposed activities (with the tasks ahead for a work team and a 'tool-box talk'). This includes a consideration of potential challenges and an examination of contingency measures that would be applied, depending on outcomes. These reviews draw on the high-levels of (hard-won) expertise of the oil workers who are used to dealing with difficult conditions, breakdowns and high-risk decisions 'routinely' day-to-day. The stakes are high: rigs can cost a million dollars a day to hire, time is always a pressure, conditions are challenging and the consequences of failure potentially catastrophic. Given this background one would think that the oil industry has contingency plans in place for everything that could possibly happen – if so, what were the particular features of the DWH incident that led to it getting out of control? In this case study our specific interest is the nature of the transition that occurred and to point out some of the kinds of insights that can be revealed by using our Approach – such as the types of tensions and mismatches that the oil-well blow-out triggered. We base our analysis of the context principally on the Commission's Report and related material. Let's start by looking at practice in this context:

A. **Patterns, Features and Characteristics of this Context.** The oil industry is used to dynamic transitions, they occur every day – such as down-hole tool failures and surface equipment down-time (cables break, pipes burst, machinery goes wrong, power fails) – these things 'just happen'. As they are inevitable, and in a way are expected, their effects can, largely, be mitigated. These events may be sudden but it is still possible to make sense of them and act accordingly – in the sense that the workers are not at a loss as to what to do because the changes are mostly the kind of smooth transitions discussed in Chapter 5. Equipment failures may seem extreme to, say, an office administrator visiting the rig, but they are commonplace to the oil workers. The workers are backed up with manuals and guides covering the operation of the rig, polices and rules concerning safety and environmental protection, and there are instructions that document best practice in check-lists provided by the companies involved.

Normally then, relationships between workers and systems were defined by these procedures and structures through an established chain-of-command. As a result, many of the interactions between people were, as the transcripts below will show, shaped by the terms used that related to the processes to be carried out. These formalised and structured operator-driven ways-of-working, imposed largely top-down through the operations management Zone (d) shown on Figure 26, were essential for the reliable, safe and repeatable control of the rig actions shown at Zone (a). These were, through training, matched by the team competencies of the workers shown at Zone (b). Other behaviours, at Zones (c) and (e) were minimised as they were not appropriate to normal operation.

So what happened on DWH such that these contingencies proved to be inadequate? It is obvious that, rather than the smooth transitions they were used to, the blow-out triggered a whole series of shock transitions where previously-held assumptions became 'invalid' in the face of the ever-new, dynamically-changing contexts. Let's look at some extracts[88] from the transcripts of the 'accident' to try to appreciate something more about the nature of the events that took place:

- 'As the Board that investigated the loss of the Columbia space shuttle noted, "complex systems almost always fail in complex ways". Though it is tempting to single out one crucial misstep or point the finger at one bad actor as the cause of the Deepwater Horizon explosion, any such explanation provides a dangerously incomplete picture of what happened—encouraging the very kind of complacency that led to the accident in the first place. Consistent with the President's [Obama] request, this [the DWH] report takes an expansive view.' (pviii)

---

88 We have made great efforts to select and use items from the [US] National Commission's *Final Report* in a balanced way to avoid, unintentionally, distorting the facts. We have also drawn material from the National Commission's *Chief Counsel's Report*.

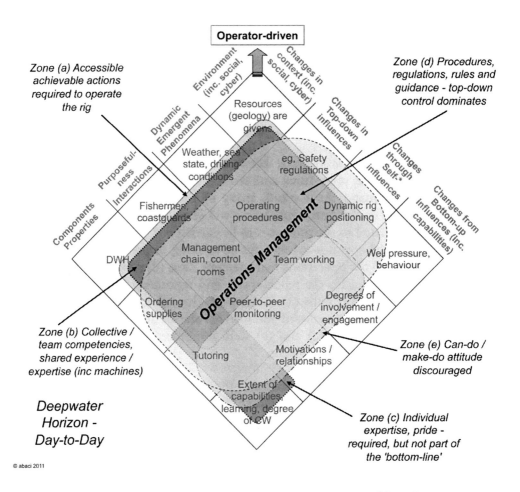

Operator-driven

Zone (a) Accessible achievable actions required to operate the rig

Zone (d) Procedures, regulations, rules and guidance - top-down control dominates

Environment (inc. social, cyber)

Changes in context (inc. social, cyber)

Dynamic Emergent Phenomena

Changes in Top-down influences

Resources (geology) are givens

Changes through Self.*

Purposeful-ness Interactions

eg. Safety regulations

Weather, sea state, drilling conditions

Changes from Bottom-up Influences (inc. capabilities)

Components Properties

Fishermen coastguards

Operating procedures

Dynamic rig positioning

Management chain, control rooms

Team working

Well pressure, behaviour

DWH

Operations Management

Ordering supplies

Peer-to-peer monitoring

Degrees of involvement / engagement

Zone (b) Collective / team competencies, shared experience / expertise (inc machines)

Tutoring

Motivations / relationships

Zone (e) Can-do / make-do attitude discouraged

Deepwater Horizon - Day-to-Day

Extent of capabilities, learning, degree of CW

Zone (c) Individual expertise, pride - required, but not part of the 'bottom-line'

© abaci 2011

Figure 26 – DWH – Extent of Control and degrees of freedom – Normal Operations.

- 'The rest of the day [of the accident] would be devoted to a series of further tests on the well—positive and negative-pressure tests—in preparation for [the planned] "temporary abandonment." [of the well while others were drilled] During the positive-pressure test, the drill crew would increase the pressure inside the steel casing and seal assembly to be sure they were intact. The negative-pressure test, by contrast, would reduce the pressure inside the well in order to simulate its state after the Deepwater Horizon had packed up and moved off location. If pressure increased inside the well during the negative-pressure test, or if fluids flowed up from the well, that would indicate a well-integrity problem—a leak of fluids into the well. Such a leak would be a worrisome sign that somewhere the casing and cement plugs had been breached—in which case remedial work would be needed to re-establish the well's integrity.' (p4)

- 'Don Vidrine, the company man coming on the evening shift, eventually said that another negative test had to be done [because the results from the previous one were ambiguous]. This time the crew members were able to get the pressure down to zero on a different pipe, the [so-called] "kill line", but still not for the drill pipe, which continued to show elevated pressure. According to BP witnesses, Anderson [a 'tool pusher'] said he had seen this before and explained away the anomalous [pressure] reading as the "bladder effect". Whether for this reason or another, the men in the [drillers' control] shack determined that no flow from the open kill line equaled a successful negative-pressure test. It was time to get on with the rest of the temporary abandonment process. Kaluza [BP's day-shift company man], his shift over, headed off duty.' (p6)

- [at the same time] 'Inside the bridge, Captain Kuchta [who had served on the Deepwater Horizon since June 2008, was in command when the vessel (rig) was "unlatched" and thus once again a maritime vessel] welcomed visitors Sims, O'Bryan, Trahan, and Winslow [executive vice-president VIPs, two each from BP and Transocean respectively]. The two dynamic-positioning officers, Yancy Keplinger and Andrea Fleytas, were also on the bridge. Keplinger was giving the visitors a tour of the bridge while Fleytas was at the desk station. The officers explained how the rig's thrusters kept the Deepwater Horizon in place above the well, showed off the radars and current meters, and offered to let the visiting BP men try their hands at the rig's dynamic-positioning video simulator.' [the presence of the VIPs was not part of the rig's normal routine]. (p7)

- 'Down in the engine control room, Chief Mechanic Douglas Brown, an Army veteran employed by Transocean [owners of DWH], was filling out the nightly log and equipment hours. He had spent the day fixing a saltwater pipe in one of the pontoons. First, he noticed an "extremely loud air leak sound". Then a gas alarm sounded, followed by more and more alarms wailing. In the midst of that noise, Brown noticed someone over the radio. "I heard the captain or chief mate, I'm not sure who, make an announcement to the standby boat, the Bankston, saying we were in a well-control situation." The vessel was ordered to back off to 500 meters. Now Brown could hear the rig's engines revving. "I heard them revving up higher and higher and higher. Next I was expecting the engine trips to take over. That did not happen. After that the power went out." Seconds later, an explosion ripped through the pitch-black control room, hurtling him against the control panel, blasting away the floor. Brown fell through into a subfloor full of cable trays and wires. A second huge explosion roared through, collapsing the ceiling on him. All around in the dark he could hear people screaming and crying for help.' (p9)

- 'He [Steve Bertone, the rig's chief engineer] went to the portside back computer, the dynamic positioning system responsible for maintaining the rig's position. "I observed that we had no engines, no thrusters, no power whatsoever. I picked up the phone which was right there and I tried calling extension 2268, which is the engine control room. There was no dial tone whatsoever." It was then that Bertone looked out to the bridge's starboard window. "I was fully expecting to see steel and pipe and everything on the rig floor." "When I looked out the window, I saw fire from derrick leg to derrick leg and as high as I could see. At that point, I realized that we had just had a blowout". ' (p10)

- 'Inside the standby generator room, Bertone flipped the switch from automatic to manual, hitting the reset and the start button. "There was absolutely no turning over of the engine. I tried it again, the reset button and the start. Again, nothing happened." He reset other functions, and turned the switch for the automatic sync on the standby generator to manual. "I ran back to the panel and again, tried the reset and the start. There was no turning over of the engine whatsoever." '(p15)

- 'By now, Winslow [a one-time assistant driller who had worked his way up to operations manager.] began to wonder why the derrick was still roaring with flames. Hadn't the blowout preventer been activated, sealing off the well and thus cutting off fuel for the conflagration? He headed to the bridge. [Captain] Kuchta said, "We've got no power, we've got no water, no emergency generator." Steve Bertone was still at his station on the bridge and he noticed Christopher Pleasant, one of the subsea engineers, standing next to the panel with the emergency disconnect switch (EDS) to the blowout preventer. Bertone hollered to Pleasant: "Have you EDSed?" Pleasant replied he needed permission. Bertone asked Winslow was it okay and Winslow said yes. Somebody on the bridge yelled, "He cannot EDS without the OIM's [offshore installation manager's] approval." Harrell [the top Transocean man on the rig when—as now—the well was latched up], still dazed, somewhat blinded and deafened, had also made it to the bridge, as had BP's Vidrine. With the rig still "latched" to the Macondo well, Harrell was in charge. Bertone yelled, "Can we EDS?" and Harrell yelled back, "Yes, EDS, EDS.". (p13)

- 'Chief Mate David Young and Bertone "hooked the life raft up and proceeded to crank it up out of its lift, rotated [it] around to the side of the rig and then drop[ped] it—drop[ped] it out so that you could inflate the raft and you could be clear of the rig." A rope attached to a balky shackling device refused to give. Bertone yelled for a knife to cut the rope. Nobody had one. No pocket knives were allowed on the rig. Williams found a gigantic nail-clipper-like device and used it to unscrew the stuck shackle, freeing the rope. The life raft moved out over the side of the rig. Young got in. Behind them, explosions punctuated the heat, noise, and dark. Thick, acrid smoke was rolling over the deck.' (p16) [The rig finally sunk 18 hours later].

These extracts from the Report and the transcripts they contain paint a picture[89] of the kind of pattern breaking that was happening which usually, though not inevitably, leads to collapse.

B. **Key aspects of Practice – Dynamics and Tensions – Insights from the Approach.** As well as the horror of the events, one gets a sense of fewer and fewer options being available to the workers, along with a degradation of influence – from being able to manoeuvre and control the whole rig as a unit reduced to just parts of it, then to only single machines and finally to where the lack of a single knife was a life-threatening issue. This reduction in this envelope of influence is one of the things that fundamentally changed people's degrees of freedom. What were the other factors? Here, based on the ways of influencing change, is a selection:

1. **Changes in the Setting**. One of the most obvious environmental changes in the context was the escape of high-pressure flammable gas from the well when the negative pressure test failed. This changed the setting from an operator-driven one in which the workers on the rig were in control, to one where the real-world imperatives were 'calling the shots' – the workers were now context-driven. Normal ways-of-working were no longer appropriate – the actions demanded by the context were mostly not achievable (shown by the extended Zone (a) on the Landscape of Change at Figure 27) and people and procedures needed to make the transition quickly to meet these new demands. Yet the new purpose and intent required (to align with the demands) were neither fully appreciated nor shared widely – leading to surprise and confusion. This meant that timescales for actions were

---

89   For an overall summary see also the *New York Times* article of the 25th December 2010 'Deepwater Horizon's Final Hours' by David Barstow, David Rohde and Stephanie Saul.

severely reduced and time-horizons had to be judged in seconds or minutes. People now experienced unfamiliar phenomena and novel dynamics. Post the blow-out transition, the context now changed again because of the explosions. Automatic systems were destroyed (or lacked power) and so could no longer assist people's capabilities – the rig was no longer functioning as a 'human-machine team'. The workers were now called upon to operate the rig systems in manual mode.

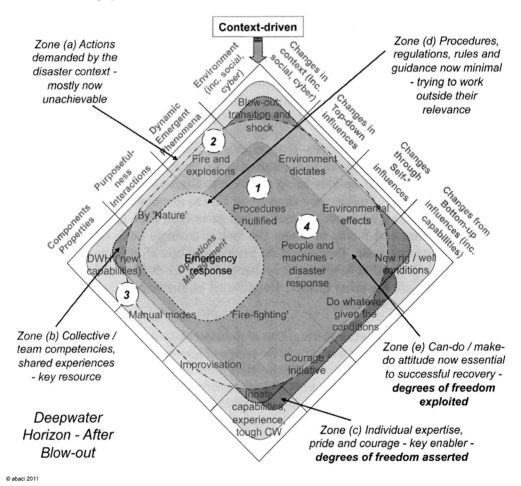

Figure 27 – DWH – Degrees of Freedom and Wiggle-room – Afterwards.

2. **Changes in Top-down Influences.** With hindsight, it may be that, actually, the procedural entanglement that had been created to regulate normal working was a contributory factor in the disaster getting out of hand. When the environment started

214

imposing damage, in a way 'top-down', these procedures were no longer 'available actions' for the control-room staff as the position of the number (1) in Figure 27 shows – so people needed to be allowed to improvise as the context required.

3. **Changes in Self-organisation etc.** In normal, everyday working there was little need for the workers to self-organise, see Zone (e) – their routine was very much set by schedules, shifts and strong organisational patterns. They knew where they would be working, whom they would be working with and, largely, what they would be doing. Most self-regulation happened automatically as the systems of the rig monitored and adjusted parameters semi-autonomously. They were prepared for certain types of challenging transitions that they would be dealt with through good training and sound 'standard[90] operational procedures' (SoPs). But, the fire on DWH was too serious – even without the explosion the operation room would still have had no option but to relinquish control because it could no longer communicate with the parts of the rig concerned or appreciate what was going on. Indeed, if they tried to intervene the mismatch between their experienced complexity in the control room and the reality could lead to them taking inappropriate actions, as shown by the number (2) in the Figure.

As the day-to-day cohesive coupling between the parts of the rig was lost, recovery relied on the actions of distributed fire units who apply 'behavioural templates' (fire drills) to regain enough local predictability to then enable global interventions to be re-exercised by the operations managers. The complexity-worthiness of the fire teams depends very much on the quality and realism[91] of this training, the authority and autonomy delegated to them and their personal qualities (initiative, courage etc.) and common sense. After the accident, everything changed – the rig became a totally different machine. Now it was essential that people self-organised to try and recover control. Yet, because of the damage, the workers could not even come together as previously

---

90   The use of the word 'standard', rather than 'standardised' is very deliberate. Enabling (interoperability) standards allow for wiggle-room as opposed to homogenous standardisation that is clamping and constraining.

91   If this training always stops short of dealing with realistic events then that's 'negative training' which holds people back. An example of this tension occurred on an airline flight across the Atlantic Ocean. The pilot and co-pilot were practicing 'loss of oxygen' drills. The drill is usually stopped at the point where a button is pressed to release oxygen masks in the passenger cabin. By 'mistake', the co-pilot *did* press the button and the masks dropped down – to the alarm of the passengers. Did the co-pilot do the 'right' thing (by completing the drill realistically) or was that 'wrong'?

exercised to form the usual fire and rescue teams – they had to work with whomever and whatever they could find, and develop what seemed to be the best purpose/intent at that time. And, with the autonomous systems disabled or malfunctioning, much of the functionality that they had previously taken for granted (concerning the stability of the rig) was no longer happening – see example number (3) on Figure 27, which indicates that the Zone (a) actions required to deal with the blow-out cannot be met by the Zone (b) collective competencies. As a result, because of the explosion and the almost complete dislocation it caused, they did not get the chance to save themselves and the rig.

4. **Changes in Bottom-up Influences.** People were, therefore, having to, literally, transition 'under fire' and were forced by the circumstances of the situation to flip from one type of complexity-worthiness to another as required. It seems from the Report that some people had neither thought about this, nor had they been trained for it (they also may not have had, or been recruited to have, the innate abilities of resourcefulness, flexibility etc.). Clearly, from the transcripts, recovering the DWH from its initial blow-out relied heavily on the personal qualities of the people – and this need was always a known factor that seems to have been discounted in the procedures and the training. As Fred Bartlit, Chief Counsel for the Commission said, Transocean's handbook was 'a safety expert's dream' and yet after reading it cover to cover he struggled to answer a basic question: 'How do you know [when] it's bad enough to act fast?'. It was never a handbook that was going to save the DWH, it was the people – working by influencing events bottom-up – trouble-shooting, number (4), and by improvising (the intersection of Zones (b), (c), (e) on Figure 27). The self-organising that had to occur relied on people having appropriate qualities.

So, what was the interplay between all the factors discussed above? When one looks at these two versions of the Landscape of Change showing the situation before (Figure 26) and after (Figure 27) the blow-out, what stands out very clearly is how fundamentally the usual 'control regime' had been disempowered and, very graphically, how key managers were now trapped into a position of paralysis as a result. But what did the Commission conclude about the way the change of context and setting had undermined normal practice and what did they recommend concerning contingencies for this type of accident in future?

C. What Happened Afterwards– Inquiry and National Commission. 'Nearly 400 feet long, the Horizon had formidable and redundant defences against even the worst blowout. It was equipped to divert surging oil and gas safely away from the rig. It had devices to quickly seal off a well blowout or to break free from it. It had systems to prevent gas from exploding and sophisticated alarms that would quickly warn the crew at the slightest trace of gas. The crew itself routinely practiced responding to alarms, fires and blowouts, and it was blessed with experienced leaders who clearly cared about safety. On paper, experts and investigators agree, the Deepwater Horizon should have weathered this blowout.' reported the *New York Times* on 25th December 2010 in the article previously mentioned. It goes on to say: 'What emerges is a stark and singular fact: crew members died and suffered terrible injuries because every one of the Horizon's defenses failed on April 20. Some were deployed but did not work. Some were activated too late, after they had almost certainly been damaged by fire or explosions. Some were never deployed at all'. Concerning these defences the news item states that 'Ms. Fleytas said it never occurred to her to use the emergency shutdown system. In any event, she explained, she had not been taught how to use it. "I don't know of any procedures," she said. [One emergency system alone was controlled by 30 buttons]. At critical moments that night, members of the crew hesitated and did not take the decisive steps needed. Communications fell apart, warning signs were missed and crew members in critical areas failed to coordinate a response.'

The result, as the interviews and records show, was paralysis. For nine long minutes, as the drilling crew battled the blowout and gas alarms eventually sounded on the bridge, no warning was given to the rest of the crew. For many, the first hint of crisis came in the form of a 'blast wave'. We have already mentioned that the paralysis which occurred was partly caused by not having trained for the possibility of a worst-case context, and partly caused by the policies, rules, SoPs and regulations the workers had to follow - and the resulting intersection and contradictions are illustrated in Figure 27. Given this analysis it is interesting to review the Commission's recommendations listed below. They are grouped in seven distinct areas:

- Improving the Safety of Offshore Operations

- Safeguarding the Environment

- Strengthening Oil Spill Response, Planning, and Capacity

- Advancing Well-Containment Capabilities

- Overcoming the Impacts of the Deepwater Horizon Spill and Restoring the Gulf

- Ensuring Financial Responsibility

- Promoting Congressional Engagement to Ensure Responsible Offshore Drilling

Almost without exception, the recommendations concern top-down policy and regulative frameworks – of which there already seem to be too many. Even the Safety section on page 231 of the Report focuses on safety procedures during normal operations rather than worst case transition events.

D. **Deductions and Lessons for Practice.** In its day-to-day operation the behaviour of the DWH rig was largely predictable and 'relaxed' – it seems at first sight that the companies involved felt that, by writing instructions to cover every contingency, they had the realities mastered. Yet, in an accident of this magnitude, because they are not written to cover the impossible, instructions are not what is required – instead, it is the human qualities of resourcefulness and, along with it, the degrees of freedom to act without unnecessary constraints in the way that the context determines. This kind of transition requires those with procedural 'positional power' to defer to those with expert power. It is interesting to speculate to what degree the presence of the four vice-presidents, on the DWH at this critical time, helped or hindered this transfer to context-driven ways-of-working. For practice, a key lesson is that contexts can switch and, along with that switch, bring fundamental changes in all the features, tensions, modifiers and options for influence that are currently active. This requires 'positive training', which demands that people make decisions involving judgement about realistic trade-offs where there is no 'right answer'. Our recommendation from the Approach would be that the implications of 'context switching' and the types of transitions they generate should be reflected in policies, regulations and procedures produced following the DWH disaster. If only the top-down aspects of influence are included then some great opportunities to enrich the space of available actions needed to mitigate another disaster will be missed. The value of self-* and bottom-up influence needs to be better appreciated.

Lost Town, East of England Development Agency

The East of England Development Agency (EEDA) is one of – at the time of writing – nine Regional Development Agencies in England. These agencies are funded through a single budget, to which various UK Government departments contribute. The aim of the agencies is the promotion of economic prosperity throughout England. In October 2003, EEDA launched an international ideas competition called Landmark East, for the creation of one or more major landmarks in order to 'put the East of England on the map – both nationally and internationally' as it states on EEDA's *Landmark East* website.

In 2004, four winning entries received funding to carry out a feasibility study for their proposal, secure finance for realising the project and for the eventual delivery of the proposed landmark. EEDA took on the role of facilitator, supporting the execution of the feasibility studies through assisting in engagement with (local) stakeholders and promoting the projects. One of the winning entries, the Lost Town Project, is the subject of this case study. The events in the various phases of the Project have been captured by Jörg Adolph in his documentary film *Lost Town*. The Project picks up on the natural dynamics of the East of England coastline, which over centuries has been severely affected through progressive coastal erosion. The proposed Lost Town Landmark by the German architects Johannes Ingrisch and Anne Niemann reflected the problem of the loss of land and livelihood as a result of the retreating coastline; they suggested a steel sculpture in form of a church, representing the lost churches of Dunwich at the site of the original location of the old town. The old town, and with it its churches, have vanished into the sea due to coastal erosion over hundreds of years, and the proposed sculpture would be placed in the sea off the Dunwich coast.

The Project was presented to the local residents in a meeting organised and facilitated by EEDA. The feasibility study carried out with the prize money concluded that the sculpture was technically viable, whereas costs were still an issue to be addressed. The more important reason for not pursuing activities in Dunwich was the complete resistance of the local population to the Project – no change was desired to the quietness of the town. However, encouraged by the supporting comments for their concept that were received, the architect team looked at alternative sites for their Project along the East of England coast and selected Walton-on-the-Naze on the Naze headland in Essex as a potential new site for the sculpture. The medieval town of Walton, once far inland, had disappeared into the sea by the 19th Century as a consequence of coastal erosion, and with it its All Saints Church. Under the Government's scheme of 'managed retreat', the Naze coastline today is decreasing by one to two metres a year. This case study, presented with kind approval by the architects Anne Niemann, Johannes Ingrisch and of Rachel Bosworth from EEDA, looks at the context and dynamics of the feasibility review for Walton-on-the-Naze, which was carried out between October 2006 and February 2007, the possibilities arising for realising the multi-million Pound Sterling Project in the town, and the tensions which came to the surface.

A. **Patterns, Features and Characteristics of this Context.** Reflecting on the Realities of this context provides a rich expression of the issues shown in Figure 28 and discussed below, in which the differences between the experienced complexity of the various 'actors' plays a significant role.

1. **The physical environment.** Walton is a place in which coastal erosion is a daily topic of discussion. Walton lies on a very distinct headland, the Naze, which is a significant landmark along the Essex coast. Walton-on-the-Naze used to be a popular seaside resort, and has a long pier and a marina, but has lost its attraction to tourists and is struggling with its economic viability. Walton-on-the-Naze is also different from Dunwich in regard to the economic situation of its residents who are not as well-off as those in Dunwich.

2. **The components of the context, the actors and their properties.** EEDA promote economic development in the region through various activities and funding. Locally elected officials (Town Mayor, Councillors) are faced with multiple expectations and objectives for the town: the economic development, the issue of coastal erosion management, planning considerations, the satisfaction of local residents with their politics, and so on. The Walton Forum has been established – with representation from local business, services and community groups with the aim of steering the regeneration of Walton. The Forum set up a Community Project office which serves as an advice and information centre for the town, among others funded by EEDA initiatives (see the Walton-on-the-Naze *Contact us* webpage for more information).

   The architects, who in their design have picked up on the coastal erosion theme, lack experience of this sort of consultation and have little local knowledge of what drives and motivates the local people and what they fear and hope for. There are the local residents who may or may not approve of the Project idea, who can see various consequences of such a project, but need to be taken on board for the idea to come to pass. An issue here is a previous 'art project', an upturned bus, which was much reviled and has made Walton people wary of such schemes.

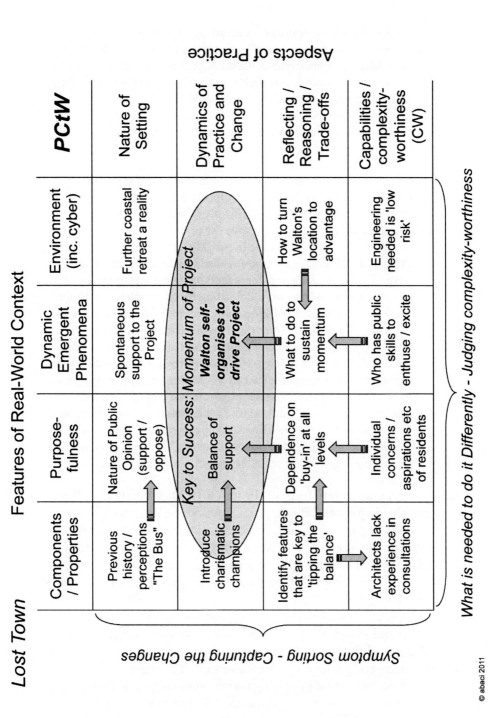

Figure 28 – Features of the Lost Town Project's Context.

Also, there are the tourists who come to Walton-on-the-Naze for seaside holidays expecting attractions and facilities for their visit. Major players in the context are potential funders for the Project execution, who could be national or international, local entities, institutions and individuals interested in art, in the topic of erosion management, conservation, history, or regional development. Thus, these potential funders might sponsor Lost Town for a variety of motivations.

3. **In terms of Purpose and Intent:** For Walton officials and representatives, the landmark sculpture is to become a tourist attraction, to draw people specifically to Walton. They hope to create economic activity, improve the reputation of and revitalize the town. The architects have to provide a feasibility study for their Project, which they want to see realised. In order to do so, they have to make the local residents feel that the sculpture is 'their Project', and they have to find funding for the implementation of their proposal if the feasibility study provides the endorsement to go ahead. Residents want their town to be a safe and living environment which provides good amenities, and where coastal erosion does not encroach on their properties. EEDA, as the initiator of the Landmark East Competition, maintains its interest in promoting economic development in the region, which the innovative idea of the Landmark East competition was to address, and – without any further financial engagement – wishes to continue to promote the Project under the, for the region, unifying theme 'management of coastal erosion'.

B. **Dynamics and Tensions of Practice in this Context – Insights from the Approach.** The Approach provides a lot of insights through the Reflecting on Doing and by considering the Conditions for Doing in Practice. Given the contextual complexity from the Reflecting on Realities, what are the options for engagement with the community-of-practice for a positive outcome of the feasibility study and the eventual implementation of Lost Town? A key insight that arises from the Approach is that the success of Lost Town depends most of all on gaining and maintaining a momentum of support for the Project to be realised, and therefore for money to be committed – the architectural and engineering issues are less important. The ongoing dynamics are influenced by the town's striving for economic recovery. This is a strong factor in the minds of the town's officials, but is it also in the mind of the residents? What are their interests, expectations and concerns, and how does the Project tap into that? An understanding of these concerns and expectations is required to reach consent in favour of the Project among the people.

Further iteration in the Reflecting on Practice loop brings up the question of who or what can drive the idea in the Town. The position of the various representative groups and institutions, their possibilities and their interests and motivations generate tensions but also can offer opportunities for bringing the desired change as shown in the Trade-off Space in Figure 29. What is their degree of collaboration, and how can the architects engage with these entities for collaboration? Does the Project clash with any other use of the environment? What are the consequences of putting up the sculptures, geographically and in the minds of people locally and in the region? Finally, there is the funding aspect of the Project, because no sponsorship is secured, but it will have to be found, the question is how?

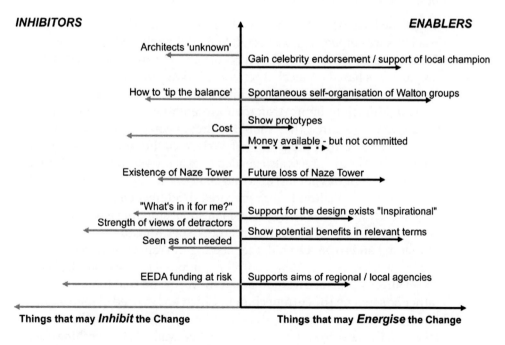

Ongoing change: "*Sustaining the Dynamic Momentum of the Lost Town Project*"

INHIBITORS   ENABLERS

Architects 'unknown'
           Gain celebrity endorsement / support of local champion

How to 'tip the balance'
           Spontaneous self-organisation of Walton groups

Cost   Show prototypes
Money available - but not committed

Existence of Naze Tower   Future loss of Naze Tower

"What's in it for me?"   Support for the design exists "Inspirational"
Strength of views of detractors
Seen as not needed   Show potential benefits in relevant terms

EEDA funding at risk   Supports aims of regional / local agencies

Things that may *Inhibit* the Change   **Things that may *Energise* the Change**

© abaci 2011

**Figure 29 – Tensions and Modifiers of the Key Aspect of Lost Town Project
– Maintaining Momentum.**

C. **What Actually Happened.** After the alternative site of Walton-on-the-Naze had been proposed as the new location for the landmark, EEDA agreed to continue to fund the initial feasibility work. Any costs incurred by the feasibility study for Walton would have to be drawn from the money that was left over from the original prize money. Support was sought from a councillor of Walton, who described how people in the town felt about the issue of the Lost Town Project as '... on the one hand there was no money from the Government to protect the coastline from the progressing coastal erosion, but there seemed to be money for an arts project'. Also, a previous art project (the upside-down bus) proposed in Walton had been rejected and not been built because it was perceived as 'laughable', whereas the Lost Town sculpture seemed to be a landmark of significance equal to the Angel of the North, near Gateshead, UK (see the Gateshead Council website *The Angel of the North* for more information). Some locals and the town officials of the town did consider Lost Town as a fantastic opportunity for an art project that would bring visitors to Walton, once a popular seaside resort but now in need of new ideas for economic development.

To get the local people on board for the idea, a meeting with the town residents was organised, backed and chaired by the Mayor of Walton. For this meeting both the Walton Forum and the architects made their preparations based on local experiences in Walton and on experiences in Dunwich respectively. The architects held a feedback session with peers in Munich to improve on their presentation of the Project. They were given advice that they should address people's 'What is in it for us?' concerns so that the people of Walton could take 'ownership' of the Project. The architects also needed to explain why Walton had been selected – that it was not just a second choice because Dunwich rejected the Project. The Walton Forum prepared to address concerns that had been raised, such as those by yachtsmen about shipping issues, by local people about parking and infrastructure issues (due to the extra influx of visitors) and so on. Overall, the meeting in Walton was a success for the Project. There were some contrary opinions – such as that the Naze Tower already provided a landmark in the town and that money should rather be spent on the current church, which was in need of renovation, but these were outweighed by those who had understood that the money raised for the Lost Town Project would not be available for anything else, that Walton was in need of something 'new', and that the town required such a project for its viability. After gaining the support of the town, EEDA signalled that they would be prepared to manage the Project after the architects had found people and donors to invest funds and time into the Project.

While the Walton Forum was seeking advice from local Members of Parliament about getting in touch with potential funders, the architects approached private companies for sponsorship. All these attempts were not fruitful and eventually the architects ran out of the time they could invest in the Project, and out of prize money to spend on project-related activities and trying to attract funds.

In November 2007, though, the Walton Forum got sight of an initiative by the UK Department for Culture, Media and Sport, which intended to make a 45-million Pound Sterling investment to generate art projects and develop rundown seaside towns. It would be a three-year programme delivered through the Commission for Architecture and the Built Environment (CABE). As this seemed a perfect opportunity to obtain substantial funding, Walton put a bid together. The bid turned out to be unsuccessful: whereas in the decision-making on funding, CABE and the Arts Council were keen on providing funding for the Project, EEDA argued that, due to budget cuts by the Government, they were unable to fund any project that had not already been agreed on – Lost Town in that climate could not be a priority for EEDA. This was the 'nail in the coffin' for the Project and, sadly, the construction of the church sculpture off the coast of Walton is still waiting to be realised.

D. **Deductions and Lessons for Practice.** After the Dunwich experience, there was the 'do-nothing' option for the architects; EEDA itself provided the suggestion that there could be a 'virtual' version of the Project on the Internet. However, a key driver for the architects to continue to pursue implementation of the real sculpture was their personal motivation – backed up by the encouragement they had received from others. The initiative was now, with consent from EEDA, with the architects who potentially had to engage in collaboration with new partners at a local level and find champions. In setting out on finding alternative sites for the landmark, Reflection on Realities of the context in the Approach would have helped the architects to identify the space-of-possibilities – especially in the light of experiences gained with the first feasibility study. From the architects' point of view, the lesson learned from the events in Dunwich was to understand how the perceptions and engagement of various interested parties may or may not influence decision-making and option-generation.

People in Dunwich held very strong viewpoints and attitudes. The introduction of the topic 'Lost Town' was considered difficult by EEDA and local officials right from the start. The context in Walton was – apart from the coastal erosion – seen as a very different one, where other conditions of the environment shaped the possibilities. Here, 'by chance' for the architects, the town welcomed the idea of the Project as a possibility for change given the economic situation. The dynamics of the feasibility study for Lost Town in the case of Walton-on-the-Naze were shaped by individual people and various groups in the town who, by collaborating, were the drivers of the dynamics. In their ongoing search for initiatives that would help the economic development of the town, the Lost Town Project was a welcome new opportunity. These local groups, and their representatives, facilitated the engagement with the local residents and considered and actively pursued the options for the funding of the Project. The majority of the population of the town took ownership of the idea as 'their' project. Hence, a lot of the changes in the context came about through the self-organisation triggered by the opportunity. The presentation of the Project to the public in Walton engaged with the ongoing dynamics. It became a sounding-board for the people's concerns – a realisation of what moved people – and this connected with what the Project could help them achieve in their endeavours for revitalising the town.

The issues surrounding the funding of the Project was one of the major modifiers of the context. The CABE opportunity came unexpectedly and changed the dynamic of the Project. Once again, it was the people in Walton who took the initiative for writing the bid. The dynamic was stopped when EEDA was unable to commit to any further funding – if more attention had been given to gaining and sustaining a popular momentum for change, then this single setback might not have been so decisive.

COMMENTS ON THE UTILITY OF THE APPROACH

These case studies have provided coverage of a number of different contexts where the challenges and opportunities of practice manifested themselves in different ways:

A. In The Fuel Crisis example the main challenge was how to deal with a structural mismatch in which one party, the Government, had little or no wiggle-room and where the other, the protesters, were, at first untouchable. The Approach illustrated this and also showed how this change issue led, though the Trade-off Space, to appropriate influences being identified and then exerted.

B. In the slum housing situation the key issue was exposing and expressing the diversity of perspectives and viewpoints so that their tensions and contradictions could be reasoned about. When, through the use of the Landscape of Change, timelines were considered it then became apparent that phasing should be determined by triggers which set the conditions for change – not by absolute time but by change criteria.

C. The Ludlow social housing case study had a different dynamic in that all concerned were equally empowered in practice, yet they had a very poor understanding of their context and so were in no position to reason about it. A version of Symptom Sorting was used to enable options to be identified, reflected upon and expressed in defendable ways.

D. The next case study looked at journalism in Lebanon and illustrated the immediacy of the context and that the principles covered in this Guide can be employed effectively, without necessarily generating any 'formal' artefacts, if the people concerned have appropriate complexity-worthiness. As an aside, plotting out the power issues between the large number of actors and entities in this context using the Trade-off Space is an interesting exercise.

E. In the Deep Water Horizon oil rig disaster case study we have examined the kinds of paralysis that can be created in a sudden transition when the network of constraints in the context can't adapt to the sudden changes that occurred. The use of the Landscape of Change, overlaid with the degrees of freedom, has provided a graphic illustration of how, in a way, what happened was, sadly, almost inevitable.

F. In the last case study, an art/architectural project called Lost Town, whilst initially successful had, over time, not been able to become a reality. The case study used Symptom Sorting and the Trade-off Space to home in on the key issue that had been missed – which was that everything depended upon gaining and maintaining the sort of positive momentum that had led to success in other projects (such as with the realisation of the Angel of the North statue in the UK).

We recognise that the Approach and the Framework we have described in this Guide are not a complete 'cure-all'. What we have provided is a sound, integrative Approach that addresses the needs of people working in complex contexts. It also responds to their requests for something tangible and pragmatic to help them do things differently and more effectively in practice as we have shown in the case studies.

So, how could our Approach be improved? As always, there is scope for better understanding of, matching with, and extension of existing techniques and ways-of-working. What we have provided is an Approach suitable for many domains of endeavour with their various natural complexities. We feel we have covered a lot of ground, bringing in our own experience as practitioners, drawing from our engagement with other practitioners and with the complexity science community. We know that more techniques and examples could have been included but felt that writing such a reference book was a separate task. Obviously, this book still needs to pass the test of practitioners 'in the field' and we welcome feedback and comment that we can incorporate, hopefully, in new editions of the Approach.

The 'whole-system' dynamics that the Approach puts to work can now be seen to be the direct concern of practitioners and not, as some might previously have considered, out of scope. As a logical extension of this Approach and of putting complexity to work in general, and as we'll show in Chapter 8, these 'dynamic energies' actually can be of use to practitioners and communities in a surprisingly practical way.

CHAPTER 8: SUMMARY AND COMMENT

REFLECTING ON COMPLEXITY DEMYSTIFIED AND PUT TO WORK

So the book is complete – but what have we actually written about? We started by saying that, in a way, people seem to have unlearned how the world works, how to engage with it and how to engage with others. Managers, in formulating plans, seem to have forgotten that they are part of the dynamics that are active in the world. Why else would they often describe the world as a place of static, non-connected objects? Why else would complexity be squeezed out – inappropriately as we have seen – into reductionist models? Why, rather than engaging with these dynamics through complexity-aware approaches to bring about change, do people 'prefer' fixed step-wise processes? We maintain that this happens, largely, because people are not aware that alternatives exist and are not confident in their use. And how does one explain that so much of it is about how to use common sense?

The Putting Complexity to Work alternative that we offer is all about being able to engage with the world as it is, and as it functions, and how to influence its interactions and its dynamics as one finds them. The Approach presented in this book supports re-learning and appreciating the natural patterns in the real-world, re-evaluating what our role in the world is, and considering how we can thus influence change – for immediate practical and mutual benefit. As the authors, we can say that it is not easy to provide a systematic approach that lives up to these challenges and to the opportunities of real-world complexity that are available across so many domains of working, as everything is dependent upon its context ...

The main theme of this Approach is, then, to work with the ever-present dynamics of change – there is no standstill in natural complexity – the dynamics are just 'there', they go on all the time and we are part of them ... Why don't we work with them more?

> C: So, in scientific terms, dynamics are generated as a result of exchanges of energy. That would mean that the sort of dynamics and phenomena we are talking about could be described as energy feedback, oscillation and so on ... whereas with the 'dance' (that we have characterised as the iterative movement of practitioners through loops), would that then be equivalent to a kind of trajectory – of flows of energy?

P: Interesting idea. Well, yes, thinking about it, we talk about potential energy in the book, for example, where people are ready to collaborate and only need some sort of catalyst to get the flow started.

C: Oh yes. That is easy to see in many situations we describe, like in the Lebanon case study. There was a lot of energy and passion there and when the journalists met in the workshop – it was like sparking a flame.

P: And the stimulation and amplification of energy is noticeable, well, in any collaboration activity that puts complexity to work. When people are motivated they bring energy into the context, when they interact it can be amplified – even changed into different forms ....

C: Such as through the TV programme that the two journalists produced, which stimulated other people's interest ...

P: Yes, exactly. And when people leave a stimulating meeting, they act like capacitors, storing the ideas and energy until later when in their enthusiasm they emit it in conversations and so on.

C: That's exciting! So putting complexity to work is about energy buzzing around – finding it, sustaining it, sharing it, working with it. But what if the energy flow is being slowed, inhibited or even stopped, say when there is no willingness for collaboration – or when it is not considered necessary?

P: I suppose physics would call that resistance, if people were deliberately trying to reduce the energy – or they might try and clamp it, by imposing rules or constraints, or damp it by disapproving of 'exuberance'. Such people are similar to being an 'earthing rod' that grounds the energy so it decays away...

C: So, imagine you were energy and ... well, hang on! Somehow practice is all about working with energy, with the dynamics it enables, with the interactions that mediate transfers of energy and with the phenomena that arise depending on the nature of the energy flows ... What would that mean to a manager, or a politician, or an economist? It would certainly be different from the kind of measures and metrics they use now ...

P: HELP!

C: Where was the energy in the Lost Town case study? All over the place in penny packets I suppose. What the Project needed to do was to provide a context which brought the energy together, generating positive feedback which generated more energy. A manager would need to identify where those packets (physicists might say 'quanta') of energy were and think about bringing them together in different ways.

P: Yes quite. Exactly as happened in the Lebanon case study. The journalists generated a 'shared energy' that no one person 'owned' and yet in which all had a hand in creating and sustaining. Eventually, it was so tangible that they were able to use it to get their way with their bosses.

C: Indeed. But, when putting complexity to work, is energy always transient, intangible – something that 'reductionist' people can ignore? That wouldn't help practitioners.

P: Let me think . . . In the Lost Town money was a key source of the energy, of enabling the space-of-possibilities to exist. So, in principle, 'energy' *can* have a tangible form – especially if it can act as a token that exerts influence. In practice, and in human terms, these forms of 'energy' are interchangeable, though the 'conversion factor' would depend on the context.

C: In Lost Town, in the end, the money that wasn't available didn't just stop the energy flow, everyone could have carried on collaborating as they had been. Instead, its absence acted as a massive damper, the dynamic slowed and the energy drained away into the ground – the Project became unviable, no longer part of people's 'achievable actions'.

P: You could think of it as 'excitation levels' I suppose. If you can get the energy up to a certain level it is self-sustaining through feedback. If the level drops then what was previously possible is now damped/blocked, the wiggle-room has gone along with some or all of the degrees of freedom.

C: That's intriguing! What about the other case studies – I'm not sure where the energy flows were in the Fuel Crisis, that seemed to be all about tensions, where the energy cancelled out. For a time there was a paralysis, a stasis, the dynamic was there but the flow wasn't. Is that what the Government realised? You worked on that one. What do you think?

P: There was a lot going on there at different levels. Once the lorry drivers started their action it induced disproportional activity among people elsewhere, which was self-organised. The Government found itself 'entrained', as it's called: they were drawn into rhythms, patterns and oscillations of behaviours against their will. Yet there was a lag (hysteresis) between what the protesters were doing and what the Government could do – and an inertia, the institutions took time to act. I suppose, thinking back, it was about slowing the momentum of the protestors to an energy level that the Government could cope with.

C: And of course, at first, they didn't have a handle on the necessary levers of power/energy.

P: True, and they were worried about reactance: that the dissonance between general public and Government would get worse if the politicians injected energy in a way that just excited the protests.

C: So what we are saying here is that thinking about putting complexity to work in energy terms really works. It's something that anyone could do using their common sense.

P: Yes, well, they'd need to understand something about the kind of complex dynamics we have already talked about but, other than that, it makes a lot of sense. But what about a crisis – that is surely very different in energy terms?

C: I don't think so. It's just about quantity and time isn't it? In other words, transitions and transformations of energy that are faster/bigger than complexity-worthiness can cope with? And than were 'expected' ...

P: There are other features and phenomena too. What's the threshold for detecting the change? The shape and nature of the change in energy – you know, smooth, turbulent etc. Ideally you'd want to reflect the energy back somehow so it has no effect, or refract it – in the sense of absorbing some of it but being able to emit it off in a different direction ... or damp it down ...

C: And in practical terms that means what exactly?

P: Erm. Well, on the DWH, pushing it back down the well wasn't viable, but the heat from the flames was deflected away from vulnerable equipment and the energy in the flow of mud from the well was diverted through a 'degasser' which also damped down some of the effect. But the experts were overwhelmed.

C: I wonder what a safety manual for oil-rig operation would look like written in the sort of energy terms we are using? It would certainly be very different from the one we have seen.

P: What about all the other 'energy qualities' we've not talked about?

C: I'd like to spend more time understanding their implications in practical terms – this idea that practitioners could 'work' in energy terms seems very promising.

P: True. And I wonder what a Masters in Business Administration (complexity-worthiness) would look like? Based on what we have been talking about, it would be interesting to think about what would need to be in such a course ...

C: So maybe an idea would be to organise another workshop, like the ECCS one ... er, how about 'Energy in Practice – Putting Complexity to Work'? Maybe some of our readers would like to take part?

This is a Guide for practitioners on putting complexity to work. It started by talking about ways-of-working, complexity science and the challenges of working in open and adaptive ways that are appropriately and dynamically matched to changing contexts. It has finished with the simple realisation that if you stop the energy flows involved in the changes you are seeking, which are part of the natural dynamics of the real-world, they may die away. Then you are blocked – and that's the end of trying to put complexity to work in that context. Whereas, if you appreciate how to engage with, foster and nurture the available energy then, in practice, you can really be surfing the opportunities!

SUPPORTING MATERIAL

LIST OF FIGURES

ABBREVIATIONS

AFP	*Agence France-Presse*
BBC	British Broadcasting Corporation
BP	Not an abbreviation (formerly British Petroleum)
BoP	Blow-out-Preventer
CA	Cellular Automata
CABE	Commission for Architecture and the Built Environment, UK
CARS	Complex Adaptive Reflexive Systems
CAS	Complex Adaptive Systems
CC	Contextual Complexity
CMMI	Capability Maturity Model Integration
CoI	Communities-of-Interest
CoP	Communities-of-Practice
CS	Complexity Science
CW	Complexity-worthiness
DNRP	Douala Neighbourhood Redevelopment Programme
DWH	Deep Water Horizon (Oil rig)
EC	Experienced Complexity
ECCS	European Conference on Complex Systems
EDS	Emergency Disconnect Switch (on the DWH rig)
EEDA	East of England Development Agency, UK
FEMA	Federal Emergency Management Agency (in the USA)
GP	General Practitioner
ICT	Information and Communication Technologies
IHMC	Institute of Human and Machine Cognition
INCOSE	International Council On Systems Engineering
IS	Influencing and Shaping
ISO	International Standards Organisation
ITU	International Telecommunication Union
NASA	National Aeronautics and Space Administration (USA)

MSP	Managing Successful Programmes
NGO	Non-Government Organisation
NHS	National Health Service (UK)
OG	Option Generation
OIM	Offshore Installation Manager
PC	Personal Computer
PCtW	Putting Complexity to Work
PI	Purpose and Intent
PPG	Planning Policy Guidance
PPS	Planning Policy Statements
RHA	Road Haulage Association
RoP	Reflecting on Practice
RoR	Reflecting on Realities
SESD	Social Eco-System Dance
SMS	Short Message Service (texting)
SoPs	Standard (not standardised!) Operational Procedures
SP	Strategies and Possibilities
TRANSIMS	TRansport ANalysis and Simulation Systems
UK	United Kingdom (of Great Britain and Northern Ireland)
UN	United Nations
UNDP	United Nations Development Programme
USA	United States of America
USJFCOM	US Joint Force Commander
USP	Unique Selling Point
VAT	Value Added Tax (UK)
VIP	Very Important Person

REFERENCES

Adolph, J. (2009) *Lost Town* [DVD], DocCollection, Munich.

AlphabetPhotography (2010) *Christmas Food Court Flash Mob, Hallelujah Chorus* [online]. Available from: http://www.youtube.com/watch?v=SXh7JR9oKVE [accessed 18 November 2010].

Ashby, W. Ross (1957) *An introduction to Cybernetics*, Chapman & Hall, London.

Asimov, I. (1981) *A Choice of Catastrophes: The Disasters That Threaten Our World.* Arrow Books Limited, London.

Barabasi, A.L.(2003) *Linked: How Everything Is Connected to Everything Else and What It Means*, Plume, London.

BBC 2 Archive (1984) *The Egg Race, Putting on the Pressure* [online], BBC Archive. Available from: http://www.bbc.co.uk/archive/great_egg_race/10805.shtml [accessed 12 December 2010].

BBC World Service (2009) *One Planet* [online], BBC iplayer (27 August 2009). Available from: http://www.bbc.co.uk/iplayer/episode/p0040kgs/One_Planet_27_08_2009 [accessed 21 November 2010].

Beautement, P. (2009) 'Putting Complexity to Work – achieving effective Human-machine Teaming'. [Poster] [online]. *European Conference on Complex Systems 2009*. Available from: http://css.csregistry.org/tiki-index.php?page=ECCS09-138&bl=y [accessed 4 February 2011].

Beautement, P. and Broenner C. (2009a) 'Complex Multi-modal Multi-level Influence Networks – Affordable Housing Case Study', in Jie Zhou (ed.), *First International Conference, Complex 2009, Shanghai, China, February 23-25, 2009, Revised Papers, Part 2*, pp. 2054-2063, Springer, Berlin Heidelberg.

Beautement, P. and Broenner C. (2009b) 'Complex Phenomena in Orchestras – Metaphors for Leadership and Enterprise', in Jie Zhou (ed.), *First International Conference, Complex 2009, Shanghai, China, February 23-25, 2009, Revised Papers, Part 2*, pp. 2184-2195, Springer, Berlin Heidelberg.

Beck, C (2009) 'Home Comforts', *The Garden*, August, 526–529.

Bennett, H.N., Bryant, P.J., Howard, N. (2001) 'Drama Theory and Confrontation Analysis' in Rosenhead J. V. and Mingers J. (eds) *Rational Analysis for a Problematic World Revisited: problem structuring methods for complexity, uncertainty and conflict*, pp. 225-248, Wiley, Chichester.

Bonabeu, E., Dorigo, M., Theraulaz, G. (1999) *Swarm Intelligence. From Natural to Artificial Systems*, Oxford University Press, New York, Oxford.

Bradshaw, J.M., Beautement, P., Breedy, M.R., Bunch, L., Drakunov, S.V., Feltovich, P.J., Foggman, R.F., Jeffers, R., Johnson, M., Kulkarni, S., Lott, J., Raj, A.K., Suri, N. and Uszok, A. (2004) 'Making Agents Acceptable to People', in Zhong, N. and Liu, J. (eds) *Intelligent Technologies for Information Analysis*, pp. 361-398, Springer, Berlin Heidelberg.

Brown, J. and Isaacs, D. (2005) *The World Café. Shaping our Futures through Conversations that matter*, Berrett-Koehler Publishers, San Francisco.

Buscell, P. (2006) 'Complexity and Change on the Reservation', *emerging – The newsletter of Plexus Institute*, April – August.

Capra, F. (1997) *The Web of Life. A New Scientific Understanding of Living Systems*, Anchor Books, New York.

Chambers, R. (2008) *Revolutions in Development Inquiry*, Earthscan, London.

Cheltenham Music Society (2010) *Cheltenham Chamber Music 2010 – 2011*, 13th November 2010, Takacs Quartet.

Cohen, J. and Stewart, I. (2000) *The Collapse of Chaos. Discovering Simplicity in a Complex World*, Penguin Books, London.

Conn, E. (2010) 'Community Engagement In The Social Eco-System Dance – Tools for Practitioners' *International Workshop on Complexity and Real World applications*. Southampton, UK, 21st-23rd July 2010. Reference with permission from the author.

Creative Clusters (2011) *Facing the Challenges of the Creative Economy* [online]. Available from: http://creativeclusters.com/ [accessed 13 March 2011].

Davies, P. (1995) *The Cosmic Blueprint – Order and Complexity at the Edge of Chaos*. Penguin, London.

Department for Communities and Local Governments *Planning Policy Guidance (PPG) and Planning Policy Statements (PPS)* [online]. Available from: http://www.communities.gov.uk/planningandbuilding/planningsystem/planningpolicy/planningpolicystatements/ [accessed 13 March 2011].

Diamond, J. (2005) *Collapse. How societies choose to fail or survive*. Penguin, London.

Dodd, L., Prins, G. and Stamp, G. (2007) 'Going from closed to open: how may we help to make it bearable?' [online], *International Conference on Complex Systems 2007*, October 28-November 2, Boston, MA. Available from: http://necsi.edu/wiki/index.php/ICCS07/95 [accessed 2 February 2011].

Drake, J. A. (1991) 'Community Assembly Mechanics and the Structure of an Experimental Species Ensemble', *The American Naturalist*, 137, 1-26.

EEDA (2005) *Landmark East* [online]. Available from: http://www.landmarkeast.org.uk/ [accessed 10 March 2011, site under construction].

Eco, U. (1984) *The role of the Reader. Explorations in the Semiotics of Texts*, Indiana University Press, Bloomington.

Epstein, P. (1999) *Notes to the Emerson String Quartet recording Dmitri Shostakovich: The String Quartets*, excerpts [online], Saint Paul Sunday PublicRadio. Available from: http://saintpaulsunday.publicradio.org/features/0004_shostakovich/epstein_notes.shtml

European Conference on Complex Systems (ECCS 2009) *The Complexity of Global Change. Public Session on Global Problems* (21 September 2009)[online], ASSYST. Available from: http://www.assystcomplexity.eu/video.jsp?video=78 [accessed 15 November 2010].

Feynman, R.P., Leighton, R.B., Sands, M. (1963) *The Feynman Lectures on Physics* Volume II, 41-12, Addison-Wesley, Reading, Mass.

Feynman, R. P. (2007) *What do you care what other people think?* Penguin Books, London.

Foreman, J. (2008) *Pakistan: Free to learn* [online], The Telegraph. Available from: http://www.telegraph.co.uk/culture/books/3671228/Pakistan-Free-to-learn.html [accessed 21 November 2010].

Gateshead Council (2011) *The Angel of the North* [online]. Available from: http://www.gateshead.gov.uk/Leisure%20and%20Culture/attractions/Angel/Home.aspx [accessed 9 March 2011]

Gladwell, M. (2001) *The Tipping Point. How little things can make a big difference*, Abacus, London.

Grisogono, A.M. (2006) *DSTO Node Report* [online], COSNet Forum, 27-28 Nov. Available from: www.complexsystems.net.au/documents/grisogono_dsto.ppt [accessed 6 March 2011].

Harris, S. (2011) *Shostakovitch's String Quartet No. 2* [online]. Available from: http://www.quartets.de/compositions/ssq02.html [accessed 16 April 2011].

Hillis, W. D. (1999) *The Pattern On The Stone: The Simple Ideas That Make Computers Work*, Basic Books, New York.

HM Treasury (2010) *Spending Challenge* [online]. Available from: http://www.hm-treasury.gov.uk/spend_spendingchallenge.htm [accessed 15 January 2011].

Hopkins, R. (2008) *The Transition Handbook: From oil dependency to local resilience*, Green Books, London.

IBM *Autonomic Computing* [online]. Available from: http://www.research.ibm.com/autonomic/ [accessed 4 February 2011]

INCOSE (2009) *SE Handbook*, Version 3 [online], INCOSE, Products & Publications. Available from: http://www.incose.org/ProductsPubs/products/sehandbook.aspx [accessed 21 March 2011].

Intervolve (2009) *factsheet DNRP* [online]. Available from: http://www.intervolve.org/images/website/factsheets/eng_factsheet_dnrp_aug_2009.jpg [accessed 8 March 2011].

ITU (2010) *The World in 2010 ICT Facts and Figures* [online]. Available from: http://www.itu.int/ITU-D/ict/material/FactsFigures2010.pdf [accessed 14 November 2010].

Jupp, D. and Ibn Ali, S. (2010) *Measuring Empowerment? Ask Them. Quantifying qualitative outcomes from people's own analysis* [online], SIDA Studies in Evaluation 2010:1. Available from: http://www.gsdrc.org/go/display&type=Document&id=3982 [accessed 5 December 2010]

Kao, J. (1997) *Jamming. The Art and Discipline of Business Creativity*, Harper Collins Publishers, New York.

Klein, N. (2008) *The Shock Doctrine*, Penguin Books, London.

Kurtz, C. F. and Snowden, D. (2003) 'The new dynamics of strategy: sense-making in a complex world', *IBM Systems Journal* Volume 42 Number 3: 462-483.

Langton, C. (1990) 'Computation at the edge of chaos', *Physica D* 42: 12–37.

Lansing, S. (2003) *Social Science Models & Tropical Disasters: When 'Emergence' Really Counts* [DVD] Santa Fe Institute, Santa Fe.

Levitt, S.D. and Dubner, S.J. (2005) *Freakonomics*, Penguin, London.

Levy, S. (1993) *Artificial Life*, Vintage Books, New York.

Lewin, R. (1993) *Complexity. Life at the Edge of Chaos*, Phoenix, London.

Lorenz, E. N. (1963) 'Deterministic Nonperiodic Flow', *Journal of the Atmospheric Sciences* 20 (2): 130–141.

Mathieson, G. (2005) *Complexity and Managing to Survive it* [online], DSTL. Available from: http://isce.edu/ISCE_Group_Site/web-content/ISCE_Events/Cork_2005/Papers/Mathieson.pdf [accessed 1 March 2011].

Mattis, N.J. (2008) 'USJFCOM Commander's Guidance for Effects-based Operations' *Parameters*, Autumn 2008, pp. 18-25 [online]. Available from: http://www.futurefastforward.com/component/content/article/902-military--intelligence/608-usjfcom-commanders-guidance-for-effects-based-operations-by-james-n-mattis-latest-update-251108?tmpl=component&print=1&page= [accessed 1 March 2011].

Mitleton-Kelly, E. (2003) 'Ten Principles of Complexity and Enabling Infrastructures', *Complex Systems and Evolutionary Perspectives of Organisations: The Application of Complexity Theory to Organisations*, pp. 3-20, Elsevier, London.

Morowitz, H. J. (2002) *The Emergence of Everything: How the World became Complex*, Oxford University Press, Oxford.

Mortenson, G. and Relin, D. O. (2007) *Three Cups of Tea: One Man's Mission to Promote Peace One School at a Time*, Penguin Books, London.

National Commission on the BP Deepwater Horizon Oil Spill and Offshore Drilling (2011) *Final Report* [online]. Available from: http://www.oilspillcommission.gov/final-report [accessed 10 March 2011].

National Commission on the BP Deepwater Horizon Oil Spill and Offshore Drilling (2011) *Chief Counsel's Report* [online]. Available from: http://www.scribd.com/doc/51073178/C21462-408-CCR-for-web [accessed 13 January 2011].

New York Times. *Deepwater Horizon's Final Hours*. [online] http://www.nytimes.com/2010/12/26/us/26spill.html?_r=1&pagewanted=all [accessed 27 December 2010]

Nicolescu, B. (2002) *Manifesto of Transdisciplinarity*, State University of New York Press, Albany.

Pearce, F. (2007) 'Climate tipping points loom large', *New Scientist* 2617: 13.

Ramalingam, B. and Jones, H. (2008) Exploring the science of complexity: Ideas and implications for development and humanitarian efforts. *Working Paper 285*, *Overseas Development Institute*, London.

Ripley, A. (2009) In case of emergency, *The Atlantic* [online]. Available from: http://www.theatlantic.com/magazine/archive/2009/09/in-case-of-emergency/7604/ [accessed 2 October 2009]

Ritchey, T. (2005) *Wicked Problems – Structuring Social Messes with Morphological Analysis* [online], Swedish Morphological Society. Available from: http://www.swemorph.com/pdf/wp.pdf [accessed 1 March 2011]

Sagan, C. (1977) *The Dragons of Eden,* Hodder and Stoughton, London.

Santa Fe Institute Library [online]. Available from: http://www.santafe.edu/library/ [accessed 1 March 2010]

Smith, R. (2005) *The Utility of Force. The Art of War in the Modern World,* Allen Lane, London.

Smuts, J.C. (1926) *Holism and Evolution,* The Macmillan Company, New York. Reprint edition 2006.

Tapscott, D. and Williams, A.D. (2006) *Wikinomics,* Atlantic Books, London.

The abaci Partnership (2009) *White Paper: Putting Complexity to Work – Supporting the Practitioners* [online], The abaci Partnership LLP. Available from: http://www.abaci.net/library/eccs09_pctw_white-paper_v1-1.pdf [accessed 10 January 2010].

The Cyc Foundation (2008) *Cyclopedia* [online]. Available from: http://www.cycfoundation.org/blog/?page_id=15 [accessed 1 March 2011].

Thompson, M. (2008) *Organising & Disorganising,* Triarchy Press Ltd, Axminster.

Treverton, G.F. (2003) *Reshaping National Intelligence for an Age of Information,* Cambridge University Press, New York.

Turner, C. (2008) *The Geography of Hope. A tour of the world we need,* Random House of Canada Ltd., Toronto.

UK Government General Act (2001) *Human Reproductive Cloning Act 2001,* [online]. Available from: http://www.legislation.gov.uk/ukpga/2001/23/contents [accessed 26 March 2011].

Varela, F. Maturana, H. Uribe, R (1974) 'Autopoiesis: the organization of living systems, its characterisation and a model'. *Biosystems* 5: 187-196.

Virginia Bioinformatics Institute at Virginia Tech (2008), *TRANSIMS* [online], Network Dynamics and Simulation Science Laboratory (NDSSL). Available from: http://ndssl.vbi.vt.edu/transims-docs.php [accessed 6 March 2011].

Wallach, J. (2005) *Desert Queen. The Extraordinary Life of Gertrude Bell: Adventurer, Adviser to Kings, Ally of Lawrence of Arabia,* Phoenix, London.

Walton-on-the-Naze. The Official Walton Website (2010) *Contact us* [online]. Available from: http://www.walton-on-the-naze.com/Contact/contact.htm [accessed 10 March 2011].

Watts, D.J. (2003) *Six Degrees: The Science of a connected Age,* W.W. Norton & Company, New York, London.

Wenger, E. (1999) *Communities of Practice. Learning, Meaning, and Identity,* Cambridge University Press, Cambridge.

Zander Stone, R. and Zander, B. (2002) *The Art of Possibility,* Penguin, London.

Literature – Recommended Reading

This is a list of books and other material that we like, but have not specifically referenced.

Alston, A.J. and Beautement, P (1999) 'Coping with Uncertainty in the Command Process' at International Command and Control (C2) Research and Technology Symposium, Rhode Island, USA. Available from: http://www.dodccrp.org/events/1999_CCRTS/pdf_files/track_1/062beaut.pdf [accessed 18 April 2011].

Bear, G. (2000) *Darwin's Radio*, Harper Collins Publishers, London.

Beautement, P., Allsopp, D., Greaves, M., Goldsmith, S., Spires, S., Thompson, S., Janicke, H. (2006) 'Autonomous Agents and Multi-agent Systems (AAMAS) for the Military Issues and Challenges' in *Lecture Notes in Computer Science*, Volume 3890/2006: 1-13, Springer, Berlin Heidelberg.

Bertalanffy von, L. (1969) *General System Theory*, George Braziller, New York.

Dörner, D. (1996) *The Logic of Failure*, Basic Books, Cambridge, MA.

Gleick, J. (1989) *Chaos*, Cardinal Books, London.

Gibson, W. (1995) *Neuromancer*, Voyager, London.

Hafner, K. and Lyon, M. (1998) *Where Wizards Stay up Late: The origins of the Internet*, Touchstone, New York.

Hofstadter, D.R. (1983) *Gödel, Escher, Bach: an Eternal Golden Braid*. Penguin Books, London.

Hollan, J., Hutchins, E. Kirsh, D. (2000) 'Distributed cognition: toward a new foundation for human-computer interaction research' in *ACM Transactions on Computer-Human Interaction (TOCHI)* – Special issue on human-computer interaction in the new millennium, Part 2, Volume 7 Issue 2: 174-196.

Kelly, K. (1994) *Out of Control*. Perseus Books, Cambridge, MA.

Lovelock, J. (1989) *The Ages of Gaia*, Oxford University Press, Oxford.

Marsay, D. (2006) 'Coalition Command and Control in the Networked Era' (Liquids as a Metaphor) [online]. Available from: http://www.dodccrp.org/events/11th_ICCRTS/html/papers/077.pdf [accessed 18 April 2011].

Nisbett, R.E. (2003) *The Geography of Thought*, Nicholas Brealey Publishing, London.

Perrow, C. (1999) *Normal Accidents*, Princeton University Press, Chichester.

Schon, D.A. (1991) *The Reflective Practitioner: How Professionals Think in Action*, Ashgate Publishing, London.

Stacey, R.D., Griffin, D. and Shaw, P. (2000) *Complexity and Management: Fad or Radical Challenge To Systems Thinking*. Routledge, London.

Stewart, R. (2006) *Occupational Hazards*, Picador, London.

Stoll, C. (1990) *The Cuckoo's Egg*, Pocket Books, New York.

Weick, K.E. and Sutcliff, K.M. (2001) *Managing the Unexpected: Assuring High Performance in an Age of Complexity*. Jossey-Bass, San Francisco.

INDEX

ABOUT TRIARCHY PRESS

Triarchy Press is an independent publishing house that looks at how organisations work and how to make them work better. We present challenging perspectives on organisations in short and pithy, but rigorously argued, books.

Other titles in the areas of organisational learning include:

Organising and Disorganising
by Michael Thompson.

Adventures in Complexity
by Lesley Kuhn

The Three Ways of Getting Things Done
by Gerard Fairtlough

Ten Things To Do in a Conceptual Emergency
by Graham Leicester and Maureen O'Hara

Economies of Life
by Bill Sharpe

In Search of the Missing Elephant
by Donald N. Michael

Through our books, pamphlets and website we aim to stimulate ideas by encouraging real debate about organisations in partnership with people who work in them, research them or just like to think about them.

Please tell us what you think about the ideas in this book at:

www.triarchypress.com/telluswhatyouthink

For more information about Triarchy Press, or to order any of our publications, please visit our website or drop us a line:

www.triarchypress.com

Twitter: @TriarchyPress ~ Facebook: www.facebook.com/triarchypress

ABOUT THE AUTHORS

Patrick Beautement, co-founder and Research Director of The *abaci* Partnership. Originally a geologist and geographer, became fascinated by 'complexity' through the inspirational teaching of Professor Igor Aleksander at Brunel University, UK in 1983 and the writings of Douglas Hofstadter in his book *Gödel, Escher, Bach: an Eternal Golden Braid*. Having grown up as one of those 'difficult children', interested in everything, it seemed natural to Patrick to think of the world as an interconnected place – and equally unnatural to him to find that some people seemed happy to see things in terms of disembodied and unrelated bits. Over time, Patrick found he had an innate ability to 'join up the dots', but he also found that he lacked an explanation for why this was a pragmatic reflection of how the world worked (or even of how the human mind could do this). This book is an attempt to explain, after many years of trying to understand it, how holistic 'joining up the dots' thinking can support practice.

Professionally, Patrick has over 25 years experience of implementing innovative studies and high-profile evaluations for government, academia and commerce and has a track record of partnering with practitioners and communities in multi-disciplinary contexts and developing tools and techniques (for understanding causal mechanisms). He has been lead facilitator for a set of UK government-sponsored workshops involving practitioners covering a three-year period and successfully collated, analysed and presented the interdependent factors in a series of detailed reports. In another Study, he was the Principal Investigator for a multinational, coalition collaboration examining crisis management and disaster response that received awards for its clarity and relevance.

Christine Broenner has been intrigued by geography all her life – she loves exploring the diversity of 'places' in the world and has lived in many countries for study and to work. It is not surprising that she chose to become a geographer (Dipl.Geogr.) and has, for almost 20 years, been involved in the design, development and use of geographic information systems in domains such as natural resources management, environmental planning, infrastructure planning, policy implementation and urban management. She has worked with practitioners in many domains, in private companies and in international research and education institutions and she has been involved in projects in Europe, as well as in technical assistance missions for development cooperation in Asia and Africa. Through these experiences, she has become particularly interested in overcoming the lack of interoperability between data, mindsets and organisations that she encounters in many of the day-to-day situations and in the wide variety of settings in which she works. Christine joined The abaci Partnership in 2008 as a Principal Consultant.

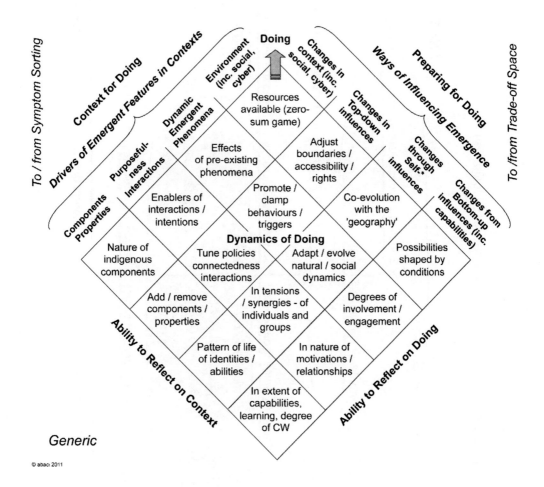

Generic

© abaci 2011

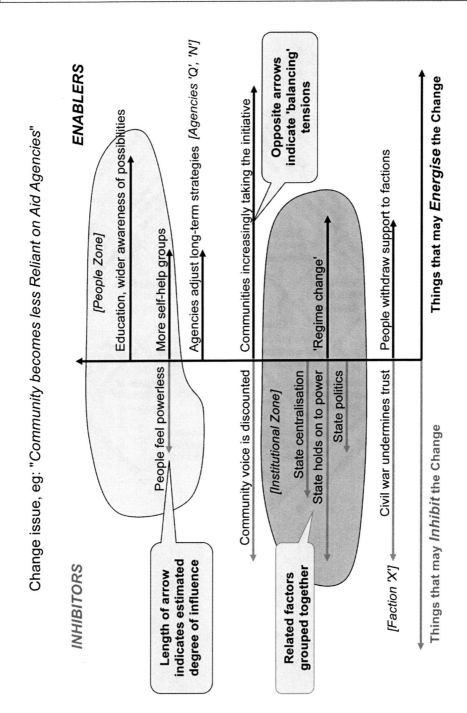

Change issue, eg: "*Community becomes less Reliant on Aid Agencies*"

ENABLERS

INHIBITORS

[People Zone]

Education, wider awareness of possibilities

More self-help groups

Agencies adjust long-term strategies *[Agencies 'Q', 'N']*

Communities increasingly taking the initiative

Opposite arrows indicate 'balancing' tensions

People withdraw support to factions

Things that may *Energise* the Change

People feel powerless

Community voice is discounted

[Institutional Zone]

State centralisation

State holds on to power

State politics

'Regime change'

Civil war undermines trust

[Faction 'X']

Things that may *Inhibit* the Change

Length of arrow indicates estimated degree of influence

Related factors grouped together

© abaci 2011

Copy of Figure 18 – Symptom Sorting – Capturing Context and Appreciating the Differences. See page 164.

[Cut out this page to enable cross-reference with other parts of the book]

Features of Real-World Context

Aspects of Practice

PCtW	Components / Properties	Purpose-fulness	Dynamic Emergent Phenomena	Environment (inc. cyber)
Nature of Setting	Components in the environment - creatures, objects, agents	Ways in which purpose set / intent is shaped by context	Ways in which context changes dynamically	Nature of natural complexity in the context
Dynamics of Practice and Change	'Role' of components in generating dynamic phenomena	Practice as changed by purpose and intent	Practice given the changing realities - patterns	Natural, ongoing background dynamics
Reflecting / Reasoning / Trade-offs	Reflecting on what entities do and could do, behaviours, relationships	Reflecting on intents, drives, values - perspectives and viewpoints	Reflecting on possibilities given the realities of change	Reflecting on givens, acknowledging realities
Capabilities / complexity-worthiness (CW)	Properties of entities as part of CW	CW aspects of personality / intent	CW aspects of dynamic change	CW aspects of capabilities available in the Environment

Circled codes across the matrix: NC, CC, EC, SP, IS, OG, PI, CW

Symptom Sorting - Capturing Changes in the Context

What is needed to do it Differently - Judging complexity-worthiness in the Context

© abaci 2011

259

Lightning Source UK Ltd.
Milton Keynes UK
178035UK00001B/3/P